THE BEST TEST PREPARATION FOR THE

CLEP

Analyzing &
Interpreting Literature

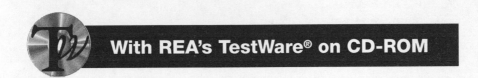

With REA's TestWare® on CD-ROM

Staff of Research & Education Association

Research & Education Association
Visit our website at
www.rea.com

Planet Friendly Publishing
✔ Made in the United States
✔ Printed on Recycled Paper
Text: 10%   Cover: 10%
Learn more: www.greenedition.org

GREEN EDITION

At REA we're committed to producing books in an Earth-friendly manner and to helping our customers make greener choices.

Manufacturing books in the United States ensures compliance with strict environmental laws and eliminates the need for international freight shipping, a major contributor to global air pollution.

And printing on recycled paper helps minimize our consumption of trees, water and fossil fuels. This book was printed on paper made with **10% post-consumer waste**. According to Environmental Defense's Paper Calculator, by using this innovative paper instead of conventional papers, we achieved the following environmental benefits:

**Trees Saved: 5 • Air Emissions Eliminated: 896 pounds
Water Saved: 891 gallons • Solid Waste Eliminated: 265 pounds**

For more information on our environmental practices, please visit us online at **www.rea.com/green**

Research & Education Association
61 Ethel Road West
Piscataway, New Jersey 08854
E-mail: info@rea.com

The Best Test Preparation for the
CLEP ANALYZING & INTERPRETING LITERATURE EXAM
With TestWare® on CD-ROM

Published 2011

Copyright © 2005 by Research & Education Association, Inc. Prior editions copyright © 2002, 2001, 1998, 1996 by Research & Education Association, Inc. All rights reserved. No part of this book may be reproduced in any form without permission of the publisher.

Printed in the United States of America

Library of Congress Control Number 2004095864

ISBN-13: 978-0-87891-343-5
ISBN-10: 0-87891-343-2

Windows® is a registered trademark of Microsoft Corporation.

REA® and TestWare® are registered trademarks of Research & Education Association, Inc.

About Research & Education Association

Founded in 1959, Research & Education Association (REA) is dedicated to publishing the finest and most effective educational materials—including software, study guides, and test preps—for students in middle school, high school, college, graduate school, and beyond.

REA's Test Preparation series includes books and software for all academic levels in almost all disciplines. REA publishes test preps for students who have not yet entered high school, as well as high school students preparing to enter college. Students from countries around the world seeking to attend college in the United States will find the assistance they need in REA's publications. For college students seeking advanced degrees, REA publishes test preps for many major graduate school admission examinations in a wide variety of disciplines, including engineering, law, and medicine. Students at every level, in every field, with every ambition can find what they are looking for among REA's publications.

REA's practice tests are always based upon the most recently administered exams, and include every type of question that can be expected on the actual exams.

REA's publications and educational materials are highly regarded and continually receive an unprecedented amount of praise from professionals, instructors, librarians, parents, and students. Our authors are as diverse as the subject matter represented in the books we publish. They are well-known in their respective disciplines and serve on the faculties of prestigious colleges and universities throughout the United States and Canada.

Today REA's wide-ranging catalog is a leading resource for teachers, students, and professionals.

We invite you to visit us at *www.rea.com* to find out how "REA is making the world smarter."

Acknowledgments

We would like to thank Pam Weston, Vice President, Publishing, for setting the quality standards for production integrity and managing the publication to completion; John Paul Cording, Vice President, Technology, for coordinating the design, development, and testing of REA's TEST*ware*® software; Project Managers Amy Jamison and Reena Shah for their software design contributions and software testing efforts; Larry B. Kling, Vice President, Editorial, for his supervision of revisions and overall direction; Anne Winthrop Esposito, Senior Editor, for coordinating revisions; Kathy Caratozzolo for typesetting revisions; and Christine Saul, Senior Graphic Artist, for designing our cover.

CONTENTS

CLEP ANALYZING AND INTERPRETING LITERATURE INDEPENDENT STUDY SCHEDULE

The following study schedule allows for thorough preparation for the CLEP Analyzing and Interpreting Literature. Although it is designed for six weeks, it can be reduced to a three-week course by collapsing each two-week period into one. Be sure to set aside enough time—at least two hours each day—to study. But no matter which study schedule works best for you, the more time you spend studying, the more prepared and relaxed you will feel on the day of the exam.

Week	Activity
1	Read and study Chapter 1, which will introduce you to the CLEP Analyzing and Interpreting Literature. Then take Practice Test 1 on TEST*ware*® to determine your strengths and weaknesses. Read the section results in the Score Report. You can then determine the areas in which you need to strengthen your skills.
2 & 3	Carefully read and study the Literature Review included in this book.
4	Take Practice Test 2 on TEST*ware*®, and after reviewing your score report, review carefully all incorrect answer explanations. If there are any types of questions or particular subjects that seem difficult to you, review those subjects by studying again the appropriate section of the Literature Review.
5	Take Practice Test 3, and after scoring your exam, review carefully all incorrect answer explanations. If there are any types of questions or particular subjects that seem difficult to you, review those subjects by studying again the appropriate section of the Literature Review.
6	Retake Practice Tests 1–3*. This will help strengthen the areas you are weak in and make you more comfortable with the different question types and testing conditions.

*Prospective examinees planning to take the Optional Free-Response Section of the CLEP Analyzing and Interpreting Literature CBT should spend Week 6 taking Practice Tests I–III in the back of this book. If you're following a three-week study schedule, use Week 3 to test yourself and study the model responses.

CHAPTER 1

PASSING THE CLEP ANALYZING & INTERPRETING LITERATURE EXAM

Chapter 1

PASSING THE CLEP ANALYZING AND INTERPRETING LITERATURE EXAM

ABOUT THIS BOOK & TEST*ware*®

This book provides you with an accurate and complete representation of the CLEP Analyzing and Interpreting Literature exam. Inside you will find a review of literature, as well as tips and strategies for test taking. Three full-length practice tests and an optional free-response section—with another three practice tests—are provided, all based on the official CLEP Analyzing and Interpreting Literature exam. Our practice tests contain every type of question that you can expect to encounter on the actual exam. Following each multiple-choice practice test, you will find an answer key with detailed explanations designed to help you more completely understand the test material. For the free-response practice tests, analysis is provided after each model essay to give you in-depth guidance on how to write your own essays.

Practice tests 1 and 2 in this book and software package are included in two formats: in printed form in this book, and in TEST*ware*® format on the enclosed CD. **We recommend that you begin your preparation by first taking the practice exams on your computer.** The software provides timed conditions, automatic scoring, and scoring information that makes it easier to target your strengths and weaknesses.

ABOUT THE EXAM

Who takes the CLEP Analyzing and Interpreting Literature exam and what is it used for?

CLEP (College-Level Examination Program) examinations are usually taken by people who have acquired knowledge outside the classroom and wish to bypass certain college courses and earn college credit. The CLEP Program is designed to reward students for learning—no matter where or how that knowledge was acquired. The CLEP is the most widely accepted credit-by-examination program in the country.

Although most CLEP candidates are adults returning to college, many graduating high school seniors, enrolled college students, and international students also take the exams to earn college credit or to demonstrate their ability to perform at the college level. There are no prerequisites, such as age or educational status, for taking CLEP examinations. However, you must meet any specific requirements of the particular institution from which you wish to receive CLEP credit.

Most CLEP examinations include material usually covered in an undergraduate course with a similar title to that of the exam (e.g., Analyzing & Interpreting Literature). However, five of the exams do not deal with subject matter covered in any particular course but rather with material taken as general requirements during the first two years of college. These general exams are College Composition or College Composition Modular, Humanities, College Mathematics, Natural Sciences, and Social Sciences and History.

Who administers the exam?

The CLEP is developed by the College Board, is administered by Educational Testing Service (ETS), and involves the assistance of educators throughout the country. The test development process is designed and implemented to ensure that the content and difficulty level of the test are appropriate.

When and where is the exam given?

The CLEP Analyzing and Interpreting Literature exam is administered each month throughout the year at more than 1,400 test centers in the U.S. and can be arranged for candidates abroad on request. To find the test center nearest you and to register for the exam, you should contact the CLEP program at:

CLEP Services
PO Box 6601
Princeton, NJ 08541-6601
Phone: (800) 257-9558
Website: www.collegeboard.com
E-mail: clep@info.collegeboard.org

Military Personnel, Veterans, and CLEP

CLEP exams are available free of charge to eligible military personnel and eligible civilian employees. All the CLEP exams are available at test centers on college campuses and military bases. In addition, the College Board has developed a paper-based version of 14 high-volume/high-pass-rate CLEP tests for DANTES Test Centers. Contact the Educational Services Officer or Navy College Education Specialist for more information. Visit the College Board website for details about CLEP opportunities for military personnel.

Eligible U.S. veterans can claim reimbursement for CLEP exams and administration fees pursuant to provisions of the Veterans Benefits Improvement Act of 2004. For details on eligibility and submitting a claim for reimbursement, visit the U.S. Department of Veterans Affairs website at *www.gibill.va.gov/pamphlets/testing.htm*.

SSD Accommodations for Students with Disabilities

Many students qualify for extra time to take the CLEP Analyzing & Interpreting Literature exam, but you must make these arrangements in advance. For information, contact:

College Board Services for Students with Disabilities
PO Box 6226
Princeton, NJ 08541-6226
Phone: (609) 771-7137 Mon.–Fri. 8 A.M. to 6 P.M. (Eastern time)
TTY: (609) 882-4118
Fax: (609) 771-7944
E-mail: ssd@info.collegeboard.org

Our TEST*ware*® can be adapted ⁀ᴐ accommodate your time extension. This allows you to practice under the same extended-time accommodations that you will receive on the actual test day. To customize your TEST*ware*® to suit the most common extensions, visit our website at *www. rea.com/ssd*.

HOW TO USE THIS BOOK

What do I study first?

Read over the course review and the suggestions for test taking, take the first practice test to determine your area(s) of weakness, and then go back and focus your study on those specific problems. Studying the reviews thoroughly will reinforce the basic skills you will need to do well on the exam. Make sure to take the practice tests to become familiar with the format and procedures involved with taking the actual exam.

To best utilize your study time, follow our Independent Study Schedule located in the front of this book. The schedule is based on a six-week program, but it can be condensed to three weeks if necessary by combining each two-week period into one.

When should I start studying?

It is never too early to start studying for the CLEP Analyzing and Interpreting Literature exam. The earlier you begin, the more time you will have to sharpen your skills. Do not procrastinate! Last-minute cramming is *not* an effective way to study, since it does not allow you the time needed to learn the test material. The sooner you learn the format of the exam, the more time you will have to familiarize yourself with it.

FORMAT OF THE CLEP ANALYZING AND INTERPRETING LITERATURE EXAM

The CLEP Analyzing and Interpreting Literature exam is composed of 80 multiple-choice questions, each with five possible answer choices, to be answered in two separately timed 45-minute sections. In this book we give you 10 additional multiple-choice questions.

The subject material on the exam is what is usually covered in a two-semester college-level class. Although knowledge of specific works is not required, the student is assumed to have an extensive background in the areas of prose, poetry, and drama. They are divided into the following percentages:

35–45% Poetry
35–45% Prose (fiction and nonfiction)
15–30% Drama

SCALED-SCORE CONVERSION TABLE

Raw Score	Scaled Score	Course Grade	Raw Score	Scaled Score	Course Grade
80	80	A	39	52	C
79	80	A	38	51	C
78	79	A	37	51	C
77	79	A	36	50	C
76	78	A	35	50	C
75	77	A	34	49	C
74	76	A	33	49	C
73	76	A	32	48	D
72	75	A	31	47	D
71	75	A	30	46	D
70	74	A	29	45	D
69	73	A	28	45	D
68	72	A	27	44	D
67	71	A	26	44	D
66	70	A	25	43	D
65	69	A	24	43	D
64	68	A	23	42	D
63	67	A	22	42	D
62	66	A	21	41	F
61	65	A	20	40	F
60	64	A	19	40	F
59	63	A	18	39	F
58	62	A	17	38	F
57	61	A	16	38	F
56	61	A	15	37	F
55	60	B	14	36	F
54	60	B	13	35	F
53	59	B	12	34	F
52	58	B	11	33	F
51	58	B	10	32	F
50	57	B	9	30	F
49	57	B	8	28	F
48	56	B	7	26	F
47	56	B	6	24	F
46	55	B	5	22	F
45	55	B	4	20	F
44	55	B	3	20	F
43	54	C	2	20	F
42	54	C	1	20	F
41	53	C			
40	53	C			

* With the advent of computer-based testing, the College-Level Examination Program uses a single across-the-board credit-granting score of 50 for all 34 CLEP computer-based exams. This table is provided for scoring REA practice tests only and recommends a minimum scaled score of 49. This score is equivalent to the score an individual would receive for having attained a C average in the corresponding college course.

The three forms of literary expression are broken down as follows:

30–45%	American Literature
50–65%	British Literature
5–15%	Works in Translation

The above areas are further divided into these time periods:

3–7%	Classical and Pre-Renaissance
20–30%	Renaissance and Seventeenth Century
35–45%	Eighteenth and Nineteenth Centuries
25–35%	Twentieth Century

ABOUT OUR COURSE REVIEW

The literature review in this book is designed to further students' understanding of the test material. It is broken down into the three exam areas of prose, poetry, and drama. Along with a discussion of the literary genres, terms, and devices found on the exam, the review also provides techniques that students can use to enhance their analytical skills.

SCORING YOUR PRACTICE TESTS

How do I score my practice tests?

The CLEP Analyzing and Interpreting Literature exam is scored on a scale of 20 to 80. To score your practice tests, count up the number of correct answers. This is your total raw score. Convert your raw score to a scaled score using the conversion table on the following page. (**Note:** The conversion table provides only an *estimate* of your scaled score. Scaled scores can and do vary over time, and in no case should a sample test be taken as a precise predictor of test performance. Nonetheless, our scoring table allows you to judge your level of performance within a reasonable scoring range.)

When will I receive my score report?

A scoring printout will be made available to you immediately after you finish. A score report for the optional free-response section (which is graded by human readers), however, will arrive about three weeks after you take the test. Your scores are reported only to you, unless you ask to have them sent elsewhere. If you want your scores reported to a college or other institution, you must ask that this be done at the time you take the exam. Since your scores are kept on file for 20 years, you may also request transcripts from ETS at a later date.

The optional 90-minute free-response section, three samples of which you will find in the back of this book, is required by some colleges in addition to the 90-minute multiple-choice test. It is graded by the faculty of the college you designate. Check with your college for details.

STUDYING FOR THE CLEP ANALYZING AND INTERPRETING LITERATURE EXAM

It is very important for you to choose the time and place for studying that works best for you. Some students may set aside a certain number of hours every morning, while others may choose to study at night before going to sleep. Other students may study during the day, while waiting on a line, or even while eating lunch. Only you can determine when and where your study time will be most effective. But be consistent and use your time wisely. Work out a study routine and stick to it!

When you take the practice tests, try to make your testing conditions as much like the actual test as possible. Turn your television and radio off, and sit down at a quiet table free from distraction. Make sure to time yourself. Start off by setting a timer for the time that is allotted for each section, and be sure to reset the timer for the appropriate amount of time when you start a new section.

As you complete each practice test, score your test and thoroughly review the explanations to the questions you answered incorrectly; however, do not review too much at one time. Concentrate on one problem area at a time by reviewing the question and explanation, and by studying our review until you are confident that you completely understand the material.

Keep track of your scores and mark them on the Scoring Worksheet. By doing so, you will be able to gauge your progress and discover general weaknesses in particular sections. You should carefully study the reviews that cover your areas of difficulty, as this will build your skills in those areas.

TEST-TAKING TIPS

Although you may not be familiar with computer-based standardized tests such as the CLEP Analyzing and Interpreting Literature exam, there are many ways to acquaint yourself with this type of examination and help alleviate your test-taking anxieties. Listed below are ways to help you become accustomed to the CLEP, some of which may be applied to other standardized tests as well.

Become comfortable with the format of the exam. CLEP computer-based tests (CBTs) are *not adaptive* but rather fixed-length tests. In a sense, this makes them kin to the familiar paper-and-pencil exam in that you have the same flexibility to go back and review your work in each section. Moreover, the format isn't very different from the paper-and-pencil CLEP. When you are practicing, simulate the conditions under which you will be taking the actual test. Stay calm and pace yourself. After simulating the test only a couple of times, you will boost your chances of doing well, and you will be able to sit down for the actual exam with greater confidence. One more thing: you're likely to see some so-called pretest questions on the CBT, but you won't know which they are and they won't be scored.

Read all of the possible answers. Just because you think you have found the correct response, do not automatically assume that it is the best answer. Read through each choice to be sure that you are not making a mistake by jumping to conclusions.

Use the process of elimination. Go through each answer to a question and eliminate as many of the answer choices as possible. By eliminating just two answer choices, you give yourself a better chance of getting the item correct, since there will only be three choices left from which to make your guess.

Work quickly and steadily. You will have only 90 minutes to work on 80 questions in each section, so work quickly and steadily to avoid focusing on any one question too long. Taking the practice tests in this book will help you learn to budget your time.

Learn the directions and format for each section of the test. Familiarizing yourself with the directions and format of the exam will save you valuable time on the day of the actual test. Familiarize yourself with the CLEP CBT screen beforehand by logging on to the College Board website. Waiting until test day to see what it looks like in the pretest tutorial risks injecting needless anxiety into your testing experience.

Be sure that your answer registers before you go to the next item. Look at the screen to see that your mouse click causes the pointer to darken the proper oval. This takes far less effort than darkening an oval on paper, but don't lull yourself into taking less care!

THE DAY OF THE EXAM

On the day of the test, you should wake up early (after a decent night's rest, one would hope) and have a good breakfast. Make sure to dress comfortably, so that you are not distracted by being too hot or too cold while taking the test. Also plan to arrive at the test center early. This will allow you to collect your thoughts and relax before the test, and will also spare you the anxiety that comes with being late. As an added incentive to make sure you arrive early, keep in mind that *no one will be allowed into the test session after the test has begun.*

Before you leave for the test center, make sure that you have your admission form and another form of identification, which must contain a recent photograph, your name, and signature (i.e., driver's license, student identification card, or current alien registration card). You will not be admitted to the test center if you do not have proper identification. Consult College Board publications (including the Collegeboard.com website) for details.

During the Exam

Once you enter the test center, follow all of the rules and instructions given by the test supervisor. If you do not, you risk being dismissed from the test and having your scores canceled.

Finally, the exam will be upon you. Here's what to expect:

♦   Scrap paper will be provided to you for all CLEP CBT examinations.

♦   At times your computer may seem to slow down. Don't worry: the built-in timer will not advance until your next question is fully loaded and visible on screen.

♦   Just as you can on a paper-and-pencil test, you'll be able to move freely between questions *within* a section.

♦   You'll have the option to mark questions and review them.

♦   You may wear a wristwatch to the test center, but it cannot make any noise, which could disturb your fellow test takers.

♦   No computers, dictionaries, textbooks, notebooks, scrap paper, briefcases, or packages will be permitted into the test center; drinking, smoking, and eating are prohibited.

After the Exam

Once you have informed the test center administrator that you've finished, you will end your session on the computer, which in turn will generate the printout of a score report. Then go home and relax—you deserve it!

CHAPTER 2
LITERATURE
REVIEW

Chapter 2

LITERATURE REVIEW

PROSE

General Rules and Ideas

Why do people write prose? Certainly such a question has a built-in counter: As opposed to writing what, poetry? One possible answer is that the person is a poor poet. The requirements and restrictions of the various genres make different demands upon a writer; most writers find their niche and stay there, secure in their private "comfort zone." Shakespeare did not write essays; Hemingway did not write poetry. If either did venture outside of his literary domain, the world took little note.

Students are sometimes confused as to what exactly is prose. Basically, prose is **not** poetry. **Prose** is what we write and speak most of the time in our everyday intercourse: unmetered, unrhymed language. Which is not to say that prose does not have its own rhythms—language, whether written or spoken, has cadence and balance. And certainly prose can have instances of rhyme or assonance, alliteration or onomatopoeia. Language is, after all, **phonic.**

Furthermore, prose may be either **fiction** or **non-fiction**. A novel (like a short story) is fiction; an autobiography is non-fiction. While a novel (or short story) may have autobiographical elements, an autobiography is presumed to be entirely factual. Essays are usually described in other terms: expository, argumentative, persuasive, critical, narrative. Essays may have elements of either fiction or non-fiction, but are generally classed as a separate subgenre.

Satire, properly speaking, is not a genre at all, but rather a **mode**, elements of which can be found in any category of literature—from poetry and drama to novels and essays. Satire is a manifestation of authorial attitude (tone) and purpose. Our discussion of satire will be limited to its use in prose.

But we have not addressed the initial question: "Why do people write prose?" The answer depends, in part, on the writer's intent. If he wishes to tell a rather long story, filled with many characters and subplots, interlaced with motifs, symbols, and themes, with time and space to develop interrelationships and to present descriptive passages, the writer generally chooses the novel as his medium. If he believes he can present his story more compactly and less complexly, he may choose the novella or the short story.

These subgenres require from the reader a different kind of involvement than does the essay. The essay, rather than presenting a story from which the reader may discern meaning through the skillful analysis of character, plot, symbol, and language, presents a relatively straightforward account of the writer's opinion(s) on an endless array of topics. Depending upon the type of essay, the reader may become informed (expository), provoked (argumentative), persuaded, enlightened (critical), or, in the case of the narrative essay, better acquainted with the writer who wishes to illustrate a point with his story, whether it is autobiographical or fictitious.

Encountering satire in prose selections demands that the reader be sensitive to the nuances of language and form, that he detect the double-edged sword of irony, and that he correctly assess both the writer's tone and his purpose.

Readers of prose, like readers of poetry, seek aesthetic pleasure, entertainment, and knowledge, not necessarily in that order. Fiction offers worlds—real and imagined—in which characters and ideas, events and language, interact in ways familiar and unfamiliar. As readers, we take delight in the wisdom we fancy we have acquired from a novel or short story. Non-fiction offers viewpoints which we may find comforting or horrifying, amusing or sobering, presented by the author rather than by his once-removed persona. Thus, we are tempted to believe that somehow the truths presented in non-fiction are more "real" than the truths revealed by fiction. But we must resist! **Truth** is not "genre-specific."

Reading prose for the CLEP: Analyzing and Interpreting Literature is really no different from reading prose for your own purposes, except for the time constraints, of course! Becoming a competent reader is a result of practicing certain skills. Probably most important is acquiring a broad reading base. Read widely; read eclectically; read actively; read avidly. The idea is not that you might stumble onto a familiar prose selection on the CLEP and have an edge in writing about it; the idea is that your familiarity with many authors and works gives you a foundation upon which to build your understanding of **whatever** prose selection you encounter on the CLEP: Analyzing and Interpreting Literature exam. So read, read, read!

Reading Novels

Most literary handbooks will define a novel as an extended fictional prose narrative, derived from the Italian *novella*, meaning "tale, piece of news." The term "novelle," meaning short tales, was applied to works such as Boccaccio's *The Decameron*, a collection of stories which had an impact on later works such as Chaucer's *Canterbury Tales*. In most European countries, the word for **novel** is **roman**, short for **romance**, which was applied to longer verse narratives (Malory's *Morte d'Arthur*), which were later written in prose. Early romances were associated with "legendary, imaginative, and poetic material"—tales "of the long ago or the far away or the imaginatively improbable"; novels, on the other hand, were felt to be "bound by the facts of the actual world and the laws of probability" (*A Handbook to Literature*, C. Hugh Holman, p. 354).

The novel has, over some 600 years, developed into many special forms which are classified by subject matter: detective novel, psychological novel, historical novel, regional novel, picaresque novel, Gothic novel, stream-of-consciousness novel, epistolary novel, and so on. These terms, of course, are not exhaustive nor mutually exclusive. Furthermore, depending on the conventions of the author's time period, his style, and his outlook on life, his *mode* may be termed **realism**, **romanticism**, **impressionism**, **expressionism**, **naturalism**, or **neo-classicism** (Holman, p. 359).

Our earlier description of a novel ("...a rather long story, filled with many characters and subplots, interlaced with motifs, symbols, and themes, with time and space to develop interrelationships and to present descriptive passages") is satisfactory for our purposes here. The works generally included on the CLEP are those which have stood the test of time in significance, literary merit, and reader popularity. New works are incorporated into the canon which is a reflection of what works are being taught in literature classes. And teachers begin to teach those works which are included frequently among the questions. So the process is circular, but the standards remain high for inclusion.

Analyzing novels is a bit like asking the journalist's five questions: what? who? why? where? and how? The **what?** is the story, the narrative, the plot and subplots. Most students are familiar with Freytag's Pyramid, originally designed to describe the structure of a five-act drama but now widely used to analyze fiction as well. The stages generally specified are

introduction or **exposition, complication, rising action, climax, falling action,** and **denouement** or **conclusion**. As the novel's events are charted, the "change which structures the story" should emerge. There are many events in a long narrative; but generally only one set of events comprises the "real" or "significant" story.

However, subplots often parallel or serve as counterpoints to the main plot line, serving to enhance the central story. Minor characters sometimes have essentially the same conflicts and goals as the major characters, but the consequences of the outcome seem less important. Sometimes the parallels involve reversals of characters and situations, creating similar yet distinct differences in the outcomes. Nevertheless, seeing the parallels makes understanding the major plot line less difficult.

Sometimes an author divides the novel into chapters—named or unnamed, perhaps just numbered. Or he might divide the novel into "books" or "parts," with chapters as subsections. Readers should take their cue from these divisions; the author must have had some reason for them. Take note of what happens in each larger section, as well as within the smaller chapters. Whose progress is being followed? What event or occurrence is being foreshadowed or prepared for? What causal or other relationships are there between sections and events? Some writers, such as Steinbeck in *The Grapes of Wrath*, use intercalary chapters, alternating between the "real" story (the Joads) and peripheral or parallel stories (the Okies and migrants in general). Look for the pattern of such organization; try to see the interrelationships of these alternating chapters.

Of course, plots cannot happen in isolation from characters, the **who?** element of a story. Not only are there major and minor characters to consider; we need to note whether the various characters are **static** or **dynamic**. Static characters do not change in significant ways—that is, in ways which relate to the story which is structuring the novel. A character may die, i.e., change from alive to dead, and still be static, unless his death is central to the narrative. For instance, in Golding's *Lord of the Flies*, the boy with the mulberry birthmark apparently dies in a fire early in the novel. Momentous as any person's death is, this boy's death is not what the novel is about. However, when Simon is killed, and later Piggy, the narrative is directly impacted because the reason for their deaths is central to the novel's theme regarding man's innate evil. A dynamic character may change only slightly in his attitudes, but those changes may be the very ones upon which the narrative rests. For instance, Siddhartha begins as a very pure and devout Hindu but is unfulfilled spiritually. He eventually does achieve spiritual contentment, but his change is more a matter of degree than of substance. He is not an evil man who attains salvation, nor a pious man who becomes corrupt. It is the process of his search, the stages in his pilgrimage, which structure the novel *Siddhartha*.

We describe major characters or "actors" in novels as **protagonists** or **antagonists**. Built into those two terms is the Greek word **agon**, meaning "struggle." The *pro*tagonist struggles **toward** or for someone or something; the *ant(i)*agonist struggles **against** someone or something. The possible conflicts are usually cited as man against himself, man against man, man against society, or man against nature. Sometimes more than one of these conflicts appears in a story, but usually one is dominant and is the structuring device.

A character can be referred to as **stock**, meaning that he exists because the plot demands it. For instance, a Western with a gunman who robs the bank will require a number of **stock** characters: the banker's lovely daughter, the tough but kindhearted barmaid, the cowardly white-shirted citizen who sells out the hero to save his own skin, and the young freckle-faced lad who shoots the bad guy from a second-story hotel window.

Or a character can be a **stereotype**, without individuating characteristics. For instance, a sheriff in a small Southern town; a football player who is all brawn; a librarian clucking over her prized books; the cruel commandant of a POW camp.

Characters often serve as **foils** for other characters, enabling us to see one or more of them better. A classic example is Tom Sawyer, the Romantic foil for Huck Finn's Realism. Or, in Lee's *To Kill a Mockingbird*, Scout as the naive observer of events which her brother Jem, four years older, comes to understand from the perspective of the adult world.

Sometimes characters are **allegorical**, standing for qualities or concepts rather than for actual personages. For instance, Jim Casey (initials "J. C.") in *The Grapes of Wrath* is often regarded as a Christ figure, pure and self-sacrificing in his aims for the migrant workers. Or Kamala, Siddhartha's teacher in the art of love, whose name comes from the tree whose bark is used as a purgative; she purges him of his ascetic ways on his road to self-hood and spiritual fulfillment.

Other characters are fully three-dimensional, "rounded," "mimetic" of humans in all their virtue, vice, hope, despair, strength, and weakness. This verisimilitude aids the author in creating characters who are credible and plausible, without being dully predictable and mundane.

The interplay of plot and characters determines in large part the **theme** of a work, the **why?** of the story. First of all, we must distinguish between a mere topic and a genuine theme or thesis; and then between a theme and contributing *motifs*. A **topic** is a phrase, such as "man's inhumanity to man"; or "the fickle nature of fate." A **theme**, however, turns a phrase into a statement: "Man's inhumanity to man is barely concealed by 'civilization.'" Or "Man is a helpless pawn, at the mercy of fickle fate." Many writers may deal with the same topic, such as the complex nature of true love; but their themes may vary widely, from "True love will always win out in the end," to "Not even true love can survive the cruel ironies of fate."

To illustrate the relationship between plot, character, and theme, let's examine two familiar fairy tales. In "The Ugly Duckling," the structuring story line is "Once upon a time there was an ugly duckling, who in turn became a beautiful swan." In this case, the duckling did nothing to merit either his ugliness nor his eventual transformation; but he did not curse fate. He only wept and waited, lonely and outcast. And when he became beautiful, he did not gloat; he eagerly joined the other members of his flock, who greatly admired him. The theme here essentially is: "Good things come to him who waits," or "Life is unfair—you don't get what you deserve, nor deserve what you get." What happens to the theme if the ugly duckling remains an ugly duckling: "Some guys just never get a break"?

Especially rewarding to examine for the interdependence of plot and theme is "Cinderella": "Once upon a time, a lovely, sweet-natured young girl was forced to labor for and serve her ugly and ungrateful stepmother and two stepsisters. But thanks to her fairy godmother, Cinderella and the Prince marry, and live happily ever after."

We could change events (plot elements) at any point, but let's take the penultimate scene where the Prince's men come to the door with the single glass slipper. Cinderella has been shut away so that she is not present when the other women in the house try on the slipper. Suppose that the stepmother or either of the two stepsisters tries on the slipper—and it fits! Cinderella is in the back room doing the laundry, and her family waltzes out the door to the palace and she doesn't even get an invitation to the wedding. And imagine the Prince's dismay when the ugly, one-slippered lady lifts her wedding veil for the consummating kiss! Theme: "There is no justice in the world, for those of low or high station"; or "Virtue is not its own reward."

Or let's say that during the slipper-test scene, the stepsisters, stepmother, and finally Cinderella all try on the shoe, but to no avail. And then in sashays the fairy godmother, who gives them all a knowing smirk, puts out her slipper-sized foot and cackles hysterically, like the mechanical witch in the penny arcade. Theme: "You can't trust anybody these days"; or, a favorite statement of theme, "Appearances can be deceiving." The link between plot and theme is very strong, indeed.

Skilled writers often employ **motifs** to help unify their works. A motif is a detail or element of the story which is repeated throughout, and which may even become symbolic. Television shows are ready examples of the use of motifs. A medical show, with many scenes alternately set in the hospital waiting room and operating room, uses elements such as the pacing, anxious parent or loved one, the gradually filling ashtray, the large wall clock whose hands melt from one hour to another. And in the operating room, the half-masked surgeon whose brow is frequently mopped by the nurse; the gloved hand open-palmed to receive scalpel, sponge, and so on; the various oscilloscopes giving read-outs of the patient's very fragile condition; the expanding and collapsing bladder manifesting that the patient is indeed breathing; and, again, the wall clock, assuring us that this procedure is taking forever. These are all **motifs**, details which in concert help convince the reader that this story occurs in a hospital, and that the mood is pretty tense, that the medical team is doing all it can, and that Mom and Dad will be there when Junior or Sissy wakes up.

But motifs can become symbolic. The oscilloscope line quits blipping, levels out, and gives off the ominous hum. And the doctor's gloved hand sets down the scalpel and shuts off the oscilloscope. In the waiting room, Dad crushes the empty cigarette pack; Mom quits pacing and sinks into the sofa. The door to the waiting room swings shut silently behind the retreating doctor. All these elements signal "It's over, finished."

This example is very crude and mechanical, but motifs in the hands of a skillful writer are valuable devices. And in isolation, and often magnified, a single motif can become a controlling image with great significance. For instance, Emma Bovary's shoes signify her obsession with material things; and when her delicate slippers become soiled as she crosses the dewy grass to meet her lover, we sense the impurity of her act as well as its futility. Or when wise Piggy, in *Lord of the Flies,* is reduced to one lens in his specs, and finally to no specs at all, we see the loss of insight and wisdom on the island, and chaos follows.

Setting is the **where?** element of the story. But setting is also the **when** element: time of day, time of year, time period or year; it is the dramatic moment, the precise intersection of time and space when this story is being told. Setting is also the atmosphere: positive or negative ambiance, calm, chaotic, Gothic, Romantic. The question for the reader to answer is whether the setting is ultimately essential to the plot/theme, or whether it is incidental; i.e., could this story/theme have been told successfully in another time and/or place? For instance, could the theme in *Lord of the Flies* be made manifest if the boys were not on an island? Could they have been isolated in some other place? Does it matter whether the "war" which they are fleeing is WWII or WWIII or some other conflict, in terms of the theme?

Hopefully, the student will see that the four elements of plot, character, theme, and setting are intertwined and largely interdependent. A work must really be read as a whole, rather than dissected and analyzed in discrete segments.

The final question, **how?**, relates to an author's style. Style involves language (word choice), syntax (word order, sentence type, and length), the balance between narration and dialogue, the choice of narrative voice (first person participant, third person with limited omniscience), use of descriptive passages, and other aspects of the actual words on the page which are basically irrelevant to the first four elements (plot, character, theme, and setting). Stylistic differences are fairly easy to spot among such diverse writers as Jane Austen, whose style is—to today's reader— very formal and mannered; Mark Twain, whose style is very casual and colloquial; William Faulkner, whose prose often spins on without punctuation or paragraphs far longer than the reader can hold either the thought or his breath; and Hemingway, whose dense but spare, pared-down style has earned the epithet, "Less is more."

Reading Short Stories

The modern short story differs from earlier short fiction, such as the parable, fable, and tale, in its emphasis on character development through scenes rather than summary: through *showing* rather than *telling*. Gaining popularity in the Nineteenth Century, the short story generally was realistic, presenting detailed accounts of the lives of middle-class personages. This tendency toward realism dictates that the plot be grounded in *probability*, with causality fully in operation. Furthermore, the characters are human with recognizable human motivations, both social and psychological. Setting—time and place—is realistic rather than fantastic. And, as Poe stipulated, the elements of plot, character, setting, style, point of view, and theme all work toward a single *unified* effect.

However, some modern writers have stretched these boundaries and have mixed in elements of nonrealism—such as the supernatural and the fantastic—sometimes switching back and forth between realism and nonrealism, confusing the reader who is expecting conventional fiction. Barth's "Lost in the Funhouse" and Allen's "The Kugelmass Episode" are two stories which are not, strictly speaking, *realistic*. However, if the reader will approach and accept this type of story on its own terms, he will be better able to understand and appreciate them fully.

Unlike the novel, which has time and space to develop characters and interrelationships, the short story must rely on flashes of insight and revelation to develop plot and characters. The "slice of life" in a short story is of necessity much narrower than that in a novel; the time span is much shorter, the focus much tighter. To attempt anything like the panoramic canvas available to the novelist would be to view fireworks through a soda straw: occasionally pretty, but ultimately not very satisfying or enlightening.

The elements of the short story are those of the novel, discussed earlier. However, because of the compression of time and concentration of effect, probably the short story writer's most important decision is **point of view**. A narrator may be *objective*, presenting information without bias or comment. Hemingway frequently uses the objective *third-person* narrator, presenting scenes almost dramatically, i.e., with a great deal of dialogue and very little narrative, none of which directly reveals the thoughts or feelings of the characters. The third-person narrator may, however, be less objective in his presentation, directly revealing the thoughts and feelings of one or more of the characters, as Chopin does in "The Story of an Hour." We say that such a narrator is fully or partially *omniscient*, depending on how complete his knowledge is of the characters' psychological and emotional makeup. The least objective narrator is the *first-person* narrator, who presents information from the perspective of a single character who is a participant in the action. Such a narrative choice allows the author to present the discrepancies between the writer's/reader's perceptions and those of the narrator.

One reason the choice of narrator, the point of view from which to tell the story, is immensely important in a short story is that the narrator reveals character and event in ways which affect our understanding of theme. For instance, in Faulkner's "A Rose for Emily," the unnamed narrator who seems to be a townsperson recounts the story out of chronological order, juxtaposing events whose causality and significance are uncertain. The narrator withholds information which would explain events being presented, letting the reader puzzle over Emily Grierson's motivations, a device common in detective fiction. In fact, the narrator presents contradictory information, making the reader alternately pity and resent the spinster. When we examine the imagery and conclude that Miss Emily and her house represent the decay and decadence of the Old South which resisted the invasion of "progress" from the North, we see the importance of setting and symbol in relation to theme.

Similarly, in Mansfield's "Bliss," the abundant description of setting creates the controlling image of the lovely pear tree. But this symbol of fecundity becomes ironic when Bertha Young belatedly feels sincere and overwhelming desire for her husband. The third-person narrator's omniscience is limited to Bertha's thoughts and feelings; otherwise we would have seen her husband's infidelity with Miss Fulton.

In O'Connor's "Good Country People," the narrator is broadly omniscient, but the reader is still taken by surprise at the cruelty of the Bible salesman who seduces Joy-Hulga. That he steals her artificial leg is perhaps poetic justice, since she (with her numerous degrees) had fully intended to seduce him ("just good country people"). The story's title, the characters' names—Hopewell, Freeman, Joy; the salesman's professed Christianity, the Bibles hollowed out to hold whiskey and condoms, add to the irony of Mrs. Freeman's final comment on the young man: "Some can't be that simple... I know I never could."

The *initiation story* frequently employs the first-person narrator. To demonstrate the subtle differences which can occur in stories which ostensibly have the same point of view and general theme, let's look at three: "A Christmas Memory" (Capote), "Araby" (Joyce), and "A & P" (Updike).

Early in "A Christmas Memory," Capote's narrator identifies himself:

> The person to whom she is speaking is myself. I am seven; she is sixty-something. We are cousins, very distant ones, and we have lived together—well, as long as I can remember. Other people inhabit the house, relatives; and though they have power over us, and frequently make us cry, we are not, on the whole, too much aware of them. We are each other's best friend. She calls me Buddy, in memory of a boy who was formerly her best friend. The other Buddy died in the 1880s, when she was still a child. She is still a child.

Buddy and his cousin, who is called only "my friend," save their meager earnings throughout the year in order to make fruitcakes at Christmas to give mainly to "persons we've met maybe once, perhaps not at all... Like President Roosevelt.... Or Abner Packer, the driver of the six o'clock bus from Mobile, who exchanges waves with us everyday...." Their gifts to one another each year are always handmade, often duplicates of the year before, like the kites they present on what was to be their last Christmas together.

Away at boarding school, when Buddy receives word of his friend's death, it "merely confirms a piece of news some secret vein had already received, severing from me an irreplaceable part of myself, letting it loose like a kite on a broken string. That is why, walking across a school campus on this particular December morning, I keep searching the sky. As if I expected to see, rather like hearts, a lost pair of kites hurrying toward heaven."

Buddy's characterizations of his friend are also self-revelatory. He and she are peers, equals, despite their vast age difference. They are both totally unselfish, joying in the simple activities mandated by their economic circumstances. They are both "children."

The story is told in present tense, making the memories from the first paragraphs seem as "real" and immediate as those from many years later. And Buddy's responses from the early years ("Well, I'm disappointed. Who wouldn't be? With socks, a Sunday school shirt, some handkerchiefs, a hand-me-down sweater and a year's subscription to a religious magazine for children, *The Little Shepherd*. It makes me boil. It really does.") are as true to his seven-year-old's perspective, as are those when he, much older, has left home ("I have a new home too. But it doesn't count. Home is where my friend is, and there I never go.").

The youthful narrator in "A & P" also uses present tense, but not consistently, which gives his narrative a very colloquial, even unschooled flavor. Like Buddy, Sammy identifies himself in the opening paragraph: "In walks these three girls in nothing but bathing suits. I'm in the third checkout slot, with my back to the door, so I don't see them until they're over by the bread." And later, "Stokesie's married, with two babies chalked up on his fuselage already, but as far as I can tell that's the only difference. He's twenty-two, and I was nineteen this April." The girls incur the wrath of the store manager, who scolds them for their inappropriate dress. And Sammy, in his adolescent idealism, quits on the spot; although he realizes that he does not want to "do this" to his parents, he tells us "... it seems to me that once you begin a gesture it's fatal not to go through with it." But his *beau geste* is ill-spent: "I look around for my girls, but they're gone, of course.... I could see Lengel in my place in the slot, checking the sheep through. His face was dark gray and his back stiff, as if he'd just had an injection of iron, and my stomach kind of fell as I felt how hard the world was going to be to me hereafter."

Like Buddy, Sammy tells his story from a perch not too distant from the events he recounts. Both narrators still feel the immediacy of their rites of passage very strongly. Buddy, however, reveals himself to be a more admirable character, perhaps because his story occurs mainly when he is seven—children tend not to be reckless in the way that Sammy is. Sammy was performing for an audience, doing things he knew would cause pain to himself and his family, for the sake of those three girls who never gave him the slightest encouragement and whom he would probably never even see again.

In "Araby," the unnamed narrator tells of a boyhood crush he had on the older sister of one of his chums: "I thought little of the future. I did not know whether I would ever speak to her or not or, if I spoke to her, how I could tell her of my confused adoration. But my body was like a harp and her words and gestures were like fingers running upon the wires." She asks the boy if he is going to Araby, a "splendid bazaar," and reveals that she cannot. He promises to go himself and bring her something. But his uncle's late homecoming delays the boy's excursion until the bazaar is nearly closed for the night, and he is unable to find an appropriate gift. Forlornly, "I turned away slowly and walked down the middle of the bazaar.... Gazing up into the darkness I saw myself as a creature driven and derided by vanity; and my eyes burned with anguish and anger." This narrator is recounting his story from much further away than either Buddy or Sammy tells his own. The narrator of "Araby" has the perspective of an adult, looking back at a very important event in his boyhood. His "voice" reflects wisdom born of experience. The incident was very painful then; but its memory, while poignant, is no longer devastating. Like Sammy, this narrator sees the dichotomy between his adolescent idealism and the mundane reality of "romance." However, the difference is in the narrator's ability to turn the light on himself; Sammy is still so close to the incident that he very likely would whip off his checker's apron again if the girls returned to the A & P. The "Araby" narrator has "mellowed" and can see the futility—and the necessity—of adolescent love.

Reading Essays

Essays fall into four rough categories: **speculative**, **argumentative**, **narrative**, and **expository**. Depending on the writer's purpose, his essay will fit more or less into one or these groupings.

The **speculative** essay is so named because, as its Latin root suggests, it *looks* at ideas; explores them rather than explains them. While the speculative essay may be said to be *meditative*, it often makes one or more points. But the thesis may not be as obvious or clear-cut as that in an expository or argumentative essay. The writer deals with ideas in an associative manner, playing with ideas in a looser structure than he would in an expository or argumentative essay. This "flow" may even produce *intercalary* paragraphs, which present alternately a narrative of sorts and thoughtful responses to the events being recounted, as in White's "The Ring of Time."

The purposes of the **argumentative** essay, on the other hand, are always clear: to present a point and provide evidence, which may be factual or anecdotal, and to support it. The structure is usually very formal, as in a debate, with counterpositions and counterarguments. Whatever the organizational pattern, the writer's intent in an argumentative essay is to persuade his reader of the validity of some claim, as Bacon does in "Of Love."

Narrative and **expository** essays have elements of both the speculative and argumentative modes. The narrative essay may recount an incident or a series of incidents and is almost always autobiographical, in order to make a point, as in Orwell's "Shooting an Elephant." The informality of the storytelling makes the narrative essay less insistent than the argumentative essay, but more directed than the speculative essay.

Students are probably most familiar with the **expository** essay, the primary purpose of which is to explain and clarify ideas. While the expository essay may have narrative elements, that aspect is minor and subservient to that of explanation. Furthermore, while nearly all essays have some element of persuasion, argumentation is incidental in the expository essay. In any event, the four categories—speculative, argumentative, narrative, and expository—are neither exhaustive nor mutually exclusive.

As non-fiction, essays have a different set of elements from novels and short stories: **voice**, **style**, **structure**, and **thought**.

Voice in non-fiction is similar to the narrator's tone in fiction; but the major difference is in who is "speaking." In fiction, the author is not the speaker—the **narrator** is the speaker. Students sometimes have difficulty with this distinction, but it is necessary if we are to preserve the integrity of the fictive "story." In an essay, however, the author speaks directly to the reader, even if he is presenting ideas which he may not actually espouse personally—as in a satire. This directness creates the writer's **tone**, his attitude toward his subject.

Style in non-fiction derives from the same elements as style in fiction: word choice, syntax, balance between dialogue and narration, voice, use of description—those things specifically related to words on the page. Generally speaking, an argumentative essay will be written in a more formal style than will a narrative essay, and a meditative essay will be less formal than an expository essay. But such generalizations are only descriptive, not prescriptive.

Structure and **thought**, the final elements of essays, are so intertwined as to be inextricable. We must be aware that to change the structure of an essay will alter its meaning. For instance, in White's "The Ring of Time," to abandon the *intercalary* paragraph organization, separating the paragraphs which narrate the scenes with the young circus rider from those which reflect on the circularity and linearity of time, would alter our understanding of the essay's thesis. Writers signal structural shifts with alterations in focus, as well as with visual clues (spacing), verbal clues—(*but, therefore, however*), or shifts in the kind of information being presented (personal, scientific, etc).

Thought is perhaps the single element which most distinguishes nonfiction from fiction. The essayist chooses his form not to tell a story but to present an idea. Whether he chooses the speculative, narrative, argumentative, or expository format, the essayist has something on his mind that he wants to convey to his readers. And it is this idea which we are after when we analyze his essay.

Often anthologized is Orwell's "Shooting an Elephant," a narrative essay recounting the writer's (presumably) experience in Burma as an officer of the British law that ruled the poverty-ridden people of a small town. Orwell begins with two paragraphs which explain that, as a white, European authority figure, he was subjected to taunts and abuse by the natives. Ironically, he sympathized with the Burmese and harbored fairly strong anti-British feelings regarding the imperialists as the oppressors rather than the saviors. He tells us that he felt caught, trapped between his position of authority which he himself resented and the hatred of those he was required to oversee.

The body of the essay—some 11 paragraphs—relates the incident with an otherwise tame elephant gone "must" which had brought chaos and destruction to the village. Only occasionally does Orwell interrupt the narrative to reveal his reactions directly, but his descriptions of the Burmese are sympathetically drawn. The language is heavily connotative, revealing the helplessness of the villagers against both the elephant and the miserable circumstances of their lives.

Orwell recounts how, having sent for an elephant gun, he found that he was compelled to shoot the animal, even though its destruction was by now unwarranted and even ill-advised, given the value of the elephant to the village. But the people expected it, demanded it; the white man realized that he did not have dominion over these people of color after all. They were in charge, not he.

To make matters worse, Orwell bungles the "murder" of the beast, which takes half an hour to die in great agony. And in the aftermath of discussions of the rightness or wrongness of his action, Orwell wonders if anyone realizes he killed the elephant only to save face. It is the final sentence of the final paragraph which directly reveals the author's feelings, although he has made numerous indirect references to them throughout the essay. Coupled with the opening paragraphs, this conclusion presents British imperialism of the period in a very negative light: "the unable doing the unnecessary to the ungrateful."

Having discovered Orwell's main idea, we must look at the other elements (voice, style, structure) to see *how* he communicates it to the reader. The voice of the first-person narrative is fairly formal, yet remarkably candid, using connotation to color our perception of the events. Orwell's narrative has many complex sentences, with vivid descriptive phrases in series, drawing our eye along the landscape and through the crowds as he ponders his next move. Structurally, the essay first presents a premise about British imperialism, then moves to a gripping account of the officer's reluctant shooting of the elephant; and ends with an admission of his own culpability as an agent of the institution he detests. Orwell frequently signals shifts between his role as officer and his responses as a humane personage with *but*, or with dashes to set off his responses to the events he is recounting.

Reading Satire

Satire is a *mode* which may be employed by writers of various genres: poetry, drama, fiction, non-fiction. It is more a perspective than a product.

Satire mainly exposes and ridicules, derides and denounces vice, folly, evil, stupidity, as these qualities manifest themselves in persons, groups of persons, ideas, institutions, customs, or beliefs. While the satirist has many techniques at his disposal, there are basically only two types of satire: gentle or harsh, depending on the author's intent, his audience, and his methods.

The terms *romanticism*, *realism*, and *naturalism* can help us understand the role of *satire*. Romanticism sees the world idealistically, as perfectible if not perfect. Realism sees the world as it is, with healthy doses of both good and bad. Naturalism sees the world as imperfect, with evil often triumphing over good. The satirist is closer to the naturalist than he is to the romantic or realist, for both the satirist and the naturalist focus on what is wrong with the world, intending to expose the foibles of man and his society. The difference between them lies in their techniques. The naturalist is very direct and does not necessarily employ humor; the satirist is more subtle, and does.

For instance, people plagued with overpopulation and starvation is not, on first glance, material for humor. Many works have treated such conditions with sensitivity, bringing attention to the plight of the world's unfortunate. Steinbeck's *Grapes of Wrath* is such a work. However, Swift's "A Modest Proposal" takes essentially the same circumstances and holds them up for our amused examination. How does the satirist make an un-funny topic humorous? And why would he do so?

The satirist's techniques—his weapons—include **irony**, **parody**, **reversal** or **inversion**, **hyperbole**, **understatement**, **sarcasm**, **wit**, and **invective**. By exaggerating characteristics, by saying the opposite of what he means, by using his cleverness to make cutting or even cruel remarks at the expense of his subject, the writer of satire can call the reader's attention to those things he believes are repulsive, despicable, or destructive.

Whether he uses more harsh (Juvenalian) or more gentle (Horatian) satire depends upon the writer's attitude and intent. Is he merely flaunting his clever intellect, playing with words for our amusement or to inflate his own sense of superiority? Is he probing the psychological motivations for the foolish or destructive actions of some person(s)? Is he determined to waken an unenlightened or apathetic audience, moving its members to thought or action? Are the flaws which the satirist is pointing out truly destructive or evil, or are they the faults we would all recognize in ourselves if we glanced in the mirror, not admirable but not really harmful to ourselves or society? Is the author amused, sympathetic, objective, irritated, scornful, bitter, pessimistic, mocking? The reader needs to identify the satirist's purpose and tone. Its subtlety sometimes makes satire a difficult mode to detect and to understand.

Irony is perhaps the satirist's most powerful weapon. The basis of irony is inversion or reversal, doing or saying the opposite or the unexpected. Shakespeare's famous sonnet beginning "My mistress' eyes are nothing like the sun..." is an ironic tribute to the speaker's beloved, who, he finally declares is "as rare/As any she belied with false compare." At the same time, Shakespeare is poking fun at the sonnet form as it was used by his contemporaries—himself included—to extol the virtues of their ladies. By selecting a woman who, by his own description, is physically unattractive in every way imaginable, and using the conventions of the love sonnet to present her many flaws, he has inverted the sonnet tradition. And then by asserting that she compares favorably with any of the other ladies whose poet-lovers have lied about their virtues, he presents us with the unexpected twist. Thus, he satirizes both the love sonnet form and its subject by using irony.

Other notable poetic satires include Koch's "Variations on a Theme by William Carlos Williams," in which he parodies Williams' "This Is Just to Say." Koch focuses on the simplicity and directness of Williams' imagery and makes the form and ideas seem foolish and trivial. In "Boom!," Nemerov takes issue with a pastor's assertion that modern technology has resulted in a concomitant rise in religious activities and spiritual values. Nemerov catalogues the instant, disposable, and extravagant aspects of Americans' lifestyles, which result in "pray as you go... pilgrims" for whom religion is another convenience, commercial rather than spiritual.

Satire in drama is also common; Wilde's "The Importance of Being Earnest" is wonderfully funny in its constant word play (notably on the name *Ernest*) and its relentless ridiculing of the superficiality which Wilde saw as characteristic of British gentry. Barrie's "The Admirable Chrichton" has a similar theme, with the added assertion that it is the "lower" or servant class which is truly superior—again, the ironic reversal so common in satire. Both of these plays are mild in their ridicule; the authors do not expect or desire any change in society or in the viewer. The satire is gentle; the satirists are amused, or perhaps bemused at the society whose foibles they expose.

Classic novels which employ satire include Swift's *Gulliver's Travels* and Voltaire's *Candide*, both of which fairly vigorously attack aspects of the religions, governments, and prevailing intellectual beliefs of their respective societies. A modern novel which uses satire is Heller's *Catch-22*, which is basically an attack on war and the government's bureaucratic bungling of men and materiel, specifically in WWII. But by extension, Heller is also viewing with contempt the unmotivated, illogical, capricious behavior of all institutions which operate by that basic law: "catch-22." Like Swift and Voltaire, Heller is angry. And although his work, like the other two, has humor, wit, exaggeration, and irony, his purpose is more than intellectual entertainment for his readers. Heller hopes for reform.

Heller's attack is frontal, his assault direct. Swift had to couch his tale in a fantastic setting with imaginary creatures in order to present his views with impunity. The audience, as well as the times, also affect the satirist's work. If the audience is hostile, the writer must veil his theme; if the audience is indifferent, he must jolt them with bitter and reviling language if he desires change. If he does not fear reprisals, the satirist may take any tone he pleases.

We can see satire in operation in two adaptations of the biblical story of King Solomon, who settled the dispute between two mothers regarding an infant: Cut the baby in two and divide it between you, he told them. The rightful mother protested and was promptly awarded the child. The story is meant to attest to the King's wisdom and understanding of parental love, in this case.

However, Twain's Huck Finn has some difficulty persuading runaway slave Jim that Solomon was wise. Jim insists that Solomon, having fathered "'bout five million chillen," was "waseful.... *He* as soon chop a chile in two as a cat. Dey's plenty mo'. A chile cr two, mo' er less, warn't no consekens to Solermun, dad fetch him!" Twain is ridiculing not only Jim's ingenuousness, as he does throughout the novel; he is also deflating time-honored beliefs about the Bible and its traditional heroes, as he earlier does with the account of Moses and the "bulrushers." While Twain's tone is fairly mild, his intent shows through as serious; Twain was disgusted with traditional Christianity and its hypocritical followers, as we see later in *Huck Finn* when young Buck Grangerford is murdered in the feud with the Shepherdsons: "I wished I hadn't ever come ashore that night to see such things."

A second satiric variation on the Solomon theme appears in Asprin's *Myth Adventures*, in the volume *Hit or Myth*. Skeebe, the narrator, realizes that he, as king pro-tem, must render a decision regarding the ownership of a cat. Hoping to inspire them to compromise, he decrees that they divide the cat between them: "Instead they thanked me for my wisdom, shook hands, and left smiling, presumably to carve up their cat." He concludes that many of the citizens of this realm "don't have both oars in the water," a conclusion very like Huck's: "I never see such a nigger. If he got a notion in his head once, there warn't no getting it out again." The citizens' unthinking acceptance of the infallibility of authority is as laughable as Jim's out-of-hand rejection of Solomon's wisdom because no wise man would "want to live in the mids' er sich a blim-blammin' all de time" as would prevail in the harem with the King's "million wives."

POETRY

Opening a book to study for an examination is perhaps the worst occasion on which to read poetry, or about poetry, because above all, poetry should be enjoyed; it is definitely "reading for pleasure." This last phrase seems to have developed recently to describe the reading we do other than for information or for study. Perhaps you personally would not choose poetry as pleasure reading because of the bad name poetry has received over the years. Some students regard the "old" poetry such as Donne's or Shelley's as effete (for "wimps" and "nerds" only, in current language), or modern poetry as too difficult or weird. It is hard to imagine that poetry was the "current language" for students growing up in the Elizabethan or Romantic eras. Whereas in our world information can be retrieved in a nanosecond, in those worlds time was plentiful to sit down, clear the mind, and let poetry take over. Very often the meaning of a poem does not come across in a nanosecond and for the modern student this proves very frustrating. Sometimes it takes years for a poem to take on meaning—the reader simply knows that the poem sounds good and it provokes an emotional response that cannot be explained. With time, more emotional experience, more reading of similar experiences, more life, the reader comes to a meaning of that poem that satisfies for the time being. In a few more years that poem may take on a whole new meaning.

This is all very well for reading for pleasure, but you are now called upon, in your present experience, to learn poetry for an important examination. Perhaps the first step in the learning process is to answer the question, "Why do people write poetry?" An easy answer is that they wish to convey an experience, an emotion, an insight, or an observation in a startling or satisfying way, one that remains in the memory for years. But why not use a straightforward sentence or paragraph? Why wrap up that valuable insight in fancy words, rhyme, paradox, meter, allusion, symbolism, and all the other seeming mumbo-jumbo that explicators of poetry use? Why not just come right out and say it like "normal people" do? An easy answer to these questions is that poetry is not a vehicle for conveying meaning alone. Gerard Manley Hopkins, one of the great innovators of rhythm in poetry, claimed that poetry should be "heard for its own sake and interest even over and above its interest or meaning." Poetry provides intellectual stimulus of course. One of the best ways of studying a poem is to consider it a jigsaw puzzle presented to you whole, an integral work of art, which can be taken apart piece by piece (word by word), analyzed scientifically, labelled, and put back together again into a whole, and then the meaning is complete. But people write poetry to convey more than meaning.

T.S. Eliot maintained that the meaning of the poem existed purely to distract us "while the poem did its work." One interpretation of a poem's "work" is that it changes us in some way. We see the world in a new way because of the way the poet has seen it and told us about it. Maybe one of the reasons people write poetry is to encourage us to *see* things in the first place. Simple things like daffodils take on a whole new aspect when we read the way Wordsworth saw them. Why did Wordsworth write that poem? His sister had written an excellent account of the scene in her journal. Wordsworth not only evokes nature as we have never seen it before, alive, joyous, exuberant, he shows nature's healing powers, its restorative quality as the scene flashes "upon that inward eye/Which is the bliss of solitude." Bent over your books studying, how many times has a similar quality of nature's power in the memory come to you? Maybe for you a summer beach scene rather than daffodils by the lake is more meaningful, but the poet captures a moment that we have all experienced. The poet's magic is to make that moment new again.

If poets enhance our power of sight they also awaken the other senses as powerfully. We can hear Emily Dickinson's snake in the repeated "s" sound of the lines:

His notice sudden is—
The Grass divides as with a Comb—
A spotted shaft is seen—

and because of the very present sense of sound, we experience the indrawn gasp of breath of fear when the snake appears. We can touch the little chimneysweep's hair "that curled like a lamb's back" in William Blake's poetry, and because of that tactile sense we are even more shocked to read that the child's hair is all shaved off so that the soot will not spoil its whiteness. We can smell the poison gas as Wilfred Owen's soldiers fumble with their gas masks; we can taste the blood gurgling in the poisoned lungs.

Poets write, then, to awaken the senses. They have crucial ideas but the words they use are often more important than the meaning. More important still than ideas and sense awakening is the poet's appeal to the emotions. And it is precisely this area that disturbs a number of students. Our modern society tends to block out emotions—we need reviews to tell us if we enjoyed a film or a critic's praise to see if a play or novel is worth our time. We hesitate to laugh at something in case it is not the "in" thing to do. We certainly do not cry—at least in front of others. Poets write to overcome that blocking (very often it is their own blocking of emotion they seek to alleviate), but that is not to say that poetry immediately sets us laughing, crying, loving, or hating. The important fact about the emotional release in poetry is that poets help us explore our own emotions, sometimes by shocking us, sometimes by drawing attention to balance and pattern, and sometimes by cautioning us to move carefully in this inner world.

Poets tell us nothing really new. They tell us old truths about human emotions that we begin to restructure anew, to reread our experiences in light of theirs, to reevaluate our world view. Whereas a car manual helps us understand the workings of a particular vehicle, a poem helps us understand the inner workings of human beings. Poets frequently write to help their emotional life—the writing then becomes cathartic, purging or cleansing the inner life, feeding that part of us that separates us from the animal. Many poets might paraphrase Byron, who claimed that he had to write or go mad. Writer and reader of poetry enter into a collusion, each helping the other to find significance in the human world, to find safety in a seemingly alien world.

This last point brings any reader of poetry to ask the next question: Why read poetry? One might contend that a good drama, novel, or short story might provide the same emotional experience. But a poem is much more accessible. Apart from the fact that poems are shorter than other genres, there is a unique directness to them which hinges purely on language. Poets can say in one or two lines what may take novelists and playwrights entire works to express. For example, Keats' lines—

Beauty is truth, truth beauty,—that is all
Ye know on earth, and all ye need to know—

studied, pondered, and opened to each reader's interpretations, linger in the memory with more emphasis than George Eliot's *Middlemarch*, or Ibsen's *The Wild Duck*, which endeavor to make the same point.

In your reading of poems remember that poetry is perhaps the oldest art and yet surrounds us without our even realizing it. Listeners thrilled to Homer's poetry; tribes chanted invocations to their gods; today we listen to pop-song lyrics and find ourselves, sometimes despite ourselves, repeating certain rhythmic lines. Advertisements we chuckle over or say we hate have a way of repeating themselves as we use the catchy phrase or snappy repetition. Both lyricists and advertisers cleverly use language, playing on the reader's/listener's/watcher's ability to pick up on a repeated sound or engaging rhythm or inner rhyme. Think of a time as a child when you thoroughly enjoyed poetry: nursery rhymes, ball-game rhythms, jump-rope patterns. Probably you had no idea of the meaning of the words ("Little Miss Muffet sat on a tuffet..." a tuffet?!) but you responded to the sound, the pattern. As adults we read poetry for that sense of sound and pattern. With more experience at reading poetry there is an added sense of pleasure as techniques are recognized: alliteration, onomatopoeia; forms of poetry become obvious—the sonnet, the rondelle. Even greater enjoyment comes from watching a poet's development, tracing themes and ideas, analyzing maturity in growth of imagery, use of rhythm.

To the novice reader of poetry, a poem can speak to the reader at a particular time and become an experience in itself. A freshman's experience after her mother's death exemplifies this. Shortly after the death, the student found Elizabeth Jenning's poem "Happy Families." Using the familiar names of the cards, Mrs. Beef and Master Bun, the poet describes how strangers try to help the family carry on their lives normally although one of the "happy family" is "missing." The card game continues although no one wants it to. At the end the players go back to their individual rooms and give way to their individual grief. The student described the relief at knowing that someone else had obviously experienced her situation where everyone in the family was putting up a front, strangers were being very kind, and a general emptiness prevailed because of that one missing family member. The poem satisfied. The student saw death through another's eyes; the experience was almost the same, yet helped the reader to reevaluate, to view a universal human response to grief as well as encourage her to deal with her own.

On reading a poem the brain works on several different levels: it responds to the sounds; it responds to the words themselves and their connotations; it responds to the emotions; it responds to the insights or learning of the world being revealed. For such a process poetry is a very good training ground—a boot camp—for learning how to read literature in general. All the other genres have elements of poetry within them. Learn to read poetry well and you will be a more accomplished reader, even of car manuals! Perhaps the best response to reading poetry comes from a poet herself, Emily Dickinson, who claimed that reading a book of poetry made her feel "as if the top of [her] head were taken off!"

Before such a process happens to you, here are some tips for reading poetry before and during the examination.

Tips for Preparation

1) Make a list of poets and poems you remember; analyze poems you liked, disliked, loved, hated, and were indifferent to. Find the poems. Reread them and for each one analyze your *feelings*, first of all, about the poetry itself. Have your feelings changed? Now what do you like or hate? Then paraphrase the *meaning* of each poem. Notice how the "magic" goes from the poem, i.e., in "To Daffodils," the poet sees many daffodils by the side of a lake and then thinks how the sight of them later comforts him.

2) Choose a poem at random from an anthology or one mentioned in this introduction. Read it a couple of times, preferably aloud, because the speaking voice will automatically grasp the rhythm and that will help the meaning. Do not become bogged down in individual word connotation or the meaning of the poem—let the poetry do its "work" on you; absorb the poem as a whole jigsaw puzzle.

3) Now take the puzzle apart. Look carefully at the title. Sometimes a straightforward title helps you focus. Sometimes a playful title helps you get an angle on the meaning. "Happy Families," of course, is an ironic title because the family playing the card game of that name is not happy.

4) Look carefully at the punctuation. Does the sense of a line carry from one to another? Does a particular mark of punctuation strike you as odd? Ask why that mark was used.

5) Look carefully at the words. Try to find the meaning of words with which you are not familiar within the context. Familiar words may be used differently: ask why that particular use. Having tapped into your memory bank of vocabulary and you are still at a loss, go to a dictionary. Once you have the *denotation* of the word, start wondering about the *connotation*. Put yourself in the poet's position and think why that word was used.

6) Look carefully at all the techniques being used. You will gain these as you progress through this section and through the test preparation. As soon as you come across a new idea—"caesura" perhaps—learn the word, see how it applies to poetry, where it is used. Be on the lookout for it in other poetry. Ask yourself questions such as why the poet used alliteration here; why the rhythm changes there; why the poet uses a sonnet form and which sonnet form is in use. Forcing yourself to ask the WHY questions, and answering them, will train the brain to read more perceptively. Poetry is not accidental; poets are deliberate people; they do things for specific reasons. Your task under a learning situation is to discover WHY.

7) Look carefully at the speaker. Is the poet using another persona? Who is that persona? What is revealed about the speaker? Why use that particular voice?

8) Start putting all the pieces of the puzzle together. The rhythm helps the meaning. The word choice helps the imagery. The imagery adds to the meaning. Paraphrase the meaning. Ask yourself simple questions: What is the poet saying? How can I relate to what is being said? What does this poem mean to me? What does this poem contribute to human experience?

9) Find time to read about the great names in poetry. Locate people within time areas and analyze what those times entailed. For example, the

Elizabethans saw a contest between secular love and love of God. The Romantics (Wordsworth, Coleridge, Keats, Shelley, Byron) loved nature and saw God within nature. The Victorians (Tennyson, Blake) saw nature as a threat to mankind and God, being replaced by the profit cash-nexus of the Industrial Age. The moderns (T.S. Eliot, Pound, Yeats) see God as dead and man as hollow, unwanted, and unsafe in an alien world. The Post-Moderns see life as "an accident," a comic/cosmic joke, fragmented, purposeless—often their topics will be political: apartheid, abortion, unjust imprisonment.

10) Write a poem of your own. Choose a particular style; use the sonnet form; parody a famous poem; express yourself in free verse on a crucial, personal aspect of your life. Then analyze your own poetry with the above ideas.

Tips for Test-Taking

You will have established a routine for reading poetry, but now you are under pressure, must work quickly, and will have no access to a dictionary. You cannot read aloud but you can do the following:

1) Internalize the reading—hear the reading in your head. Read through the poem two or three times following the absorbing procedure.

2) If the title and poet are supplied, analyze the title as before and determine the era of the poetry. Often this pushes you toward the meaning.

3) Look carefully at the questions which should enable you to "tap into" your learning process. Answer the ones that are immediately clear to you: form, technique, language perhaps.

4) Go back for another reading for those questions that challenge you— theme or meaning perhaps—analyze the speaker or the voice at work— paraphrase the meaning—ask the simple question "What is the poet saying?"

5) If a question asks you about a specific line, metaphor, opening or closing line, mentally highlight and re-read it, focusing on each crucial word. Internalize another reading emphasizing this area—analyze again the options you have for your answers.

6) Do not waste time on an answer that eludes you. Move on to another item and let the poetry do its "work." Very often the brain will continue working on the problem on another level of consciousness. When you go back to the difficult question, it may well become clear.

7) If you still are not sure of the answer, choose the option that you *feel* is the closest to correct.

Go home, relax, forget about the examination—read your favorite poem!

Verse and Meter

As children reading or learning poetry in school, we referred to each section of a poem as a verse. We complained we had ten verses to learn for homework. In fact the word **verse** strictly refers to a line of poetry, perhaps from the original Latin word "versus": a row or a line, and the notion of turning, "vertere," to turn or move to a new idea. In modern use we refer to poetry often as "verse" with the connotation of rhyme, rhythm, and meter; but we still recognize verse because of the positioning of lines on the page, the breaking of lines that distinguish verse from prose.

The verses we learned for homework are in fact known as **stanzas:** a grouping of lines with a metrical order and often a repeated rhyme which we know as the **rhyme scheme.** Such a scheme is shown by letters to show the repeating sounds. Byron's "Stanzas" will help you recall the word, see the use of a definite rhyme, and how to mark it:

"Stanzas"

(When a man hath no freedom to fight for at home)

When a man hath no freedom to fight for at home,	*a*
Let him combat for that of his neighbors;	*b*
Let him think of the glories of Greece and of Rome,	*a*
And get knocked on the head for his labors.	*b*
To do good to mankind is the chivalrous plan,	*c*
And is always as nobly requited;	*d*
Then battle for freedom wherever you can,	*c*
And, if not shot or hanged, you'll get knighted.	*d*

The rhyme scheme is simple: *abab* and your first question should be "Why such a simple, almost sing-song rhyme?" The simplicity reinforces the **tone** of the poem: sarcastic, cryptic, cynical. There is almost a sneer behind the words "And get knocked on the head for his labors." It is as if the poet sets out to give a lecture or at least a homily along the lines of: "Neither a lender nor a borrower be," but then undercuts the seriousness. The **irony** of the poem rests in the fact that Byron joined a freedom fighting group in Greece and died, not gloriously, but of a fever. We shall return to this poem for further discussion.

Certain types of rhyme are worth learning. The most common is the **end rhyme**, which has the rhyming word at the end of the line, bringing the line to a definite stop but setting up for a rhyming word in another line later on, as in "Stanzas": home… Rome, a perfect rhyme. **Internal rhyme** includes at least one rhyming word within the line, often for the purpose of speeding the rhythm or making it linger. Look at the effect of Byron's internal rhymes mixed with half-rhymes: "combat… for that"; "Can/And… hanged" slowing the rhythm, making the reader dwell on the harsh long "a" sound, prolonging the sneer which almost becomes a snarl of anger. **Slant rhyme**, sometimes referred to as half, off, near, or approximate rhyme, often jolts a reader who expects a perfect rhyme; poets thus use such a rhyme to express disappointment or a deliberate let-down. **Masculine rhyme** uses one-syllable words or stresses the final syllable of polysyllabic words, giving the feeling of strength and impact. **Feminine rhyme** uses a rhyme of two or more syllables, the stress not falling upon the last syllable, giving a feeling of softness and lightness, one can see that these terms for rhyme were written in a less enlightened age! The terms themselves for the rhymes are less important than realizing or at least appreciating the effects of the rhymes.

If the lines from "Stanzas" had been unrhymed and varying in metrical pattern, the verse would have been termed **free**, or to use the French term, *"Vers libre,"* not to be confused with **blank verse**, which is also unrhymed but has a strict rhythm. The Elizabethan poets Wyatt and Surrey introduced blank verse, which Shakespeare uses to such good effect in his plays, and later, Milton in the great English epic *Paradise Lost*. Free verse has become associated with "modern" poetry, often adding to its so-called obscurity because without rhyme and rhythm, poets often resort to complicated syntactical patterns, repeated phrases, awkward cadences, and parallelism. Robert Frost preferred not to use it because, as he put it, "Writing free verse is like playing tennis with the net down," suggesting that free verse is easier than rhymed and metrical. However, if you have ever tried writing such verse, you will know the problems. (Perhaps a good exercise after your learning about meter is to write some "free" verse.) T.S. Eliot, who uses the form most effectively in "The Journey of the Magi," claimed that no *"vers"* is *"libre"* for the poet who wanted to do a good job.

Such a claim for the artistry and hard work behind a poem introduces perhaps the most difficult of the skills for a poet to practice and a reader to learn: meter. This time the Greeks provide the meaning of the word from *"metron,"* meaning measure. **Meter** simply means the pattern or measure of stressed or accented words within a line of verse. When studying meter a student should note where stresses fall on syllables—that is why reading aloud is so important, because it catches the natural rhythm of the speaking voice—and if an absence of stressed syllables occurs there is always an explanation why. We "expect" stressed and unstressed syllables because that is what we use in everyday speech. We may stress one syllable over another for a certain effect, often using the definite article "THE well known author..." or the preposition "Get OUT of here!" Usually, however, we use a rising and falling rhythm, known as **iambic rhythm**. A line of poetry that alternates stressed and unstressed syllables is said to have **iambic meter**. A line of poetry with ten syllables of rising and falling stresses is known as **iambic pentameter**, best used by Shakespeare and Milton in their blank verse. The basic measuring unit in a line of poetry is called a **foot**. An **iambic foot** has one unstressed syllable followed by a stressed marked by ∪. Pentameter means "five-measure." Therefore, **iambic pentameter** has five groups of two syllables, or ten beats, to the line. Read aloud the second and fourth, sixth and eighth lines of "Stanzas," tapping the beat on your desk or your palm, and the ten beat becomes obvious. Read again with the stresses unstressed and stressed (or soft and loud, short or long, depending on what terminology works for you) and the iambic foot becomes clear.

Tapping out the other alternate lines in this poem, you will not find ten beats but twelve. The term for this line is **hexameter**, or six feet, rather than five. Other line-length names worth learning are:

monometer	one foot	**dimeter**	two feet
trimeter	three feet	**tetrameter**	four feet
heptameter	seven feet	**octameter**	eight feet

Other foot names worth learning are:

the **anapest** marked ∪ ∪ /, the most famous anapestic line being:

∪ ∪ /   ∪ ∪   / ∪   ∪ /   ∪   ∪   /

"Twas the night before Christmas, when all through the house..."

the **trochee**, marked / ∪, the most memorable trochaic line being:

/ ∪   / ∪   / ∪   / ∪

"Double double toil and trouble..."

the **dactyl** marked / ∪ ∪, the most often quoted dactylic line being:

/   ∪ ∪ / ∪ ∪

"Take her up tenderly..."

Old English poetry employs a meter known as **accentual meter**, with four stresses to the line without attention to the unstressed syllables. Contemporary poets tend not to use it, but one of the greatest innovators in rhythm and meter, Gerard Manley Hopkins, used it as the "base line" for his counterpointed "Sprung Rhythm." Living in the Nineteenth Century, Hopkins produced poetry that even today strikes the reader as "modern," in that the rhymes and rhythms often jar the ear, providing stressed syllables where we expect unstressed and vice versa. The rhythm was measured by feet of from one to four syllables, and any number of unstressed syllables. Underneath the rhythm we hear the "regular" rhythm we are used to in speech, and an intriguing counterpoint develops. One stanza from "The Caged Skylark" will show the method at work:

As a dare-gale skylark scanted in a dull cage
Man's mounting spirit in his bone-house, mean house, dwells—
That bird beyond the remembering his free fells;
This in drudgery, day-labouring-out life's age.

The stress on "That" and "This" works particularly well to draw attention to the two captives: the skylark and Man. The accentual meter in the second line reinforces the wretchedness of the human condition. No reader could possibly read that line quickly, nor fail to put the full length of the syllable on "dwells." The dash further stresses the length and the low pitch of the last word.

If at first the terms for meter are new and strange, remember that what is most important is not that you mindlessly memorize the terminology but are able to recognize the meter and analyze why the poet has used it in the particular context of the poem. For example, Shakespeare did not want the lyrical fall and rise of the iamb for his witches around the cauldron, so he employs the much more unusual trochee to suggest the gloom and mystery of the heath in "Macbeth." Many poets will "mix and match" their meter and your task as a student of poetry is to analyze why. Perhaps the poet sets up the regular greeting card meter, rising and falling rhythm, regular end-stopped rhyme. If the poet abruptly changes that pattern, there is a reason. If the poet subtly moves from a disruptive meter into a smooth one, then analyze what is going on in the meaning. If the poet is doing "a good job" as T.S. Eliot suggested, then the rhyme, rhythm, and meter should all work together in harmony to make the poem an integral whole. Answer the test essay questions to practice the points in this section and the integrity of a poem as a single unit will become clearer.

Figurative Language and Poetic Devices

It will be becoming ever more obvious that a poem is not created from mere inspiration. No doubt the initial movement for a poem has something of divine intervention: the ancients talked of being visited by the Muse of Poetry; James Joyce coined the word "epiphany" for the clear moment of power of conception in literature, but then the poet sets to, working at the expression to make it the best it can be.

Perhaps what most distinguishes poetry from any other genre is the use of figurative language—figures of speech—used through the ages to convey the poet's own particular world-view in a unique way. Words have **connotation** and **denotation**, **figurative** and **literal** meanings. We can look in the dictionary for denotation and literal meaning, but figurative language works its own peculiar magic, tapping into shared experiences within the psyche. A simple example involves the word "home." If we free-associated for awhile among a group of 20 students, we would find a number of connotations for the word, depending on the way home was for us in our experiences: comforting, scary, lonely, dark, creepy, safety, haven, hell…. However, the denotation is quite straightforward: a house or apartment or dwelling that provides shelter for an individual or family. Poets include in their skill various figures of speech to "plug into" the reader's experiences, to prompt the reader to say "I would have never thought of it in those terms but now I see!"

The most important of these skills is perhaps the **metaphor**, which compares two unlike things, feelings, or objects, and the **simile**. Metaphors are more difficult to find than **similes**, which also compare two dissimilar things but always use the words "as if" (for a clause) or "like" (for a word or phrase). Metaphors suggest the comparison; the meaning is implicit. An easy way to distinguish between the two is the simple example of the camel. **Metaphor:** the camel is the ship of the desert. **Simile**: a camel is like a ship in the desert. Both conjure up the camel's almost sliding across the desert, storing up its water as a ship must do for survival for its passengers, and the notion of the vastness of the desert parallels the sea. The metaphor somehow crystallizes the image. Metaphors can be *extended* so that an entire poem consists of a metaphor, or unfortunately they can be *mixed*. The latter rarely happens in poetry unless the poet is deliberately playing with his readers and provoking humor.

Start thinking of how many times you use similes in your own writing or speech. The secret is, as Isaac Babel once said, that similes must be "as precise as a slide rule and as natural as the smell of dill." The precision and naturalness coming together perfectly often set up an equation of comparison. A student once wrote "I felt torn apart by my loyalty to my mother and grandmother, like the turkey wishbone at Thanksgiving." We have all experienced divided loyalties. Using the graphic wishbone-tearing idea, something we have all done at Thanksgiving or have seen done lets us more easily relate to the student's experience. Another student wrote of his friends waiting for the gym class to begin "like so many captive gazelles." Again, the visual point of comparison is important but also the sense of freedom in the idea of gazelle, the speed, the grace; juxtaposing that freedom with the word "captive" is a master stroke that makes a simile striking.

The same student went on to an *extended simile* to state precisely and naturally his feelings upon going into a fistfight: "I was like the kid whose parents were killed by the crooked sheriff, waiting for high noon and the showdown that would pit a scared kid with his father's rusty old pistol against the gleaming steel of a matched pair, nestled in the black folds of the sheriff's holsters. I knew there was no way out. Surrounded by friends, I marched out into the brilliant sun, heading for the back fields of the playground, desperately trying to polish the rusty old gun." Although this student was writing in prose, his use of figurative language is poetic. He plugs into readers' movie experience with the central idea of the showdown at high noon, an **allusion** that involves the reader on the same plane as the writer. The notion of the black holster extends the allusion of the old cowboy films where the "baddies" wore black hats and rode black horses. The use of the word "nestled" provokes some interesting connotations of something soft and sweet like a kitten nestling into something. But then the gun is an implement of destruction and death; maybe "nestles" takes on the connotation of how a snake might curl in the sun at the base of a tree. The metaphor then ends with the child going out into the sun. The "rusty gun" in context of the essay was in fact the outmoded ideas and morals his father and old books had inculcated in him. All in all a very clever use of figurative language in prose. If the same concept had been pursued in poetry, the metaphor would have moved more speedily, more subtly—a poet cannot waste words—and of course would have employed line breaks, rhythm, and meter.

Personification is a much easier area than metaphor to detect in poetry. Usually the object that is being personified—referred to as a human with the personal pronoun sometimes, or possessing human attributes—is capitalized, as in this stanza from Thomas Gray's "Ode on a Distant Prospect of Eton College":

Ambition this shall tempt to rise,
Then whirl the wretch from high,
To bitter Scorn a sacrifice,
And grinning Infamy.
The stings of Falsehood those shall try,
And hard Unkindness' altered eye,
That mocks the tear it forced to flow;
And keen Remorse with blood defiled,
And moody Madness laughing wild
Amid severest woe.

As the poet watches the young Eton boys, he envisions what the years have to offer them, and the qualities he sees he gives human status. Thus, Ambition is not only capable of tempting, an amoral act, but also of "whirling," a physical act. Scorn is bitter, Infamy grinning, and so on. Coleridge employs a more visual personification in "The Ancient Mariner," for the sun whom he describes as:

...the Sun (was) flecked with bars
(Heaven's Mother send us grace!)
As if through a dungeon-grate he peered
With broad and burning face.

More so than with Gray's more formal personification, Coleridge's supplies an image that is precise—we can see the prisoner behind the bars, and what's more this particular prisoner has a broad and burning face... of course because he is the sun! The personification brings us that flash of recognition when we can say "Yes, I see that!"

The word **image** brings us to another important aspect of figurative language. Not a figure of speech in itself, the image plays a large role in poetry because the reader is expected to **imagine** what the poet is evoking, through the senses. The image can be **literal**, wherein the reader has little adjustment to make to see or touch or taste the image; a **figurative image** demands more from readers, almost as if they have to be inside the poet's imagination to understand the image. Very often this is where students of poetry, modern poetry particularly, find the greatest problems because the poetry of **imagism**, a term coined by Ezra Pound, is often intensely personal, delving into the mind of the poet for the comparison and connection with past memories that many readers cannot possibly share. Such an image is referred to as *free*, open to many interpretations. This concept suits the post-modern poet who feels that life is fragmented, open to multi-interpretations—there is no fixed order. Poets of the Elizabethan and Romantic eras saw the world as whole, steady, *fixed*, exactly the word used for their type of images. Readers of this poetry usually share the same response to the imagery. For example, the second stanza of Keats' "Ode to a Nightingale" sets up the taste imagery of a

> draught of vintage that hath been
> Cooled a long age in the deep-delvéd earth,
> Tasting of Flora and the country green,
> Dance, and Provençal song, and sunburnt mirth!
> O for a beaker of the warm South,
> Full of the true, the blushful Hippocrene,
> With beaded bubbles winking at the brim,
> And purple-stainéd mouth;

Even though Flora and Hippocrene are not names we are readily familiar with, the image of the cool wine, the taste, the look, the feeling evoked of the South and warmth, all come rushing into our minds as we enter the poet's imagination and find images in common.

Blake's imagery in "London" works in a similar way but as readers we have to probe a little harder, especially for the last line of the last stanza:

> But, most thro' midnight streets I hear
> How the youthful Harlot's curse
> Blasts the new-born Infant's tear,
> And blights with plagues the Marriage hearse.

Notice how the "Marriage hearse" immediately sets up a double image. Marriage we associate with happiness and joy; hearse we associate with death and sorrow. The image is troubling. We go back to the previous lines. The harlot curses her (?) new-born—the curse of venereal disease—that child marries and carries the disease to marriage? Or the young man consorting with the harlot passes on the disease to his marriage partner? Marriage then becomes death? The image is intriguing and open to interpretation.

Image in figurative language inevitably leads to **symbol**. When an object, an image, or a feeling takes on larger meaning outside of itself, then a poet is employing a symbol, something which stands for something greater. Because mankind has used symbols for so long, many have become **stock** or **conventional**: the rose standing for love; the flag standing for patriotism, love of one's country (thus the controversy over flag-burning today); the color yellow standing for corruption (hence Gatsby's Daisy Buchanan—the white-dressed virginal lady with the center core of carelessness); the bird for freedom; the sea for eternity; the cross for suffering and sacrifice. If you are not versed in the Christian tradition, it might be useful to read its symbols because the older poetry dwells on the church and the trials of loving God and loving Woman—the latter also has become a symbol deteriorating over the ages from Eve to the Madonna to Whore.

If the symbol is not conventional then it may carry with it many interpretations, depending on the reader's insight. Some students "get carried away" with symbolism, seeing more in the words than the poets do! If the poet is "doing a good job," the poetry will steer you in the "right" direction of symbolism. Sometimes we are unable to say what "stands for" what, but simply that the symbol evokes a mood; it suggests an idea to you that is difficult to explain. The best way to approach symbolism is to understand a literal meaning first and then shift the focus, as with a different camera lens, and see if the poet is saying something even more meaningful. Blake again supplies an interesting example. In his poem "The Chimney Sweeper" he describes the young child's dream of being locked up in "coffins of black." Literally of course coffins are brown wood, the color of mourning is black. Shift the focus then to the young child chimney sweeper, so young he can barely lisp the street cry "Sweep" so it comes out "'weep! 'weep! 'weep! 'weep!" (a symbolic line in itself). Your reading of the Industrial Age's cruelty to children who were exploited as cheap, plentiful, and an expendable labor force will perhaps have taught you that children were used as chimney brushes—literally thrust up the thin black chimneys of Victorian houses and factories, where very often they became trapped, suffocated, sometimes burned to death if fires were set by unknowing owners. Now the black coffins stand for the black-with-soot chimneys the little children had to sweep, chimneys which sometimes became their coffins. The realization of the symbol brings a certain horror to the poem. In the dream an Angel releases the children who then run down "a green plain leaping, laughing.../And wash in a river, and shine in the sun." The action is of course symbolic in that in real life the children's movements were restricted, living in monstrous cities where green plains would be enjoyed only by the rich, and totally limited by the size of the chimneys. They were always black with soot. They rarely saw the sun, never mind shone in it! Again, the symbolism adds something to the poem. In many students there have been reactions of tears and anger when they *see* the symbolism behind such simple lines.

The idea of reading about the Industrial Age brings us to an important part of figurative language, briefly mentioned before: **allusion**. Poets tap into previous areas of experience to relate their insights, to draw their readers into shared experiences. Remember how the student writer alluded to old cowboy movies, the classic "high noon." Poets will refer to history, myth, other older poems, plays, music, heroes, famous people. Allusion is becoming more and more difficult for the modern student because reading is becoming more and more a lost art. Core courses in schools have become hotbeds of controversy about what students should know. Fortunately modern poets are shifting their allusions so that contemporary readers can appreciate and join in with their background of knowledge. However, be aware that for the examination in poetry it will be useful to have a working knowledge of, at least a passing acquaintance with, "oldness." Think of areas of history that were landmarks: the burning of Catharge; Hannibal's elephants; Caesar's greatness; Alexander the Great; the first World War and its carnage of young men; the Second World War and the Holocaust. Think of the great Greek and Roman myths: the giving of fire to the world; the entrance of sin into the world; the labyrinth; the names associated with certain myths (Daedalus, Hercules, the Medusa). You may never have a question on the areas you read but your background for well-rounded college study will already be formulated.

If we now return to more specific figures of speech and other poetic devices, you may feel you can immediately get to grips with these rather than read for background! Alphabetical order may help in your studying:

Alliteration: the repetition of consonants at the beginning of words that are next door to each other or close by. The Hopkins' stanza quoted earlier provides some fine examples: "skylark scanted"; "Man's mounting... mean house"; "free fells"; "drudgery, day-labouring-out life's age." Always try to understand the reason for the alliteration. Does it speed or slow the rhythm? Is it there for emphasis? What does the poet want you to focus on?

Apostrophe: the direct address of someone or something that is not present. Many odes begin this way. Keats' "Ode to a Grecian Urn" for example: "Thou still unravished bride of quietness," and "Ode to Psyche": "O Goddess! hear these tuneless numbers."

Assonance: the repetition of vowel sounds usually internally rather than initially. "Her goodly eyes like sapphires shining bright." Here the poet, Spenser, wants the entire focus on the blue eyes, the crispness, and the light.

Bathos: deliberate anticlimax to make a definite point or draw attention to a falseness. The most famous example is from Pope's "Rape of the Lock": "Here thou, great Anna! whom three realms obey, /Dost sometimes counsel take—and sometimes tea."

The humor in the bathos is the fact that Anna is the Queen of England—she holds meetings in the room Pope describes but also indulges in the venerable English custom of afternoon tea. The fact that <u>tea</u> should rhyme with <u>obey</u> doubles the humor as the elongated vowel of the upper-class laconic English social group is also mocked.

Caesura: the pause, marked by punctuation (/) or not within the line. Sometimes the caesura (sometimes spelled cesura) comes at an unexpected point in the rhythm and gives the reader pause for thought.

Conceits: very elaborate comparisons between unlikely objects. The metaphysical poets such as John Donne were criticized for "yoking" together outrageous terms, describing lovers in terms of instruments, or death in terms of battle.

Consonance: similar to slant rhyme—the repetition of consonant sounds without the vowel sound repeated. Hopkins again frequently uses this as in "Pied Beauty": "All things counte<u>r</u>, o<u>r</u>iginal, spa<u>r</u>e, st<u>r</u>ange;... a<u>d</u>azzle, <u>d</u>im."

Diction: the word for word choice. Is the poet using formal or informal language? Does the poetry hinge on slang or a dialect? If so what is the purpose? Are the words "highfalutin" or low-brow? As always, the diction needs examining and questions like these answering.

Enjambment: the running-on of one line of poetry into another. Usually the end of lines are rhymed so there is an end-stop. In more modern poetry, without rhyme, often run-on lines occur to give a speedier flow, the sound of the speaking voice or a conversational tone.

Hyperbole: refers to large overstatement often used to draw attention to a mark of beauty or a virtue or an action that the poet disagrees with. Donne's instruction to the woman he is trying to seduce not to kill the flea, by contrasting her reluctance with "a marriage" of blood within a flea, reinforces the hyperbole used throughout the poem:

> Oh stay, three lives in one flea spare,
> Where we almost, yea, more than married are.

The example is also good for an unexpected caesura for emphasis at the second pause.

Irony: plays an important role in voice or tone, inferring a discrepancy between what is said and what is meant. A famous example is Shelley's "Ozymandias," which tells of the great ruler who thought that he and his name would last forever, but the traveller describes the huge statue in ruins with the inscription speaking truer than the ruler intended: "My name is Ozymandias, king of kings: /Look on my works, ye Mighty, and despair!"

Metonymy: the name for something closely related to it which then takes on a larger meaning. "You can't fight City Hall" has taken on the meaning of fighting against an entire bureaucracy. "You can't go home again" suggests that you can never emotionally return to your roots.

Onomatopoeia: a device in which the word captures the sound. In many poems the words are those in general use: the whiz of fireworks; the crashing of waves on the shore; the booming of water in an underground seacave. However, poets like Keats use the device to superb effect in, for example, "To Autumn," when he describes the gleaner sitting by the cider press watching the last "oozings hours by hours"... one can hear the last minute drops squeezed from the apples.

Oxymoron: a form of paradox in which contradictory words are used next to each other: "painful pleasure," "sweet sorrow."

Paradox: a situation or action or feeling that appears to be contradictory but on inspection turns out to be true or at least make sense. "The pen is mightier than the sword" at first glance is a contradiction of reality. One can hardly die by being stabbed by a pen... but in the larger world view the words of men, the signing of death warrants, and the written issuing of commands to the gas chambers have killed. Or reason has prevailed by men writing out their grievances and as a result lives have been saved. Paradox always opens up the doors of thinking.

Pun: a play on words often for humorous or sarcastic effect. The Elizabethans were very fond of them; many of Shakespeare's comedies come from punning. Much of Donne's sexual taunting involves the use of the pun.

Sarcasm: when verbal irony is too harsh, it moves into the sarcastic realm. It is the "lowest form of wit" of course but can be used to good effect in the tone of a poem. Browning's dramatic monologues make excellent use of the device.

Synecdoche: when a part of an object is used to represent the entire thing or vice versa. When we ask someone to give us a hand, we would be horrified if they cut off the hand; what we want is the person's help, from all of the body!

Syntax: the ordering of words into a particular pattern. If a poet shifts words from the usual word order, you know you are dealing with an older style of poetry (Shakespeare, Milton) or a poet who wants to shift emphasis onto a particular word.

Tone: the voice or attitude of the speaker. Remember that the voice need not be that of the poet's. He or she may be adopting a particular tone for a purpose. Your task is to analyze if the tone is angry, sad, conversational, abrupt, wheedling, cynical, affected, satiric, etc. Is the poet including you in a cozy way by using "you," or is he accusing "you" of what he is criticizing? Is the poet keeping you at a distance with coldness and third person pronouns. If so, why? The most intriguing of voices is Browning's in his **dramatic monologues**: poems that address another person who remains silent. Browning brought this type of poetry to an art. Think of all the variations of voices and attitudes and be prepared to meet them in poetry.

Types of Poetry

Having begun to grasp that poetry contains a great deal more than what initially meets the eye, you should now start thinking about the various types of poetry. Of course, when reading for pleasure, it is not vital to recognize that the poem in hand is a sonnet or a villanelle, but for the exam you may well be asked to determine what sort of poem is under scrutiny. Certainly in discussing a poem it is also useful to know what "breed" you are dealing with because the form may dictate certain areas of rhyme or meter and may enhance the meaning.

The pattern or design of a poem is known as **form**, and even the strangest, most experimental poetry will have some type of form to it. Allen Ginsberg's "A Supermarket in California" caused a stir because it didn't read like poetry, but on the page there is a certain form to it. Some poets even try to match the shape of the poem to the subject. Find in anthologies John Hollander's "Swan and Shadow" and Dorthi Charles' "Concrete Cat." Such visual poems are not just fun to look at and read but the form adds to the subject and helps the reader appreciate the poet's world view. **Closed form** will be immediately recognizable because lines can be counted and shape determined. The poet must keep to the recognized form, in number of lines, rhyme scheme, and/or meter. **Open form** developed from "vers libre," which name some poets objected to as it suggested that there was little skill or craft behind the poem, simply creativity, as the name suggests, gives a freedom of pattern to the poet.

The most easily recognized closed form of poetry is the **sonnet**, sometimes referred to as a **fixed form**. The sonnet always has 14 lines, but there are two types of sonnets, the Petrarchan or Italian, and the

Shakespearean or English. The word sonnet in fact comes from the Italian word "sonnetto" meaning a "little song," and Petrarch, the Fourteenth Century Italian poet, took the form to its peak with his sonnets to his loved one Laura. This woman died before he could even declare his love, and such poignant, unrequited love became the theme for many Elizabethan sonnets. As a young man might telephone a young woman for a date in today's society, the Elizabethan would send a sonnet. The Petrarchan sonnet is organized into two groups: eight lines and six—the **octave** and the **sestet**. Usually the rhyme scheme is is abbaabba-cdecde, but the sestet can vary in its pattern. The octave may set up a problem or a proposition, and then the answer or resolution follows in the sestet after a turn or a shift. The Shakespearean sonnet organizes the lines into three groups of four lines: **quatrains** and a **couplet** (two rhyming lines). The rhyming scheme is always abab cdcd efef gg, and the turn or shift can happen at one of three places or leave the resolution or a "twist in the tail" at the end.

Couplet, mentioned earlier, leads us to a closed form of poetry that is very useful for the poet. It is a two-line stanza that usually rhymes with an end rhyme. If the couplet is firmly end-stopped and written in iambic pentameter, it is known as an **heroic couplet**, after the use was made of it in the English translations of the great classical or heroic epics such as *The Iliad* and *The Odyssey*. Alexander Pope became a master of the heroic couplet, sometimes varying to the 12-syllable line from the old French poetry on Alexander the Great. The line became known as the **Alexandrine**. Pope gained fame first as a translator of the epics and then went on to write **mock-heroic** poems like "The Rape of the Lock," written totally in heroic couplets which never become monotonous, as a succession of regularly stepped-out couplets can, because he varied the place of the caesura and masterfully employed enjambment.

Rarely in an exam will you be presented with an **epic** because part of the definition of the word is vastness of size and range. However, you may be confronted with an excerpt and will need to recognize the structure. The translation will usually be in couplets and the meter regular with equal line lengths, because originally these poems were sung aloud or chanted to the beat of drums. Because of their oral quality, repetition plays an important part, so that if the bard, or singer, forgot the line, the audience, who had heard the stories many times before, could help him out. The subject deals with great deeds of heroes: Odysseus (Ulysses), Hector, and Aeneus, their adventures and their trials; the theme will be of human grief or pride, divided loyalties—but all "writ large." The one great English epic *Paradise Lost* is written by Milton and deals with the story of Adam and Eve and the Fall. Adam thus becomes the great hero. The huge battle scenes of

The Iliad are emulated in the War of the Heavens when Satan and his crew were expelled into Hell; the divided loyalties occur when Adam must choose between obedience to God and love for his wife.

On much simpler lines are the **ballads**, sometimes the earliest poems we learn as children. Folk or popular ballads were first sung as early as the Fifteenth Century and then handed down through generations until finally written down. Usually the ballads are anonymous and simple in theme, having been composed by working folk who originally could not read or write. The stories—a ballad is a story in a song—revolve around love and hate and lust and murder, often rejected lovers, knights, and the supernatural. As with the epic, and for the same reason, repetition plays a strong part in the ballad and often a repeated refrain holds the entire poem together. The form gave rise to the **ballad stanza**, four lines rhyming abcb with lines 1 and 3 having eight syllables and lines 2 and 4 having six. Poets who later wrote what are known as **literary ballads** kept the same pattern. Read Coleridge's "Ancient Mariner" and all the elements of the ballad come together as he reconstructs the old folk story but writes it in a very closed form.

The earlier poetry dealt with narrative. The "father of English poetry," Geoffrey Chaucer, told stories within a story for the great *Canterbury Tales*. The Elizabethans turned to love and the humanistic battle between love of the world and love of God. Wordsworth and Coleridge marked a turning point by not only using "the language of men" in poetry but also by moving away from the narrative poem to the **lyric**. The word comes again from the Greek, meaning a story told with the poet playing upon a lyre. Wordsworth moves from story to emotion, often "emotion recollected in tranquillity" as we saw in "Daffodils." Although sometimes a listener is inferred, very often the poet seems to be musing aloud.

Part of the lyric "family" is the **elegy**, a lament for someone's death or the passing of a love or concept. The most famous is Thomas Gray's "Elegy Written in a Country Churchyard," which mourns not only the passing of individuals but of a past age and the wasted potential within every human being, no matter how humble. Often **ode** and elegy become synonymous, but an ode, also part of the lyric family, is usually longer, dealing with more profound areas of human life than simply death. Keats' odes are perhaps the most famous and most beloved in English poetry.

More specialized types of poetry need mentioning so that you may recognize and be able to explicate how the structure of the poem enhances the meaning or theme. For example the **villanelle**: a courtly love poem structure from medieval times, built on five three-line stanzas known as

tercets, with the rhyme scheme aba, followed by a four-line stanza, and a **quatrain** which ends the poem abaa. As if this were not pattern and order enough, the poem's first line appears again as the last line of the 2nd and 4th tercets; *and* the third line appears again in the last line of the 3rd and 5th tercets; *and* these two lines appear again as rhyming lines at the end of the poem! The most famous and arguably the best villanelle, as some of the older ones can be so stiff in their pattern that the meaning is inconsequential, is Dylan Thomas' "Do not go gentle into that good night." The poem stands on its own with a magisterial meaning of mankind raging against death, but when one appreciates the structure also, the rage is even more emphatic because it is so controlled. A poem well worth finding for "reading for pleasure." In James Joyce's *A Portrait of the Artist as a Young Man*, writing a villanelle on an empty cigarette packet turns the young boy, Stephen Daedalus, dreaming of being an artist, into a poet, a "real" artist.

Said to be the most difficult of all closed forms is the **sestina**, also French, sung by medieval troubadours, a "song of sixes." The poet presents six six-line stanzas, with six end-words in a certain order, then repeats those six repeated words in any order in a closing tercet. Find Elizabeth Bishop's "Sestina" or W.H. Auden's "Hearing of Harvests Rotting in the Valleys" and the idea of six images running through the poet's head and being skillfully repeated comes across very clearly. You might even try working out a sestina for yourself.

Perhaps at this stage an **epigram** might be more to your liking and time scale because it is short, even abrupt, a little cynical and always to the point. The cynical Alexander Pope mastered the epigram, as did Oscar Wilde centuries later. Perhaps at some stage we have all written **doggerel**, rhyming poetry that becomes horribly distorted to fit the rhymes, not through skill but the opposite. In contrast **limericks** are very skilled: five lines using the anapest meter with the rhyme scheme: aabba. Unfortunately, they can deteriorate into types such as "There was a young lady from....," but in artful hands such as Shakespeare's (see Ophelia's mad song in *Hamlet*: "And will he not come again?") and Edward Lear's, limericks display fine poetry. Finally, if you are trying to learn all the different types of closed-form poetry, you might try an **aubade**—originally a song or piece of music sung or played at dawn—a poem written to the dawn or about lovers at dawn—the very time when poetic creation is extremely high!

Although the name might suggest open-form, **blank verse** is in fact closed-form poetry. As we saw earlier, lines written in blank verse are unrhymed and in iambic pentameter. Open-form poets can arrange words on the page in any order, not confined by any rhyme pattern or meter. Often it seems as if words have spilled onto the page at random with a direct address to the readers, as if the poets are cornering them in their room, or simply chatting over the kitchen table. The lines break at any point—the dash darts in and out—the poets are talking to the audience with all the "natural" breaks that the speaking voice will demonstrate. Open-form poets can employ rhyme, but sometimes it seems as if the rhyme has slipped into the poem quite easily—there is no wrenching of the word "to make it rhyme." Very often there is more internal rhyme as poets play with words, often giving the sensation they are thinking aloud. Open-form poetry is usually thought of as "modern," at least post-World War I, but the use of space on the page, the direct address of the voice, and the use of the dash clearly marks Emily Dickinson as an open-form poet, but she lived from 1830-1886.

DRAMA AND THEATER

The Glass Menagerie by Tennessee Williams begins when one of its four characters, Tom, steps into the downstage light and addresses the audience directly as though he were the chorus from a much earlier play. "I have tricks in my pocket, I have things up my sleeve," says Tom. "But I am the opposite of a stage magician. He gives you illusion that has the appearance of truth. I give you truth in the pleasant disguise of illusion."

To sit among the audience and watch a skillful production of *The Glass Menagerie* is to visit Tom's paradoxical world of theater, a magic place in which known imposters and stagecraft trickery create a spectacle which we know is illusion but somehow recognize as truth. Theater, as a performed event, combines the talents and skills of numerous artists and craftspersons, but before the spectacle must come the playwright's work, the pages of words designating what the audience sees and hears. These words, the written script separate from the theatrical performance of them, is what we call *drama*, and the words give the spectacle its significance because without them the illusion has neither frame nor content. Truth requires boundaries and substance. When Shakespeare's Hamlet advises actors just before their performance, he places careful emphasis on the importance of the words, cautioning the players to speak them "trippingly on the tongue." If all actions are not suited to the words, Hamlet adds, the performance will fail because the collaborative purpose combining the dramatist's literary art and the actors' performing art "is to hold as 'twere the mirror up to Nature."

Although drama is literature written to be performed, it closely resembles the other genres. In fact, both poetry and prose also can be performed; but as captivating as these public readings sometimes are, only performed drama best creates the immediate living "illusion as truth" Tom promises. Like fiction and narrative poetry, drama tells a tale—that is, it has plot, characters, and setting—but the author's voice is distant, heard only through the stage directions and perhaps some supplementary notes. With rare exceptions, dialogue dominates the script. Some drama is poetry, such as the works of Shakespeare and Molière, and all plays resemble poems as abstractions because both forms are highly condensed, figurative expressions. Even in Henrik Ibsen's social realism, the dramatic action is metaphorical.

A scene set inside a house, for instance, requires a room with only three walls. No audience complains, just as no movie audience feels betrayed by film characters' appearing ridiculously large. Without a thought, audiences employ what Samuel Taylor Coleridge called "a willing suspension of disbelief"; in other words, they know that the images before them are not real but rather representations, reflections in the mirror of which Hamlet speaks, not the real world ("Nature").

A play contains conflict which can be enacted immediately on the stage without any alterations in the written word. **Enacted** means performed by an actor or actors free to use the entire stage and such theatrical devices as sets, costumes, makeup, special lighting, and props for support. This differs from the oral interpretation of prose or poetry. No matter how animated, the public reader is not acting. This is the primary distinction between drama and other literary forms. Their most obvious similarity is that any form of literature is a linguistic expression. There is, however, one other feature shared by all kinds of narratives: the pulsating energy which pushes the action along is generated by human imperfection. We speak of tragic characters as having "flaws," but the same is true about comic characters as well. Indeed, nothing is more boring either on a stage or in a written text than a consistently flawless personality, because such characters can never be congruent with the real people of our everyday experiences. The most fundamental human truth is human frailty.

Although it can be argued that a play, like a musical composition, must be performed to be realized, the script's linguistic foundation always gives the work potential as a literary experience. Moreover, there is never a "definitive" interpretation. The script, in a sense, remains unfinished because it never stops inviting new variations, and among those invited to participate are individual readers whose imaginations should not be discounted. For example, when *Death of a Salesman* was originally produced, Lee J. Cobb played Willy Loman. Aside from the character's age, Dustin Hoffman's Willy in the revival 40 years later bore hardly any physical resemblance to Cobb's. Yet both portrayals "worked." The same could be said about the Willys created by the minds of the play's countless readers. Quite capable of composing its own visions and sounds, the human imagination is the original mirror, the place where all human truths evolve from perceived data.

Hamlet's mirror and Tom's truthful illusions are figures of speech echoing drama's earliest great critic, Aristotle, who believed art should create a **mimesis**, the Greek word for "imitation." For centuries this "mimetic theory" has asserted that a successful imitation is one which reproduces natural objects and actions in as realistic portrayal as possible. Later, this notion of imitation adopted what has been called the "expressive theory," a variation allowing the artist a freer, more individual stylized approach. A drama by Ibsen, for example, attempts to capture experience as unadorned raw sense, the way it normally appears to be. This is realistic imitation. As 20th century drama moved toward examinations of people's inner consciousness as universal representations of some greater human predicament, new expressive styles emerged. The diversity in the works of Eugene O'Neill, Samuel Beckett, and Harold Pinter illustrate how dramatists' imitations can disrupt our sense of the familiar as their plays become more personally expressive. But the theater of Aristotle's time was hardly "realistic" in today's objective sense. Instead, it was highly stylized and full of conventions derived from theater's ritualistic origins. The same is true of medieval morality plays and the rigid formality of Japanese Kabuki theater, yet these differ greatly from each other and from ancient Greek and Roman dramas. In other words, imitating "what's out there" requires only that the form be consistent with itself, and any form is permissible.

Plot Structure

As with other narrative types, a play's **plot** is its sequence of events, its organized collection of incidents. At one time it was thought that all the actions within a play should be contained within a single 24-hour period. Few lengthy plays have plots which cover only the period of time enacted on the stage. Most plays condense and edit time much as novels do. Decades can be reduced to two hours. Included in the plot is the **exposition**, the revealing of whatever information we need in order to understand the impending conflict. This exposed material should provide us with a sense of place and time (**setting**), the central participants, important prior incidents, and the play's overall mood. In some plays such as Shakespeare's, the exposition comes quickly. Notice, for instance, the opening scenes in *Macbeth,* *Hamlet,* and *Romeo and Juliet*: not one presents us with a central character, yet each—with its witches or king's ghost or street brawl—clearly establishes an essential tension heralding the main conflict to come. These initial expositions attack the audience immediately and are followed by subsequent events in chronological order. Sophocles' *Oedipus Rex* works somewhat differently, presenting the central character late in the myth from which the play is taken. The exposition must establish what has come previously, even for an audience familiar with the story, before the plot can advance. Like Shakespeare, Sophocles must start his exposition at the beginning, but he takes a longer (though not tedious) time revealing the essential facts. Arthur Miller, in his *Death of a Salesman,* continuously interrupts the central action with dislocated expositions from earlier times as though the past were always in the present. He carefully establishes character, place, mood, and conflict throughout the earliest scenes; however, whatever present he places on stage is always caught in a tension between the audience's anticipation of the future and its suspicions of the past. The plots in plays like *Oedipus Rex* and *Death of a Salesman* tend not to attack us head-on but rather to surround us and gradually close in, the circle made tighter by each deliberately released clue to a mysterious past.

Conflict requires two opposing forces. We see, for instance, how King Lear's irresponsible abdication and conceited anger are countered by Goneril and Regan's duplicity and lusts for power. We also see how Creon's excessive means for restoring order in Thebes is met by Antigone's allegiance to personal conscience. Fairly soon in a play we must experience some incident that incites the fundamental conflict when placed against some previously presented incident or situation. In most plays the conflict's abrasive conditions continuously chafe and even lacerate each other. The play's tempo might provide some interruptions or variations in the pace; nevertheless, conflicts generate the actions which make the characters' worlds worse before they can get better. Any plot featuring only repetitious altercations, however, would soon become tiresome. Potentially, anything can happen in a conflict. The **complication** is whatever presents an element capable of altering the action's direction. Perhaps some new information is discovered or a previously conceived scheme fails, creating a reversal of what had been expected. The plot is not a series of similar events but rather a compilation of related events leading to a culmination, a **crisis**.

In retrospect we should be able to accept a drama's progression of actions leading to the crisis as inevitable. After the crisis comes the **resolution** (or **denouement**), which gives the play its concluding boundary. This does not mean that the play should offer us solutions for whatever human issues it raises. Rather, the playwright's obligation is to make the experience he presents to us seem filled within its own perimeters. George Bernard Shaw felt he had met this obligation when he ended *Pygamalion* with his two principal characters, Higgins and Eliza, utterly incapable of voicing any romantic affection for each other; and the resolution in Ibsen's *A Doll's House* outraged audiences a hundred years ago and still disturbs some people today, even though it concludes the play with believable consequences.

Terms such as **exposition**, **complication**, **crisis**, and **resolution**, though helpful in identifying the conflict's currents and directions, at best only artificially define how a plot is molded. If the play provides unity in its revelations, these seams are barely noticeable. Moreover, any successful creative composition clearly shows that the artist accomplished much more than merely plugging components together to create a finished work. There are no rules which all playwrights must follow, except the central precept that the play's unified assortment of actions be complete and contained within itself. *Antigone*, for instance, depicts the third phase of Sophocles' *Oedipus* trilogy, although it was actually written and performed before *Oedipus Rex* and *Oedipus at Colonus*. And although a modern reader might require some background information before starting, *Antigone* gives a cohesive dramatic impact independent from the other two plays.

Character

Essential to the plot's success are the characters who participate in it. Midpoint in *Hamlet* when Elsinore Castle is visited by the traveling theater company, the prince joyously welcomes the players, but his mood quickly returns to bitter depression shortly after he asks one actor to recite a dramatic passage in which the speaker recalls the fall of Troy and particularly Queen Hecuba's response to her husband's brutal murder. The player, caught by the speech's emotional power, becomes distraught and cannot finish. Left alone on stage, Hamlet compares the theatrical world created by the player with Hamlet's "real" world and asks: "What's Hecuba to him, or he to Hecuba,/That he should weep for her!" Under ordinary circumstances Hamlet's anxiety would not overshadow his Renaissance sensibilities, because he knows well that fictional characters always possess the potential to move us. As though by instinct, we know the same. We read narratives and go to the theater precisely because we want to be shocked, delighted, thrilled, saddened, titillated, or invigorated by "a dream of passion." Even though some characters are more complex and interesting than others, they come in countless types as the playwright's delegates to our imaginations and as the imitations of reality seeking our response.

Antigone begins with two characters, Antigone and Ismene, on stage. They initiate the exposition through their individual reactions to a previous event, King Creon's edict following the battle in which Thebes defeated an invading army. Creon has proclaimed Eteocles and the others who recently died defending Thebes as heroes worthy of the highest burial honors; in addition, Creon has forbidden anyone, on penalty of death, from burying Poloneices and the others who fell attacking the city. Since Antigone, Ismene, Polyneices, and Eteocles are the children of Oedipus and Iocaste, the late king and queen, conflict over Creon's law seems imminent. These first two characters establish this inevitability. They also reveal much about themselves as individuals.

ANTIGONE:… now you must prove what you are:
A true sister, or a traitor to your family.

ISMENE: Antigone, are you mad! What could I possibly do?

ANTIGONE: You must decide whether you will help me or not.

ISMENE: I do not understand you. Help you in what?

ANTIGONE: Ismene, I am going to bury him. Will you come?

ISMENE: Bury him! You have just said the new law forbids it.

ANTIGONE: He is my brother. And he is your brother, too.

ISMENE: But think of the danger! Think what Creon will do!

ANTIGONE: Creon is not strong enough to stand in my way.

ISMENE: Ah sister!
Oedipus died, everyone hating him
For what his own search brought to light, his eyes
Ripped out by his own hand; and Iocaste died,
His mother and wife at once: she twisted the cords
That strangled her life; and our two brothers died,
Each killed by the other's sword. And we are left:
But oh, Antigone,
Think how much more terrible than these
Our own death would be if we should go against Creon
And do what he has forbidden! We are only women,
We cannot fight with men, Antigone!
The law is strong, we must give in to the law
In this thing, and in worse. I beg the Dead
To forgive me, but I am helpless: I must yield
To those in authority. And I think it is dangerous business
To be always meddling.

ANTIGONE: If that is what you think,
I should not want you, even if you asked to come.
You have made your choice, you can be what you want to be.
But I will bury him; and if I must die,
I say that this crime is holy: I shall lie down
With him in death, and I shall be as dear
To him as he to me.
It is the dead,
Not the living, who make the longest demands:
We die for ever...
You may do as you like,
Since apparently, the laws of the gods mean nothing to you.

ISMENE: They mean a great deal to me; but I have no strength
To break laws that were made for the public good.

ANTIGONE: That must be your excuse, I suppose. But as for me,
I will bury the brother I love.

ISMENE: Antigone, I am so afraid for you!

ANTIGONE: You need not be:
You have yourself to consider, after all.

ISMENE: But no one must hear of this, you must tell no one!
I will keep it a secret, I promise!

ANTIGONE: Oh tell it! Tell everyone!
Think how they'll hate you when it all comes out
If they learn that you knew about it all the time!

ISMENE: So fiery! You should be cold with fear.

ANTIGONE: Perhaps. But I am doing only what I must.

ISMENE: But can you do it? I say that you cannot.

ANTIGONE: Very well: when my strength gives out, I shall do no more.

ISMENE: Impossible things should not be tried at all.

ANTIGONE: Go away, Ismene:
I shall be hating you soon, and the dead will too,
For your words are hateful. Leave me my foolish plan:
I am not afraid of the danger; if it means death,
It will not be the worst of deaths—death without honor.

ISMENE: Go then, if you feel that you must.
You are unwise,
But a loyal friend to those who love you.

[Exit into the palace. ANTIGONE goes off...]

Reading the Play

All we know about Antigone and Ismene in this scene comes from
what they say; therefore, we read their spoken words carefully. However,
we must also remain attentive to dramatic characters, propensity for not
revealing all they know and feel about a given issue, and often characters
do not recognize all the implications in what they say. We might be helped
by what one says about the other, yet these observations are not necessarily accurate or sincere. Even though the previous scene contains fewer
abiguities than some others in dramatic literature, we would be oversim-
plifying to say the conflict here is between one character who is "right"
and another who is "wrong." Antigone comes out challenging, determined
and unafraid, whereas Ismene immediately reacts fearfully. Antigone brims
with the self-assured power of righteousness while Ismene expresses vul-
nerability. Yet Antigone's boast that "Creon is not strong enough to stand
in my way" suggests a rash temperament. We might admire her courage,
but we question her judgment. Meanwhile, Ismene can evoke our sympathies with her burden of family woes, at least until she confesses her
helplessness and begs the Dead to forgive her, at which point we realize
her objections stem from cowardice and not conscience.

Although we might remain unsettled by Antigone's single-mindedness,
we soon find ourselves sharing her disdain for Ismene's trepidation, particularly when Ismene rationalizes her position as the more responsible
and labels unauthorized intervention in royal decisions as "meddling" against
the "public good." Soon, as we realize the issue here demands moral
conscience, we measure Ismene far short of what is required. Quickly
though, Ismene is partly redeemed by her obvious concern for Antigone's
well-being: "I am so afraid for you." Unaffected, Antigone retorts with
sarcasm and threats, but her demeanor never becomes so impetuously
caustic that we dismiss her as a conceited adolescent. In fact, we are
touched by her integrity and devotion, seeing no pretensions when she
says: "I am not afraid of the danger: if it means death,/It will not be the
worst of deaths—death without honor." Ismene's intimation that loyalty
and love are unwise counters Antigone's idealism enough to make us
suspect that the stark, cruel world of human imperfection will not tolerate
Antigone's solitary rebellion, no matter how selfless her motivation. At

the same time we wonder how long Ismene could remain neutral if Antigone were to clash with Creon.

What immediately strikes us about Antigone and Ismene is that each possesses a sense of self, a conscious awareness about her existence and her connection with forces greater than herself. This is why we can identify with them. It may not always feel reassuring, yet we too can define our existence by saying "I am, and I am not alone." As social creatures, a condition about which they have had no choice, both Antigone and Ismene have senses of self which are touched by their identification with others: each belongs to a family, and each belongs to a civil state. Indeed, much of the play's conflict focuses on which identification should be stronger. Another connection influences them as well—the unbreakable tie to truth. This truth, or ultimate reality, will vary from play to play, and not all characters ever realize it is there, and few will define it the same way. Still, the universe which characters inhabit has definition, even if the resolution suggests a great human absurdity in our insufficient capacity to grasp this definition or, worse, asserts the only definition is the absence of an ultimate reality. With Antigone, we see how her sense of self cannot be severed from its bonds to family obligations and certain moral principles.

Characters with a sense of self and an identity framed by social connections and unmitigated truths dwell in all good narratives. As readers we wander within these connecting perimeters, following the plot and sensing a commentary about life in general. This commentary, the **theme,** places us within the mirror's image along with the characters and their actions. We look and see ourselves. The characters' universe is ours, the playwright would have us believe, for a while at least. If his art succeeds, we do believe him. But reading literary art is no passive experience; it requires active work. And since playwrights seldom help us decide *how* characters say what they do or interrupt to explain *why* they say what they do, what personal voice he gives through stage directions deserves special attention, because playwrights never tell as much as novelists; instead they show. Our reading should focus on the tone of the dialogue as much as on the information in what is said. Prior to the Nineteenth Century, dramatists relied heavily on poetic diction to define their characters. Later playwrights provided stage directions which detail stage activities and modify dialogue. Modern writers usually give precise descriptions for the set and costume design and even prescribe particular background music. But no matter when a play was written or what its expressive style is, our role as readers and audience is to make judgments about characters in action, just as we make judgments about Antigone and Ismene the first time we see them. We should strive to be "fooled" by the truthful illusion by activating our sensitivities to human imperfections and the potential conflicts such flaws can generate. And, finally, as we peer into the playwright's mirror, we seek among the populated reflections shadows of ourselves.

Types of Plays

When Polonius presents the traveling players to Hamlet, he reads from the theater company's license, which identifies them as

> The best actors in the world, either for tragedy, comedy, history, pastoral, pastoral-comical, historical-pastoral, tragical-historical, tragical-comical-historical-pastoral, scene individable or poem unlimited...

Shakespeare's sense of humor runs through this speech which sounds like a parody of the license granted Shakespeare's own company by James I, authorizing "the Arte and faculty of playing Comedies, Tragedies, histories, Enterludes, moralls, pastoralls, Stageplaies and Such others..." for the king's subjects and himself. The joke is on those who think all plays somehow can be categorized according to preconceived definitions, as though playwrights follow literary recipes. The notion is not entirely ridiculous, to be sure, since audiences and readers can easily tell a serious play from a humorous one, and a play labeled "tragedy" or "comedy" will generate certain valid expectations from us all, regardless of whether we have read a word by Aristotle or any other literary critic. Still, if beginning playwrights had to choose between writing according to some rigid strictures designating the likes of a "tragical-comical-historical-pastoral" or writing a play unrestricted by such rules (a "poem unlimited"), they would probably choose the latter.

All plays contain thought—its accumulated themes, arguments, and overall meaning of the action—together with a mood or tone, and we tend to categorize dramatic thought into three clusters: the serious, the comic, and the seriocomic. These distinctions echo the primitive rites from which theater evolved, religious observances usually tied to seasonal cycles. In the course of a year numerous situations could arise which would initiate dramatic, communal prayers of supplication or thanksgiving. Indeed, for humanity to see its fate held by the will of a god is to see the intricate unity of flesh and spirit, a paradox ripe for representation as dramatic conflict. And if winter's chill brings the pangs of tragedy and summer's warmth the delight of comedy, the year becomes a metaphor for the overall human condition, which contains both. Thus, in our attempts to interpret life's complexities, it is tempting to place the art forms representing it in precise, fixed designations. From this can come critical practices which ascertain how well a work imitates life by how well it adheres to its designated form. Of course, such a critical system's rigidity would limit the range of possible human experiences expressed on stage to a narrow few, but then the range could be made elastic enough to provide for possible variations and combinations. Like the old Ptolomaic theories which held the earth as the center of the universe, these precepts could work for a while. After a few centuries, though, it would become clear that there is a better way of explaining what a play's form should be—not so much fixed as organic. In other words, we should think of a play as similar to a plant's growing and taking shape according to its own design. This analogy works well because the plant is not a mechanical device constructed from a predetermined plan, yet every plant is a species and as such contains qualities which identify it with others. So just as Shakespeare could ridicule overly precise definitions for dramatic art, he could still write dramas which he clearly identified as tragedies, comedies, or histories, even though he would freely mix two or more of these together in the same play. For the purpose of understanding some of the different perspectives available to the playwright's examining eye, we will look at plays from different periods which follow the three main designations Shakespeare used, followed by a fourth which is indicative of modern American drama. A knowledge of *The Importance of Being Earnest*, *Othello*, *A Man for All Seasons*, and *Death of a Salesman* will be helpful.

Comedy

The primary aim of comedy is to amuse us with a happy ending, although comedies can vary according to the attitudes they project, which can be broadly identified as either **high** or **low**, terms having nothing to do with an evaluation of the play's merit. Generally, the amusement found in comedy comes from an eventual victory over threats or ill fortune. Much of the dialogue and plot development might be laughable, yet a play need not be funny to be comic. **Farce** is low comedy intended to make us laugh by means of a series of exaggerated, unlikely situations that depend less on plot and character than on gross absurdities, sight gags, and coarse dialogue. The "higher" a comedy goes, the more natural the characters seem and the less boisterous their behavior. The plots become more sustained, and the dialogue shows more weighty thought. As with all dramas, comedies are about things that go wrong. Accordingly, comedies create deviations from accepted normalcy, presenting incongruities which we might or might not see as harmless. If these incongruities make us judgmental about the involved characters and events, the play takes on the features of **satire**, a rather high comic form implying that humanity and human institutions are in need of reform. If the action triggers our sympathy for the characters, we feel even less protected from the incongruities as the play tilts more in the direction of **tragi-comedy**. In other words, the action determines a figurative distance between the audience and the play. Such factors as characters' personalities and the plot's predictability influence this distance. The farther away we sit, the more protected we feel and usually the funnier the play becomes. Closer proximity to believability in the script draws us nearer to the conflict, making us feel more involved in the action and less safe in its presence. It is a rare play that can freely manipulate its audience back and forth along this plane and still maintain its unity. Shakespeare's *The Merchant of Venice* is one example.

A more consistent play is Oscar Wilde's *The Importance of Being Earnest*, which opened in 1895. In the following scene, Lady Bracknell questions Jack Worthing, who has just announced that Lady Bracknell's daughter, Gwendolyn, has agreed to marry him. Being satisfied with Jack's answers concerning his income and finding his upper-class idleness and careless ignorance about world affairs an asset, she queries him about his family background. In grave tones, the embarrassed Jack reveals his mysterious lineage. His late guardian, Thomas Cardew—"an old gentleman of a very charitable and kindly disposition"—had found the baby Jack in an abandoned handbag.

LADY BRACKNELL: A hand-bag?

JACK (very seriously): Yes, Lady Bracknell. I was in a hand-bag—a somewhat large, black leather hand-bag, with handles to it—an ordinary hand-bag in fact.

LADY BRACKNELL: In what locality did this Mr. James, or Thomas, Cardew come across this ordinary hand-bag?

JACK: In the cloak-room at Victoria Station. It was given him in mistake for his own.

LADY BRACKNELL: The cloak-room at Victoria Station?

JACK: Yes. The Brighton line.

LADY BRACKNELL: The line is immaterial, Mr. Worthing. I confess I feel somewhat bewildered by what you have just told me. To be born, or at any rate bred, in a hand-bag, whether it had handles or not, seems to me to display a contempt for the ordinary decencies of family life that reminds one of the worst excesses of the French Revolution. And I presume you know what that unfortunate movement led to? As for the particular locality in which the hand-bag was found, a cloak-room at a railway station might serve to conceal a social indiscretion—has probably, indeed, been used for that purpose before now—but it could hardly be regarded as an assured basis for recognized position in good society.

JACK: May I ask you then what would you advise me to do? I need hardly say I would do anything in the world to ensure Gwendolyn's happiness.

LADY BRACKELL: I would strongly advise you, Mr. Worthing, to try and acquire some relations as soon as possible, and to make a definite effort to produce at any rate one parent, of either sex, before the season is over.

JACK: Well, I don't see how I could possibly manage to do that. I can produce the hand-bag at any moment. It is in my dressing-room at home. I really think that should satisfy you, Lady Bracknell.

LADY BRACKNELL: Me, sir! What has it to do with me? You can hardly imagine that I and Lord Bracknell would dream of allowing our only daughter—a girl brought up with the utmost care—to marry into a cloak-room, and form an alliance with a parcel. Good morning, Mr. Worthing!

(LADY BRACKNELL sweeps out in majestic indignation.)

This dialogue between Lady Bracknell and Jack is typical of what runs throughout the entire play. It is full of exaggerations, in both the situation being discussed and the manner in which the characters, particularly Lady Bracknell, express their reactions to the situation. Under other circumstances a foundling would not be the focus of a comedy, but we are relieved from any concern for the child since the adult Jack is obviously secure, healthy, and, with one exception, carefree. Moreover, we laugh when Lady Bracknell exaggerates Jack's heritage by comparing it with the excesses of the French Revolution. On the other hand, at the core of their discussion is the deeply ingrained and oppressive notion of English class consciousness, a mentality so flawed it almost begs to be satirized. Could there be more there than light, witty entertainment?

Tragedy

The term "tragedy" when used to define a play has historically meant something very precise, not simply a drama which ends with unfortunate consequences. This definition originated with Aristotle, who insisted that the play be an imitation of complex actions which should arouse an emotional response combining fear and pity. Aristotle believed that only a certain kind of plot could generate such a powerful reaction. Comedy, as we have seen, shows us a progression from adversity to prosperity. Tragedy must show the reverse; moreover, this progression must be experienced by a certain kind of character, says Aristotle, someone whom we can designate as the **tragic hero**. This central figure must be basically good and noble: "good" because we will not be aroused to fear and pity over the misfortunes of a villain, and "noble" both by social position and moral stature because the fall to misfortune would not otherwise be great enough for tragic impact. These virtues do not make the tragic hero perfect, however, for he must also possess **hamartia**—a tragic flaw—the frailty which leads him to make an error in judgment which initiates the reversal in his fortunes, causing his death or the death of others or both. These dire consequences become the hero's **catastrophe**. The most common tragic flaw is **hubris**, an excessive pride that adversely influences the protagonist's judgment.

Often the catastrophic consequences involve an entire nation because the tragic hero's social rank carries great responsibilities. Witnessing these events produces the emotional reaction Aristotle believed the audience should experience, the **catharsis**. Although tragedy must arouse our pity for the tragic hero as he endures his catastrophe and must frighten us as we witness the consequences of a flawed behavior which anyone could exhibit, there must also be a purgation, "a cleansing," of these emotions which should leave the audience feeling not depressed but relieved and almost elated. The assumption is that while the tragic hero endures a crushing reversal somehow he is not thoroughly defeated as he gains new stature though suffering and the knowledge that comes with suffering. Classical tragedy insists that the universe is ordered. If truth or universal law is ignored, the results are devastating, causing the audience to react emotionally; simultaneously, the tragic results prove the existence of truth, thereby reassuring our faith that existence is sensible.

Sophocles' plays give us some of the clearest examples of Aristotle's definition of tragedy. Shakespeare's tragedies are more varied and more modern in their complexities. *Othello* is one of Shakespeare's most innovative and troublesome extensions of tragedy's boundaries. The title character commands the Venetian army and soon becomes acting governor of Cypress. He is also a Moor, a dark-skinned African whose secret marriage to the beautiful Desdemona has infuriated her father, a wealthy and influential Venetian, whose anger reveals a racist element in Venice which Othello tries to ignore. Iago hates Othello for granting a promotion to Cassio which Iago believes should rightfully be his. With unrelenting determination and malicious deception, Iago attempts to persuade Othello that Desdemona has committed adultery with Cassio. The following excerpt catches Iago in the early stages of his successful manipulation:

IAGO: In Venice they [wives] do let heaven see pranks
They dare not show their husbands; their best conscience
Is not to leave 't undone, but keep 't unknown.

OTHELLO: Dost thou say so?

IAGO: She did deceive her father, marrying you;
And when she seem'd to shake and fear your looks,
She lov'd them most.

OTHELLO: And so she did.

IAGO: Why, go to, then;
She that so young could give out such a seeming,
To see her father's eyes up close as oak,
He thought 'twas witchcraft; but I am much to blame;
I humbly do beseech you of your pardon
For too much loving you.

OTHELLO: I am bound to thee forever.

IAGO: I see, this hath a little dash'd your spirits.

OTHELLO: Not a jot, not a jot.

IAGO: I' faith, I fear it has.
I hope you will consider what is spoke
Comes from my love. But I do see you're mov'd;
I am to pray you not to strain my speech
To grosser issues nor to larger reach
Than to suspicion.

OTHELLO: I will not.

IAGO: Should you do so, my lord,
My speech should fall into such vile success
As my thoughts aim not at. Cassio's my worthy friend—
My lord, I see you're mov'd.

OTHELLO: No, not much mov'd:
I do not think but Desdemona's honest.

IAGO: Long live she so! and long live you to think so!

OTHELLO: And yet, how nature erring from itself,—

IAGO: Ay, there's the point: as, to be bold with you,
Not to affect many proposed matches
Of her own clime, complexion, and degree,
Whereto, we see, in all things nature tends;
Foh! one may smell in such, a will most rank,
Foul disproportion, thoughts unnatural.
But pardon me; I do not in position
Distinctly speak of her, though I may fear
Her will, recoiling to her better judgment,
May fall to match you with her country forms
And happily repent.

OTHELLO: Farewell, farewell:
If more thou dost perceive, let me know more;
Set on thy wife to observe. Leave me, Iago.

IAGO: My lord, I take my leave. (Going)

OTHELLO: Why did I marry? This honest creature, doubtless,
Sees and knows more, much more, than he unfolds.

Notice that Iago speaks much more than Othello. This is typical of their conversations, as though Iago were the superior of the two. Dramatically, for Iago's machinations to compel our interests we must perceive in Othello tragic proportions, both in his strengths and weaknesses; otherwise, *Othello* would slip into a malevolent tale about a rogue and his dupe. Much of the tension in this scene emanates from Othello's reluctance either to accept Iago's innuendos immediately or to dismiss them. This confusion places him on the rack of doubt, a torture made more severe because he questions his own desirability as a husband. Consequently, since Iago is not the "honest creature" he appears to be and Othello is unwilling to confront openly his own self-doubts, Iago becomes the dominant personality—a situation which a flawless Othello would never tolerate.

History

The playwright's raw data can spring from any source. A passion play, for instance, is a dramatic adaptation of the Crucifixion as told in the gospels. A history play is a dramatic perspective of some event or series of events identified with recognized historical figures. Television docudramas are the most recent examples. Among the earliest histories were the chronicle plays which flourished during Shakespeare's time and often relied on *Chronicles* by Raphael Holinshed, first published in 1577. Holinshed's volumes and similar books by others glorified English history and were very popular throughout the Tudor period, especially following the defeat of the Spanish Armada. Similarly, Shakespeare's *Henry V* and *Henry VIII* emphasize national and religious chauvinism in their treatments of kings who, from a more objective historical perspective appear less than nobly motivated. These plays resemble romantic comedies with each one's protagonist defeating some adversary and establishing national harmony through royal marriage. *King Lear* and *Macbeth*, on the other hand, movingly demonstrate Shakespeare's skill at turning historical figures into tragic heroes.

Ever since the Sixteenth Century history plays have seldom risen above the level of patriotic whitewash and political propaganda. Of course there are notable exceptions to this trend: Robert Bolt's *A Man for All Seasons* is one. The title character, Sir Thomas More, is beheaded at the play's conclusion, following his refusal to condone Henry VIII's break from the Roman Catholic Church and the king's establishment of the Church of England with the monarch as its head. Henry wants More to condone these actions because the Pope will not grant Henry a divorce from Queen Catherine so that he can marry Anne Boleyn, who the king believes will bear him the male heir he desperately wants. The central issue for us is not whether More's theology is valid but whether any person of conscience can act freely in a world dominated by others far less principled. In Henry's only scene he arrives at Sir Thomas' house hoping his Lord Chancellor will not disappoint him:

[music in background]

HENRY: Son after son she's borne me, Thomas, all dead at birth, or dead within a month; I never saw the hand of God so clear in anything... I have a daughter, she's a good child, a well-set child—But I have no son. (He flares up) It is my bounden duty to put away the Queen, and all the Popes back to St. Peter shall not come between me and my duty! How is it that you cannot see? Everybody else does.

MORE: (Eagerly) Then why does Your Grace need my poor support?

HENRY: Because you are honest. What's more to the purpose, you're known to be honest... There are those like Norfolk who follow me because I wear the crown, and there are those like Master Cromwell who follow me because they are jackals with sharp teeth and I am their lion, and there is a mass that follow me because it follows anything that moves— and there is you.

MORE: I am sick to think how much I must displease Your Grace.

HENRY: No, Thomas, I respect your sincerity. Respect? Oh, man, it's water in the desert... How did you like our music? That air they played, it had a certain—well, tell me what you thought of it.

MORE: (Relieved at this turn; smiling) Could it have been Your Grace's own?

HENRY: (Smiles back) Discovered! Now I'll never know your true opinion. And that's irksome, Thomas, for we artists, though we love praise, yet we love truth better.

MORE: (Mildly) Then I will tell Your Grace truly what I thought of it.

HENRY: (A little disconcerted) Speak then.

MORE: To me it seemed—delightful.

HENRY: Thomas—I chose the right man for Chancellor.

MORE: I must in fairness add that my taste in music is reputably deplorable.

(From *A Man for All Seasons* by Robert Bolt. Copyright © 1960, 1962 by Robert Bolt. Reprinted by permission of Random House Inc.)

To what extent Henry and More discussed the king's divorce and its subsequent events nobody knows, let alone what was actually said, although we can be certain they spoke an English distinctively different from the language in the play. Bolt's imagination, funnelled through the dramatist's obligation to tell an interesting story, presides over the historical data and dictates the play's projections of More, Henry, and the other participants. Thus, we do not have "history"; instead, we have a dramatic perception of history shaped, altered, and adorned by Robert Bolt, writing about Sixteenth Century figures from a 1960 vantage point. But as the scene above shows, the characters' personalities are not simple reductions of what historical giants should be. Henry struts a royal self-assurance noticeably colored by vanity and frustration; yet although he lacks More's wit and intelligence, the king clearly is no fool. Likewise, as troubled as More is by the controversy before him, he projects a formidable power of his own. *A Man for All Seasons* succeeds dramatically because Bolt provides only enough historical verisimilitude to present a context for the characters' development while he allows the resultant thematic implications to touch all times, all seasons. When we read any history play, we should search for similar implications; otherwise, the work can never become more than a theatrical précis with a narrow, didactic focus.

Modern Drama

From the 1870s to the present, the theater has participated in the artistic movements reflecting accumulated theories of science, social science, and philosophy which attempt to define reality and the means we use to discern it. First caught in a pendulum of opposing views, modern drama eventually synthesized these perspectives into new forms, familiar in some ways and boldly original in others. Henrik Ibsen's plays began the modern era with their emphasis on **realism**, a seeking of truth through direct observation using the five senses. As objectively depicted, contemporary life received a closer scrutiny than ever before, showing everyday people in everyday situations. Before Ibsen, theatrical sets were limited, with rare exceptions, to castles and country estates. After Ibsen the farmhouse and city tenement were suitable for the stage. Ibsen's work influenced many others, and from realism came two main variations. The first, **naturalism**, strove to push realism towards a direct transformation of life on stage, a "slice of life" showing how the scientific principles of heredity and environment have shaped society, especially in depicting the plights of the lower classes. The second variation, **expressionism**, moved in a different direction and actually denied realism's premise that the real world could be objectively perceived; instead—influenced by Sigmund Freud's theories about human behavior's hidden, subconscious motivations and by other modernist trends in the arts, such as James Joyce's fiction and Picasso's paintings—expressionism imitated a disconnected dream-like world filled with psychological images at odds with the tangible world surrounding it. While naturalism attempts to imitate life directly, expressionism is abstract and often relies on symbols.

A modern play can employ any number of elements found in the spectrum between these extremes as well as suggest divergent philosophical views about whether humanity has the power to change its condition or whether any of its ideas about the universe are verifiable. Moreover, no work of art is necessarily confined within a particular school of thought. It is quite possible that seemingly incongruent forms can appear in the same play and work well. *The Glass Menagerie, A Man for All Seasons*, and *Death of a Salesman* feature characters and dialogue indicative of realistic drama, but the sets described in the stage directions are expressionistic, offering either framed outlines of places or distorted representations. Conventions from classical drama are also available to the playwright. As previously noted, Tom acts as a Greek chorus as well as an important character in his play; the same is true of the Common Man, whose identity changes from scene to scene. Playwrights Eugene Ionesco and Harold Pinter have created characters speaking and behaving in extraordinary ways while occupying sets which are typically realistic. In short, anything is possible in modern drama, a quality which is wholly compatible with the diversity and unpredictability of Twentieth Century human experiences.

In a sense, all good drama is modern. No label about a play's origin or form can adequately describe its content. Establishing the people, places, and thought within the play is crucial to our understanding. For the characters to interest us, we must perceive the issues that affect their lives, and eventually we will discover why the characters' personalities and backgrounds, together with their social situations, inevitably converge with these issues and create conflicts. We must also stay aware of drama's kinship with lyric poetry's subjective mood and tone, a quality dominating all plays regardless of the form. *Death of a Salesman* challenges the classical definitions of tragedy by giving us a modern American, Willy Loman, who is indeed a "low man," a person of little social importance and limited moral fiber. His delusionary values have brought him at age 64 to failure and despair, yet more than ever he clings to his dreams and painted memories for solace and hope. Late one night, after Willy has returned from an aborted sales trip, his rambling conversation with his wife Linda returns to the topic which haunts him the most, his son Biff.

WILLY: Biff is a lazy bum!

LINDA: They're sleeping. Get something to eat. Go on down.

WILLY: Why did he come home? I would like to know what brought him home.

LINDA: I don't know. I think he's still lost, Willy. I think he's very lost.

WILLY: Biff Loman is lost. In the greatest country in the world a young man with such—personal attractiveness, gets lost. And such a hard worker. There's one thing about Biff—he's not lazy.

LINDA: Never.

WILLY (with pity and resolve): I'll see him in the morning; I'll have a nice talk with him. I'll get him a job selling. He could be big in no time. My God! Remember how they used to follow him around in high school? When he smiled at one of them their faces lit up. When he walked down the street... (He loses himself in reminiscences.)

LINDA (trying to bring him out of it): Willy, dear, I got a new kind of American-type cheese today. It's whipped.

WILLY: Why do you get American cheese when you know I like Swiss?

LINDA: I just thought you'd like a change—

WILLY: I don't want change! I want Swiss cheese. Why am I always being contradicted?

LINDA (with a covering laugh): I just thought it would be a surprise.

WILLY: Why don't you open a window in here, for God's sake?

LINDA (with infinite patience): They're all open dear.

WILLY: The way they boxed us in here. Bricks and windows, windows and bricks.

LINDA: We should have bought the land next door.

WILLY: The street is lined with cars. There's not a breath of fresh air in the neighborhood. The grass don't grow any more, you can't raise a carrot in the backyard. They should've had a law against apartment houses. Remember those two beautiful elms out there? When I and Biff hung the swing between them?

LINDA: Yeah, like a million miles from the city.

WILLY: They should've arrested the builder for cutting those down. They massacred the neighborhood. (Lost) More and more I think of those days, Linda. This time of year it was lilac and wisteria. And then the peonies would come out, and the daffodils. What fragrance in this room!

LINDA: Well, after all, people had to move somewhere.

WILLY: No, there's more people now.

LINDA: I don't think there's more people. I think—

WILLY: There's more people! That's what's ruining this country! Population is getting out of control. The competition is maddening! Smell the stink from that apartment house! And another on the other side... How can they whip cheese?

In Arthur Miller's stage directions for *Death of a Salesman*, the Loman house is outlined by simple framing with various floors represented by short elevated platforms. Outside the house the towering shapes of the city angle inward presenting the crowded oppressiveness Willy complains about. First performed in 1949, the play continues to make a powerful commentary on modern American life. We see Willy as more desperate than angry about his condition, which he defines in ways as contradictory as his assessments of Biff. In his suffocating world so nebulously delineated, Willy gropes for peace while hiding from truth; and although his woes are uniquely American in some ways, they touch broader, more universal human problems as well.

PRACTICE
TEST 1

This test is also on CD-ROM in our special interactive CLEP Analyzing & Interpreting Literature TEST*ware*®. It is highly recommended that you first take this exam on computer. You will then have the additional study features and benefits of enforced timed conditions, individual diagnostic analysis, and instant scoring. See page 2 for guidance on how to get the most out of our CLEP Analyzing & Interpreting Literature book and software.

CLEP ANALYZING AND INTERPRETING LITERATURE
Test 1

(Answer sheets appear in the back of this book.)

TIME: 90 Minutes
             80 Questions

DIRECTIONS: Each of the questions or incomplete statements below is followed by five possible answers or completions. Select the best choice in each case and fill in the corresponding oval on the answer sheet.

QUESTIONS 1–4

Me Deare Deare Lord, I know not what to say:
    Speech is too Course a web for me to cloath
My Love to thee in or it to array,
    Or make a mantle. Wouldst thou not such loath?
5   Thy Love to mee's too great, for mee to shape
    A Vesture for the Same at any rate.

When as thy Love doth Touch my Heart down tost
    It tremblingly runs, seeking thee its all,
And as a Child when it his nurse hath lost
10   Runs seeking her, and after her doth Call.
    So when thou hidst from me, I seek and sigh.
    Thou saist return return Oh Shulamite.

Rent out on Use thy Love thy Love I pray.
    My Love to thee shall be thy Rent and I
15 Thee Use on Use, Intrest on intrest pay.

There's none Extortion in such Usury.
I'le pay thee Use on Use for't and therefore
    Thou shalt become the greatest Usurer.
But yet the principall I'le neer restore.
20   The Same is thine and mine. We shall not Jar.
    And so this blessed Usury shall be
    Most profitable both to thee and mee.

And shouldst thou hide thy shining face most fair
    Away from me. And in a sinking wise
25 My trembling beating heart brought nigh t'dispare
    Should cry to thee and in a trembling guise
    Lord quicken it. Drop in its Eares delight
    Saying Return, Return my Shulamite.

"Meditation 146, Second Series," by Cotton Mather

1. The poem as a whole expresses

    (A) man's distress over his search for God.

    (B) man's inability to communicate effectively with God.

    (C) God's great love for mankind.

    (D) the patience God exhibits when dealing with mankind.

    (E) the speaker's sorrow at man's inability to love God.

2. In stanza one the speaker

    (A) complains about God's distance from man.

    (B) expresses that God's love for him is too great and too demanding.

    (C) says that his words are inadequate to express his feelings.

    (D) feels wrapped in a coarse web of sin and deceit.

    (E) fears that he will never love God as God loves him.

3. Which of the following words does NOT support the metaphor of the speaker's words being mere wrapping for his love to God?

    (A) "web" (line 2)   (D) "loath" (line 4)

    (B) "array" (line 3)   (E) "Vesture" (line 6)

    (C) "mantle" (line 4)

4. Which of the following is the BEST statement of meaning in stanzas 3 and 4?

(A) The narrator is accusing God of being parsimonious with his love.

(B) The narrator is thanking God for showing man how to earn enough money to have a good life.

(C) The narrator knows that his term on this planet is but "rented" space and time.

(D) The narrator expresses his belief that too much concentration on money will "Jar" the relationship between man and God.

(E) The narrator hopes that this kind of "Usury" will be profitable to both man and God.

QUESTIONS 5–9

But the Divell as hee affecteth Deitie, and seeketh to have all the complements of Divine honor applied to his service, so hath he among the rest possessed also most Poets with his idle fansies. For in lieu of solemne and devout mat-
5   ter, to which in duety they owe their abilities, they now busy themselves in expressing such passions, as onely serve for testimonies to how unwoorthy affections they have wedded their wils. And because the best course to let them see the errour of their workes, is to weave a new webbe in their
10   owne loom; I have heere layd a few course threds together, to invite some skillfuller wits to goe forward in the same, or to begin some finer peece, wherin it may be seene, how well verse and vertue sute together. Blame me not (good Cosen) though I send you a blamewoorthy present, in which the
15   most that can commend it, is the good will of the writer, neither Arte nor invention, giving it any credite. If in mee this be a fault, you cannot be faultless that did importune mee to committe it, and therefore you must bear part of the penance, when it shall please sharpe censures to impose it. In
20   the meane time with many good wishes I send you these few ditties, add you the Tunes, and let the Meane, I pray you, be still a part in all your Musicke.

From "The Author to his Loving Cosen," by Robert Southwell

5. In the author's view, poets should write about

    (A) the devil putting on Godly attributes.

    (B) the honor and duty due to God.

    (C) fantasies that help the reader to relax.

    (D) love and passion pertaining to women.

    (E) serious matters pertaining to God.

6. The author criticizes poets because

    I.   they waste their abilities on poems that deal with loving women instead of loving God.

    II. they write about love in such a way that shows they disdain marriage.

    III. their love poems show that worldly passion has got the better of them.

    (A) I only   (D) I and II only

    (B) I and III only   (E) I, II, and III

    (C) II only

7. What best describes the role of the author in the figure of speech used to describe his purpose?

    (A) He personifies the writer struggling to put across his web of ideas.

    (B) He plays the weaver in the extended metaphor about the loom and weaving, trying to encourage better poetry.

    (C) He plays the role of the new poet weaving new ideas for the old poets to copy.

    (D) He plays the role of the weaver trying to put back old techniques such as alliteration into the poetry of his days.

    (E) He personifies the role of the old jaded writer trying to encourage younger poets to write better rhyming poetry.

8. Why does the author send the book to his "cosen"?

    (A) He wants him to share in the praise if it is good.

(B)   He wants him to share in the blame if it is criticized.

(C)   The cousin asked him to write it.

(D)   He wants the cousin to learn from the book of poems.

(E)   The cousin is a patron who will promote the book.

9.   The author's voice changes from

(A)   lecturing to praising.   (D)   harsh to gentle.

(B)   didactic to pedantic.   (E)   arrogant to pleasant.

(C)   critical to encouraging.

QUESTIONS 10–13

Kilgore Trout became Billy's favorite living author, and science fiction became the only sort of tales he could read.

5   Rosewater was twice as smart as Billy, but he and Billy were dealing with similar crises in similar ways. They both had found life meaningless, partly because of what they had seen in war. Rosewater, for instance, had shot a fourteen-year-old fireman, mistaking him for a German soldier. So it goes. And Billy had seen the greatest massacre in

10   European history, which was the fire-bombing of Dresden. So it goes.

So they were trying to re-invent themselves and their universe. Science fiction was a big help.

Rosewater said an interesting thing to Billy one

15   time about a book that wasn't science fiction. He said that everything there was to know about life was in *The Brothers Karamazov*, by Feodor Dostoevsky. "But that isn't *enough* any more," said Rosewater.

Another time Billy heard Rosewater say to a psy-

20   chiatrist, "I think you guys are going to have to come up with a lot of wonderful *new* lies, or people just aren't going to want to go on living."

From Slaughterhouse-Five, by Kurt Vonnegut, Jr.

10.   As it is used in the context of this passage, "science fiction" (lines 2, 13) suggests which of the following?

I.   A metaphoric contrast between real and fantasy lives

II.   A metaphor for a secure and stable life

III.   A metaphor suggesting we need lies to survive life

(A) I only

(B) II only

(C) III only

(D) I and III only

(E) I, II, and III

11.   As it is used in lines 9 and 11, the sentence "So it goes" suggests

   (A) verbal irony.

   (B) apparent empathy toward tragedy.

   (C) sensitivity toward tragedy.

   (D) excuses for accidents.

   (E) a verbal "shrug of the shoulders."

12.   It can be inferred from the context that the book *The Brothers Karamazov* (lines 16–17)

   (A) is a science fiction book.

   (B) is about people "trying to re-invent themselves and their universe" (lines 12–13).

   (C) is not a science fiction book.

   (D) represents a type of fiction that answers life's questions.

   (E) represents fantasy or escape fiction.

13.   All of the following are suggested by Rosewater's comments in lines 15–22 EXCEPT

   (A) survival requires beliefs which mask reality.

   (B) life is meaningful only if confronted directly.

   (C) life is meaningless without fantasies.

   (D) psychiatrists and novelists provide useful lies to help us survive.

   (E) old solutions do not solve new problems.

QUESTIONS 14–20

OEDIPUS:

    One day at dinner, a man who had drunk too much
Insulted me by saying I was not
My father's son. In spite of being angry,
I managed to control myself. Next day
5   I asked my parents, who were both indignant
That he had leveled such a charge against me.
This was a satisfaction, yet the thing
Still Rankled, for the rumor grew widespread.
At last I went to Delphi secretly.
10   Apollo gave no answer to my question
But sent me off, anguished and terrified,
With fearful prophecies that I was fated
To be my mother's husband, to bring forth
Children whom men could not endure to see,
15   And to take my father's life. When I heard this
I turned and fled, hoping to find at length
Some place where I could know of Corinth only
As a far distant land beneath the stars,
Some place where I would never have to see
20   The infamies of this oracle fulfilled.
And as I went on, I approached the spot
At which you tell me Laius met his end.
Now this, Jocasta, is the absolute truth.
When I had come to where the three roads fork,
25   A herald met me, walking before a carriage,
Drawn by two colts, in which a man was seated,
Just as you said. The old man and the herald
Ordered me off the road with threatening gestures.
Then as the driver pushed me to one side,
30   I struck him angrily. And seeing this
The old man, as I drew abreast, leaned out
And brought his drivers two-pronged goad down hard
Upon my head. He paid a heavy price
For doing that. With one blow of my staff
35   I knocked him headlong from his chariot
Flat on his back. Then every man of them
I killed. Now if the blood of Laius flowed
In that old stranger's veins, what mortal man
Could be more wretched, more accursed than I?

40   I whom no citizen or foreigner
     May entertain or shelter, I to whom
     No one may speak, I, I who must be driven
     From every door. No other man has cursed me.
     I have brought the curse upon myself.
45   The hands that killed him now pollute his bed!
     Am I not vile, foul, utterly unclean?
     For I must fly and never see again
     My people or set foot in my own land,
     Or else become the husband of my mother
50   And put to death my father Polybus,
     To whom I owe my life and upbringing.
     Men would be right in thinking that such things
     Have been inflicted by some cruel fate.
     May the gods' high and holy majesty
55   Forbid that I should see that day. No! No!
     Rather than be dishonored by a doom
     So dreadful may I vanish from the earth.

   From "Oedipus the King," by Sophocles

14. The dramatic style of speech in this passage is one of a

   (A) soliloquy.   (D) dialogue.

   (B) monologue.   (E) poetic drama.

   (C) dramatic lyric.

15. The "This" of line 7 refers to

   (A) the satisfaction.

   (B) the drunken man.

   (C) the charge against the speaker.

   (D) the indignance of the speaker's parents.

   (E) the anger of the speaker.

16. The word "infamies" in line 20 reaffirms

   (A) the speaker's anger.

   (B) his parents denial.

   (C) the fact that the rumor was circulating.

(D) the speaker's visit to Delphi.

(E) the speaker's unanswered question.

17. The dominant feeling expressed by Oedipus in this passage is one of

(A) guilt and horror.   (D) anger and denial.

(B) timidity and fearfulness.   (E) remorse and resentment.

(C) confusion and sorrow.

18. The remark made by Oedipus, "He paid a heavy price / For doing that" (lines 33–34) allows the reader to infer

(A) that he reproached the drunken man who originally spread the rumor.

(B) Oedipus did not heed the advice of the herald.

(C) Oedipus was a brave man.

(D) Oedipus charged them with a fine for his insult.

(E) Oedipus could be quickly incited to violence when physically provoked.

19. At what point in the plot does this passage MOST seem to be located?

(A) Exposition   (D) Climax

(B) Rising action   (E) Resolution

(C) Falling action

20. The final 19 lines of the passage (lines 39–57) intimate that Oedipus will follow what specific course of action?

(A) He will return to Polybus and Merope.

(B) He intends to commit suicide.

(C) He intends to punish himself by ostracization.

(D) He will consult the gods.

(E) He will make restitution for his actions.

QUESTIONS 21–27

Monday, 29 January, 1932

Something has happened to me, I can't doubt it any more. It came as an illness does, not like an ordinary certainity, not like anything evident. It came cunningly, little by little; I felt a little strange, a little put out, that's all.

5 Once established it never moved, it stayed quiet, and I was able to persuade myself that nothing was the matter with me, that it was a false alarm. And now, it's blossoming.

I don't think the historian's trade is much given to psychological analysis. In our work we have to do only

10 with sentiments in the whole to which we give genetic titles such as Ambition and Interest. And yet if I had even a shadow of self-knowledge, I could put it to good use now.

For instance, there is something new about my hands, a certain way of picking up my pipe or fork. Or else

15 it's the fork which now has a certain way of having itself picked up, I don't know. A little while ago, just as I was coming into my room, I stopped short because I felt in my hand a cold object which held my attention through a sort of personality. I opened my hand, looked: I was simply

20 holding the door knob. This morning in the library, when the Self-Taught Man came to say good morning to me, it took me ten seconds to recognize him. I saw an unknown face, barely a face. Then there was this hand like a fat white worm in my own hand. I dropped it almost immediately

25 and the arm fell back flabbily.

There are a great number of suspicious noises in the streets, too.

So a change *has* taken place during these last few weeks. But where? It is an abstract change without object.

30 Am I the one who has changed? If not, then it is this room, this city and this nature; I must choose.

From "Nausea," by Jean-Paul Sartre

21. What literary form best describes this passage?

(A) Autobiography   (D) Biography

(B) Memoir   (E) Prose poem

(C) Diary

22. What term LEAST describes the tone of the author?

    (A) Introspective   (D) Determined

    (B) Listless   (E) Languid

    (C) Confused

23. What is "blossoming" in line 7?

    (A) The speaker's illness

    (B) The speaker's strange feeling

    (C) The belief that the oddness is a false alarm

    (D) The stagnant, quiet uncertainty

    (E) The speaker's job as a historian

24. The second paragraph is BEST interpreted to mean

    (A) the speaker is unhappy with his career choice.

    (B) he believes that one should seek psychological counseling upon entering the trade.

    (C) the speaker is criticizing his job because it is mindless.

    (D) the speaker is lamenting his lack of self-knowledge which is unnecessary to his job.

    (E) the speaker thinks the sentimental titles of his works are silly.

25. The metaphor "fat white worm" (lines 23–24) reveals the speaker's attitude to be one of

    (A) revulsion.   (D) disregard.

    (B) condescension.   (E) betrayal.

    (C) indifference.

26. The speaker's observance that "there is something new about my hands" (lines 13–14) MOST emphasizes his

    (A) new found love of self.

    (B) lack of familiarity with his own body.

    (C) narcissistic egomania.

(D)   a sudden self-consciousness.

(E)   a desire for change.

27.   The last paragraph suggests that the speaker is confused because

(A)   the sudden changes are in his imagination.

(B)   his room seems altered.

(C)   he is not at ease with the city or the strange sounds in the street.

(D)   although he is certain about the transformation, it is not obvious or tangible.

(E)   he cannot choose between the city and the country.

QUESTIONS 28–32

In short, I went on thus for a long time (I may say it
without boasting), faithfully minding my business, till it
became more and more evident that my townsmen would
not after all admit me into the list of town officers, nor
5   make my place a sinecure with a moderate allowance. My
accounts, which I can swear to have kept faithfully, I have,
indeed, never got audited, still less accepted, still less paid
and settled. However, I have not set my heart on that.
Not long since, a strolling Indian went to sell bas-
10   kets at the house of a well-known lawyer in my neighborhood. "Do you wish to buy any baskets?" he asked. "No,
we do not want any," was the reply. "What!" exclaimed the
Indian as he went out the gate, "do you mean to starve us?"
Having seen his industrious white neighbors so well off, —
15   that the lawyer had only to weave arguments, and, by some
magic, wealth and standing followed, — he had said to
himself: I will go into business; I will weave baskets; it is a
thing which I can do. Thinking that when he had made the
baskets he would have done his part, and then it would be
20   the white man's to buy them. He had not discovered that it
was necessary for him to make it worth the other's while to
buy them, or at least make him think that it was so, or to
make something else which it would be worth his while to
buy. I too had woven a kind of basket of a delicate texture,
25   but I had not made it worth anyone's while to buy them.
Yet not the less, in my case, did I think it worth my while

to weave them, and instead of studying how to make it worth men's while to buy my baskets, I studied rather how to avoid the necessity of selling them. The life which men
30   praise and regard as successful is but one kind. Why should we exaggerate any one kind at the expense of others?

From Walden, by Henry David Thoreau

28.   As it is used in the passage, the word "sinecure" (line 5) means

    (A) a job or position.   (D) wealth.

    (B) a partial cure for illness.   (E) insecurity.

    (C) a mathematical term.

29.   The narrator uses the story about the Indian (lines 9–24) trying to sell his baskets as

    (A) allusion.   (D) paradox.

    (B) metaphor.   (E) simile.

    (C) image.

30.   As used by the narrator, the effect of such phrases as "without boasting" (line 2), "faithfully minding my business" (line 2), "accounts, which I can swear to have kept faithfully" (line 6), and "never got audited" (line 7) is to

    (A) indicate the narrator's success in business.

    (B) mock the ethics of his business partners.

    (C) satirize the language of business.

    (D) stress the narrator's ethical stance.

    (E) reveal his townspeople's inattention to his abilities.

31.   The idea in lines 29–31 is presented in which of the following ways?

    (A) As a categorical statement of truth

    (B) As a question to suggest the absolute truth about success

    (C) As a rhetorical question to prod the reader into thinking about different ways to be successful

(D) As a rejection of anything but the conventional measure of success

(E) As a comparison between the Indian and the lawyer

32. As it is used in context, the phrase "Yet not the less, in my case, did I think it worth my while to weave them" (lines 26–27), suggests all of the following about the narrator's character EXCEPT his

(A) idealistic philosophy.

(B) studied indifference about his image.

(C) relative indifference to wealth.

(D) whimsical behavior.

(E) relative indifference toward community status.

QUESTIONS 33–39

      Sir Anthony. Madam, a circulating library in a town is as an evergreen tree of diabolical knowledge! It blossoms through the year! — And depend on it. Mrs. _____, that they who are so fond of handling the leaves,

5   will long for the fruit at last.

      Mrs. _____ Fie, Fie, Sir Anthony! you surely speak laconically.

      Sir Anthony. Why, Mrs. _____, in moderation now, what would you have a woman know?

10   Mrs. _____ Observe me, Sir Anthony. I would by no means wish a daughter of mine to be a progeny of learning; I don't think so much learning becomes a young woman; for instance, I would never let her meddle with Greek or Hebrew, or algebra, or simony, or fluxions, or

15   paradoxes, or such inflammatory branches of learning— neither would it be necessary for her to handle any of your mathematical, astronomical, diabolical instruments. —But, Sir Anthony, I would send her, at nine years old, to a boarding school, in order to learn a little ingenuity, and

20   artifice. Then, sir, she should have a supercilious knowl- edge in accounts;—and as she grew up, I would have her instructed in geometry, that she might know something of the contagious countries; but above all, Sir Anthony, she

should be mistress of orthodoxy, that she might not mis-
25 spell, and mispronounce words so shamefully as girls usually do; and likewise that she might reprehend the true
meaning of what she is saying. This, Sir Anthony, is what I
would have a woman know; and I don't think there is a
superstitious article in it.
30   Sir Anthony. Well, well, Mrs. _____, I will dispute the point no further with you; though I must confess,
that you are a truly moderate and polite arguer, for almost
every third word you say is on my side of the question...

From <u>The Rivals</u>, *Act I Sc. ii, by Richard Sheridan*

33. Mrs. _____'s last name gave rise to which of the following
dictionary terms?

(A) Homonym

(D) Synonym

(B) Altruism

(E) Synecdoche

(C) Malapropism

34. Which best describes what Mrs. _____ does to words?

(A) She changes the meaning to something outrageous.

(B) She chooses the wrong meaning.

(C) She gives a word close in meaning that sounds the same.

(D) She gives a word close in sound that gives a ridiculous meaning.

(E) She gives a word close in sound but often wrong in meaning.

35. All of the following words Mrs. _____ uses wrongly EXCEPT

(A) fluxions.

(D) contagious.

(B) laconically.

(E) orthodoxy.

(C) ingenuity.

36. What device does Sir Anthony use to describe a circulating library?

(A) A mixed metaphor

(D) An extended metaphor

(B) Personification

(E) Pathetic fallacy

(C) An extended simile

37. What best describes Sir Anthony's meaning behind the notion of the "leaves" and the "fruit"?

(A) Those who leaf quickly through books will never learn from the tree of knowledge.

(B) Those who read evil books will become evil.

(C) Those who read books about exciting adventures will want to experience the same.

(D) Those who read novels that look exciting will want to read more and more.

(E) Those who choose a book by its cover will be disappointed at length.

38. What best describes the meaning behind Sir Anthony's concluding speech?

(A) Mrs. _____ has in fact agreed with everything he has said so he has enjoyed the argument.

(B) Because Mrs. _____ does not understand him, there has been no argument.

(C) He loves this type of argument because he wins.

(D) He admires Mrs. _____'s powers of debating in an argument.

(E) He knows Mrs. _____ has not understood him and gone against most of her own argument.

39. What words best describe Sir Anthony's tone in his concluding speech?

(A) Droll and dry

(B) Amused but angry

(C) Sarcastic but amused

(D) Whimsical and weary

(E) Laconic and sardonic

QUESTIONS 40–45

      I looked at the sea of yellow faces above the garish clothes—faces all happy and excited over this bit of fun, all certain that the elephant was going to be shot. They were watching me as they would watch a conjuror about to per-
5 form a trick. They did not like me, but with the magical rifle in my hands, I was momentarily worth watching. And suddenly I realized that I would have to shoot the elephant after all. The people expected it of me and I had got to do it; I could feel their two thousand wills pressing me for-
10 ward, irresistibly. And it was at this moment, as I stood there with the rifle in my hands, that I first grasped the hollowness, the futility of the white man's dominion in the East. Here was I, the white man with his gun, standing in front of an unarmed native crowd — seemingly the leading
15 actor of the piece; but in reality I was only an absurd pup-pet pushed to and fro by the will of those yellow faces behind. I perceived in this moment that when the white man turns tyrant it is his own freedom he destroys. He becomes a sort of hollow posing dummy, the conventional-
20 ized figure of a sahib. For it is the condition of his rule that he shall spend his life in trying to impress the "natives," and so in every crisis he has got to do what the "natives" expect of him.

From Shooting an Elephant and Other Essays, by George Orwell

40. The controlling metaphor of the piece involves

    (A) the stage and acting.

    (B) magic and mystery.

    (C) the thrill of the hunt.

    (D) the crowd's will.

    (E) the ventriloquist's dummy.

41. The narrator must shoot the elephant for the following reasons EXCEPT

    (A) he is willed by the crowd.

    (B) his role of sahib demands it.

(C) he must impress the natives.

(D) his role of policeman demands it.

(E) the people expect it.

42. The resolution to kill the elephant symbolizes the

(A) power yet stupidity of the white man in the East.

(B) domination of the white man in the East.

(C) prejudice the white man has toward the natives.

(D) emptiness of the role the white man plays in the East.

(E) role of the sahib as clown.

43. Which of the following BEST explains why the people are "happy and excited"?

(A) They love and respect the narrator who will put on a show.

(B) They hate but respect the role of sahib who will perform for them.

(C) They are on a feast day of revelry to watch this show.

(D) They scorn the narrator but anticipate his prowess in the show-down with the elephant.

(E) They dislike the narrator and hope to see his downfall in a show of arms.

44. The narrator uses the personal pronoun frequently and the term "white man" to show his

(A) scorn of the rabble.

(B) distancing himself from the situation.

(C) realization that he stands for many.

(D) fear of the rabble.

(E) awareness that he stands alone.

45. Which word best describes the tone of the passage?

(A) Furious   (D) Sardonic

(B) Philosophic   (E) Disillusioned

(C) Amused

QUESTIONS 46–49

> In Breughel's *Icarus*, for instance: how everything turns away
> Quite leisurely from the disaster; the plowman may
> Have heard the splash, the forsaken cry,
> But for him it was not an important failure; the sun shone
> 5   As it had to on the white legs disappearing into the green
> Water; and the expensive delicate ship that must have seen
> Something amazing, a boy falling out of the sky,
> Had somewhere to get to and sailed calmly on.

"Musée des Beaux Arts," by W.H. Auden

46. The technique used between lines 1–2 is

    (A) alliteration.   (D) personification.

    (B) enjambment.   (E) bathos.

    (C) onomatopoeia.

47. What examples are given for "everything turns away"?

    I.   The boy

    II. The plowman and the ship

    III. The plowman and the painter

    (A) I only   (D) II only

    (B) I and III only   (E) I and II only

    (C) III only

48. Which of the following most clearly expresses the poem's meaning?

    (A) Society's blatant disregard for life

    (B) People's inhumanity toward others

    (C) Society's indifference to suffering

(D)   A courageous attempt to escape the bounds of society

(E)   Society's contempt for the weak and failure

49.   The words "for instance" give the poem a(n)

(A)   didactic tone.   (D)   conversational tone.

(B)   ironic tone.   (E)   regular rhythm.

(C)   irregular scansion.

QUESTIONS 50–53

> Perchance he for whom this bell tolls may be so ill
> as that he knows not it tolls for him; and perchance I may
> think myself so much better than I am, as that they who are
> about me and see my state may have caused it to toll for
> 5   me, and I know not that. The church is catholic, universal,
> so are all her actions; all that she does belongs to all. When
> she baptizes a child, that action concerns me; for that child
> is thereby connected to that body which is my head too, and
> ingrafted into that body whereof I am a member. And when
> 10   she buries a man, that action concerns me: all mankind is of
> one author and is one volume; when one man dies, one
> chapter is not torn out of the book, but translated into a
> better language; and every chapter must be so translated.

From "For Whom the Bell Doth Toll," by John Donne

50.   How is the writer most like the person for whom the bell tolls?

(A)   He does not realize that he has tolled the bell for others.

(B)   He thinks the bell tolls for himself.

(C)   He fears that the bell tolls for himself.

(D)   He does not realize that others may have caused the bell to toll
for him.

(E)   They both know the bell tolls for them.

51.   How is the poet related to the child who is baptized?

(A)   There is no relation except that they are both members of the
church.

(B) Their membership in the true church makes them brothers.

(C) There is no relationship whatsoever.

(D) The child is his brother regardless of what the church does to him.

(E) After the child's baptism they are members of the same metaphorical body.

52. The final line of the passage indicates that

(A) all will die and go to a better place.

(B) it is impossible to know what will happen to us at death.

(C) there is no better place than this.

(D) change is inevitable in the world.

(E) all men will die eventually.

53. Which of the following describes the tone of this passage?

I. Playful

II. Ironic

III. Condescending

IV. Serious

(A) I and III only

(B) IV only

(C) II only

(D) None of these

(E) I and II only

QUESTIONS 54–58

One speaks the glory of the British Queen,
And one describes a charming Indian screen;
A third interprets motions, looks, and eyes;
At every word a reputation dies.
5 Snuff, or the fan, supply each pause of chat,

With singing, laughing, ogling, and all that.
Meanwhile, declining from the noon of day,
The sun obliquely shoots his burning ray;
The hungry judges soon the sentence sign,
10   And wretches hang that jurymen may dine;

From "The Rape of the Lock" (Canto 3 lines 13–22), by Alexander Pope

54. The last two lines suggest that this society

(A) takes pride in its justice system.

(B) speedily administers justice for humanitarian reasons.

(C) sentences the wrong people to death.

(D) sentences people for the wrong reasons.

(E) believes in the jury system.

55. Lines 1–6 suggest that this society

I. indulges in gossip that slanders the Queen.

II. engages in serious discussions about affairs of state.

III. engages in gossip that ruins reputations.

(A) I and III only   (D) I, II, and III

(B) III only   (E) I only

(C) II only

56. The juxtaposition in lines 1 and 2 suggests that the people

(A) talk of trivia.

(B) revere the monarchy and Indian screens equally.

(C) are Imperialists.

(D) are Royalists.

(E) talk of serious matters.

57. The word "obliquely" (line 8) in this context could mean all of the following EXCEPT

(A) perpendicularly.

(B)   at a steep angle.

(C)   a pun on hidden meanings.

(D)   a pun on stealth.

(E)   a suggestion of the amoral standing of this society.

58.   The change in voice from the first half of the excerpt into the second is best described as one from

(A)   light to dark.

(B)   amused to critical.

(C)   light-hearted to sarcastic.

(D)   criticism to acceptance.

(E)   amused to sadness.

QUESTIONS 59–63

Be that as it may, I could not help thinking, as I looked at the works of Shakespeare on the shelf, that the Bishop was right at least in this; it would have been impossible, completely and entirely, for any woman to have writ-
5   ten the plays of Shakespeare in the age of Shakespeare. Let me imagine, since facts are hard to come by, what would have happened had Shakespeare a wonderfully gifted sister, called Judith, let us say. Shakespeare himself went, very probably—his mother was an heiress—to grammar school,
10   where he learnt Latin—Ovid, Virgil, and Horace—and the elements of grammar and logic. He was, as well known, a wild boy who poached rabbits, perhaps shot a deer, and had, rather sooner than he should have done, to marry a woman in the neighborhood, who bore him a child rather
15   quicker than was right. That escapade sent him to seek his fortune in London. He had, it seemed, a taste for the theater; he began by holding horses at the stage door. Very soon he got work in the theater, became a successful actor, and lived at the hub of the universe, meeting everybody,
20   knowing everybody, practicing his art on the boards, exercising his wits in the streets, and even getting access to the palace of the queen. Meanwhile his extraordinary sister, let us suppose, remained at home. She was adventurous, as imaginative, as agog to see the world as he was. But she
25   was not sent to school. She had no chance of learning

grammar and logic, let alone of reading Horace and Virgil. She picked up a book now and then, one of her brother's perhaps, and read a few pages. But then her parents came home and told her to mend the stockings or mind the stew
30 and not moon about with books and papers. They would have spoken sharply but kindly, for they were substantial people who knew the conditions of life for a woman and loved their daughter—indeed, more likely than not she was the apple of her father's eye.

From "A Room of One's Own," by Virginia Woolf

59. The speaker most believes women in Shakespeare's time were denied creative expression because

(A) they were mentally inferior.

(B) they had little time due to household responsibilities.

(C) they were constrained by social conventions which designated a woman's inferior position.

(D) they did not know how to read Latin.

(E) they obeyed their parents.

60. It may be inferred from line 10 that Ovid, Virgil, and Horace were

(A) Shakespeare's professors.

(B) instructors of Latin.

(C) instructors of grammar and logic.

(D) fellow classmates.

(E) famous Latin writers.

61. Lines 13–15 may be best interpreted to mean

(A) Shakespeare's wife was from the same town.

(B) Shakespeare's first child was premature.

(C) Shakespeare was forced to marry a local girl that he impregnated.

(D) Shakespeare did not want to get married.

(E) Shakespeare was too young to get married.

62. In context, the word "agog" in line 24 means

    (A) eager.   (D) disappointed.

    (B) intimidated.   (E) deserving.

    (C) expecting.

63. In this passage, the speaker mostly attempts to

    (A) persuade the audience that women need more rights.

    (B) complain about the freedoms denied to women yet enjoyed by men.

    (C) reveal the tragic story of Judith Shakespeare.

    (D) show the audience that women can do anything a man can do.

    (E) illustrate how the lives of men and women at this time were different as a function of gender roles.

QUESTIONS 64–70

She had suffered badly during the period of poverty. Nothing, however, could shake the curious, sullen, animal pride that dominated each member of the family. Now, for Mabel, the end had come. Still she would not cast about her.
5   She would follow her own way just the same. She would always hold the keys of her own situation. Mindless and persistent, she endured from day to day. Why should she think? Why should she answer anybody? It was enough that this was the end, and there was no way out. She need not
10 pass any more darkly along the main street of the small town, avoiding every eye. She need not demean herself any more, going into the shops and buying the cheapest food. This was at an end. She thought of nobody, not even of herself. Mindless and persistent, she seemed in a sort of ec-
15 stasy to be coming nearer to her fulfillment, her own glorifi-cation, approaching her dead mother, who was glorified.
In the afternoon, she took a little bag, with shears and sponge and a small scrubbing-brush, and went out. It was a gray, wintry day, with saddened dark green fields and
20 an atmosphere blackened by the smoke of foundries not far off. She went quickly, darkly along the causeway, heeding nobody, through the town to the churchyard.

There she always felt secure, as if no one could see her, although as a matter of fact she was exposed to the stare of everyone who passed along under the churchyard wall. Nevertheless, once under the shadow of the great looming church, among the graves, she felt immune to the world, reserved within the thick churchyard wall as in another country.

Carefully, she clipped the grass from the grave, and arranged the pinky-white, small chrysanthemums in the tin cross. When this was done, she took an empty jar from a neighboring grave, brought water, and carefully, most scrupulously sponged the marble headstone and coping-stone.

It gave her sincere satisfaction to do this. She felt in immediate contact with the world of her mother. She took minute pains, went through the park in a state bordering on pure happiness, as if in performing this task she came into a subtle, intimate connection with her mother. For the life she followed here in the world was far less real than the world of death she inherited from her mother.

From "The Horse Dealer's Daughter," by D. H. Lawrence

64. The tone of the author towards Mabel is

(A) sympathetic.

(B) sarcastic.

(C) horrified.

(D) patronizing.

(E) uninterested.

65. The author implies that Mabel's questioning

(A) is an act of information gathering.

(B) is an expression of self-doubt.

(C) is a defiant expression of self-assurance.

(D) is simply an attempt by the author to indicate what she is thinking.

(E) is an attempt by the author to gain the reader's sympathy for her situation.

66. The second paragraph of this selection is remarkable stylistically in that it

    (A) portrays a woman more involved with death than with life.

    (B) sustains a pattern of death imagery almost throughout.

    (C) concentrates on seemingly unimportant minor details.

    (D) uses natural description to portray Mabel's despair.

    (E) is written in a style unlike the surrounding paragraphs.

67. The author's placement of the description of Mabel's bag in the same paragraph with the description of the landscape

    (A) underscores the stylistic challenges the author typically presents to the reader.

    (B) indicates that Mabel is as intent on eliminating the grime of her life as she is in "scrubbing" the soot off her mother's grave.

    (C) foreshadows her impending suicide.

    (D) is meant to indicate the disorder of her mind; no well-adjusted person would go out in this weather.

    (E) reinforces the picture of Mabel as a character who gives no outward indication of her "dark" intentions.

68. The churchyard wall represents for Mabel

    (A) the boundary between the living and the dead.

    (B) a border between her native land and that of foreigners.

    (C) a mere physical obstacle of little consequence.

    (D) a forbidding symbol of death.

    (E) a religious boundary, representing hallowed ground.

69. Which of the following best describes the movement in this passage?

    (A) From the crowded world of her house to the solitary world of the graveyard

    (B) From the careworn world of the town to the carefree world of death

    (C) From the solitary world of her house to communion with her mother at the graveyard

(D) From the earthly connections of her house to the otherworldly in the graveyard

(E) From the critical world of the town to the liberating world of the graveyard

70. In line 19, "saddened dark green fields" is an example of which of the following?

(A) Hyperbole

(B) Irony

(C) Personification

(D) Apostrophe

(E) Metaphor

QUESTIONS 71–77

DO NOT GO GENTLE INTO THAT GOOD NIGHT

Do not go gentle into that good night,
Old age should burn and rave at close of day;
Rage, rage against the dying of the light.

Though wise men at their end know dark is right,
5   Because their words had forked no lightning they
Do not go gentle into that good night.

Good men, the last wave by, crying how bright
Their frail deeds might have danced in a green bay,
Rage, rage against the dying of the light.

10   Wild men who caught and sang the sun in flight,
And learn, too late, they grieved it on its way,
Do not go gentle into that good night.

Grave men, near death, who see with blinding sight
Blind eyes could blaze like meteors and be gay,
15   Rage, rage against the dying of the light.

And you, my father, there on the sad height,
Curse, bless, me now with your fierce tears, I pray.
Do not go gentle into that good night.
Rage, rage against the dying of the light.

By Dylan Thomas

71. In the context of the first stanza, lines 2 and 3 express the belief that

    (A) old people should be less complaining.

    (B) old people should vent their anger regularly, and thus prolong their lives.

    (C) old people should fight against death in every way.

    (D) old people should fight against losing the will to live.

    (E) old people should be expected to be bitter and disappointed.

72. The "dying of the light" (lines 3, 15, 19) refers metaphorically to

    (A) the passage of time.

    (B) the aging of the body.

    (C) the aging of the spirit.

    (D) death.

    (E) the loss of the will to live.

73. The use of the word "rage" throughout the poem has the greatest effect in

    (A) increasing the emotional intensity of the statement.

    (B) providing closure at the end of every stanza.

    (C) providing "stock" figures with a vivid emotional reaction.

    (D) providing the poet's audience with a clear statement of the poem's message.

    (E) reinforcing the "curse" of the last stanza.

74. The fifth stanza is notable for its evident

    (A) hyperbole.   (D) sexual innuendo.

    (B) irony.   (E) paradox.

    (C) synecdoche.

75. The poem indicates that the poet's father

    (A) is at the same time wise, good, wild, and near death.

(B)   is old, only.

(C)   is already dead.

(D)   is watching his son prepare for death.

(E)   is already raging against death.

76.   The poet "pray(s)" to his father to "bless" him because the poet implies he

(A)   is near death himself.

(B)   is afraid of death.

(C)   is in need of a last blessing from his father.

(D)   knows he will have to face death sometime in the future.

(E)   is unsure of his own feelings about death.

77.   The battle of color and light within each of the four middle stanzas has the effect of

(A)   portraying life as good and death as evil.

(B)   emphasizing the ongoing conflict between good and evil.

(C)   underscoring the frustration each individual feels as he confronts death.

(D)   reinforcing the cosmic imagery throughout.

(E)   imbuing the confrontation with a vivid, "living" quality.

QUESTIONS 78–82

"I'd like to clear away the lion business," Macomber said. "It's not very pleasant to have your wife see you do something like that."

I should think it would be even more unpleasant to

5   do it, Wilson thought, wife or no wife, or to talk about it having done it. But he said, "I wouldn't think about that any more. Any one could be upset by his first lion. That's all over."

But that night after dinner and a whisky and soda by

10   the fire before going to bed, as Francis Macomber lay on his cot with the mosquito bar over him and listened to the

night noises it was not all over. It was neither all over nor was it beginning. But more than shame he felt cold, hollow fear in him. The fear was still there like a cold slimy hollow

15 in all the emptiness where once his confidence had been and it made him feel sick. It was still there with him now.

It had started the night before when he had wakened and heard the lion roaring somewhere up along the river. It was a deep sound and at the end there were sort of cough-

20 ing grunts that made him seem just outside the tent, and when Francis Macomber woke in the night to hear it he was afraid. He could hear his wife breathing quietly, asleep. There was no one to tell he was afraid, nor to be afraid with him, and, lying alone, he did not know the Somali proverb

25 that says a brave man is always frightened three times by a lion; when he first sees his track, when he first hears him roar and when he first confronts him. Then while they were eating breakfast by lantern light out in the dining tent, be-fore the sun was up, the lion roared again and Francis

30 thought he was just at the edge of camp.

"Sounds like an old-timer," Robert Wilson said, looking up from his kippers and coffee. "Listen to him cough."

"Is he very close?"

35 "A mile or so up the stream."

"Will we see him?"

"We'll have a look."

"Does his roaring carry that far? It sounds as though he were right in camp."

40 "Carries a hell of a long way,'' said Robert Wilson. "It's strange the way it carries. Hope he's a shootable cat. The boys said there was a very big one about here."

"If I get a shot, where should I hit him," Macomber asked, "to stop him?"

45 "In the shoulders," Wilson said. "In the neck if you can make it. Shoot for bone. Break him down."

"I hope I can place it properly," Macomber said.

"You shoot very well," Wilson told him. "Take your time. Make sure of him. The first one in is the one that

50 counts."

From "The Short Happy Life of Francis Macomber," by Ernest Hemingway

78. Which of the following best indicates the subject of the passage?

    (A) Dealing with the apprehension of an impending confrontation

    (B) Coping with life in the wild

    (C) Dealing with a previous failure of courage

    (D) Coping with marital difficulties

    (E) Dealing with culture shock in a new situation

79. The passage is most stylistically notable for

    (A) clear and precise descriptions of time placement.

    (B) clear and precise descriptions of fear.

    (C) clear and precise descriptions of geography and climate.

    (D) clear and precise descriptions of camp life.

    (E) clear and precise descriptions of the sounds of nature.

80. The chief effect of Hemingway's seemingly casual attention to punctuation and sentence length in this passage is to

    (A) contribute to a "stream of consciousness" atmosphere.

    (B) indicate that the personalities he is describing are marginally educated.

    (C) indicate that Macomber's emotional turmoil is great.

    (D) imply that these passages are not as important as those that will come later.

    (E) create a sense of detachment in the reader.

Please Note: This is where the actual CLEP exam would end. We provide 10 extra questions for practice purposes.

---

81. Throughout the passage, Hemingway implies that the most important difference between Macomber and Wilson is that

    (A) Wilson is brave while Macomber is a coward.

    (B) Macomber is dependent on his wife, while Wilson lives independently.

    (C) Wilson is African while Macomber is an outsider.

(D) Macomber is expressive, while Wilson is more restrained.

(E) Wilson is experienced, while Macomber is inexperienced.

82. The nature of the dialogue between the men at the end of the passage is most indicative of

(A) Macomber's limited attention and Wilson's complete absorption.

(B) Macomber's curiosity and Wilson's casual interest.

(C) Macomber's fear and Wilson's bravery.

(D) Wilson's delight and Macomber's dread.

(E) Macomber's limited experience and Wilson's complete knowledge.

QUESTIONS 83–86

Their encreasing passion quite terrified us; and Mrs. Mirvan was beginning to remonstrate with the Captain, when we were all silenced by what follows.

"Let me go, villain that you are, let me go, or I'll promise you I'll get you put to prison for this usage; I'm no
5 common person, I assure you, and, *ma foi*, I'll go to Justice Fielding about you; for I'm a person of fashion, and I'll make you know it, or my name i' n't Duval."

I heard no more: amazed, frightened, and unspeakably shocked, an involuntary exclamation of *Gracious*
10 *Heaven*! escaped me, and, more dead than alive, I sunk into Mrs. Mirvan's arms. But let me draw a veil over a scene too cruel for a heart so compassionately tender as yours; it is sufficient that you know this supposed foreigner proved to be Madame Duval, — the grandmother of your Evelina!

15 O, Sir, to discover so near a relation in a woman who had thus introduced herself! — what would become of me, were it not for you, my protector, my friend, and my refuge?

My extreme concern, and Mrs. Mirvan's surprise, immediately betrayed me. But I will not shock you with the
20 manner of her acknowledging me, or the bitterness, the *grossness* — I cannot otherwise express myself, — with which she spoke of those unhappy past transactions you have so pathetically related to me. All the misery of a much-injured parent, dear, though never seen, regretted,
25 though never known, crowded so forcibly upon my memory, that they rendered this interview — one only excepted — the most afflicting I can ever know.

When we stopt at her lodgings, she desired me to accompany her into the house, and said she could easily procure
30 a room for me to sleep in. Alarmed and trembling, I turned to
Mrs. Mirvan, "My daughter, Madam," said that sweet woman,
"cannot so abruptly part with her young friend; you must allow a little time to wean them from each other."

"Pardon me, Ma'am," answered Madame Duval,
35 (who, from the time of her being known somewhat softened
her manners) "Miss can't possibly be so nearly connected to
this child as I am."

By Fanny Burney

83. Mrs. Duval's threat of sending the Captain to prison is

(A) justified, given the Captain's behavior.

(B) unjustified, as the Captain is obviously teasing.

(C) a sign to the others that they should interfere in the escalating hostilities.

(D) something that undermines her protests of not being a common person.

(E) absurd, because she is only making an idle threat.

84. To whom is Evelina probably writing?

(A) Mrs. Mirvan's son

(B) Her grandfather

(C) Her guardian

(D) The father of her closest friend

(E) Her own father

85. What piece of information suggests that the meeting between Madame Duval and the others had been planned?

(A) The shocking grossness with which her grandmother speaks of the past

(B) Madame Duval's failure to be surprised at discovering her granddaughter

(C) Madame Duval's already having lodgings and being easily able to procure a room for Evelina

    (D)   Mrs. Mirvan's plea to let Evelina spend one more night with the Mirvans

    (E)   The Captain's not being able to apologize gracefully for his rudeness

86.   Evelina's reaction to meeting Madame Duval makes it clear that

    (A)   Evelina has known of Madame Duval's existence but has not cared to seek her out.

    (B)   Madame Duval has merely pretended to be a foreigner.

    (C)   this scene is the worst one Evelina has ever endured.

    (D)   Evelina is prepared to love her newly found relative.

    (E)   everyone involved would have been better off if the meeting had never taken place.

QUESTIONS 87–90

My daddy's face is a study. Winter moves into it and presides there. His eyes become a cliff of snow threatening to avalanche; his eyebrows bend like black limbs of leafless trees. His skin takes on the pale, cheerless yellow of winter
5   sun; for a jaw he has the edges of a snowbound field dotted with stubble; his high forehead is the frozen sweep of the Erie, hiding currents of gelid thoughts that eddy in darkness. Wolf killer turned hawk fighter, he worked night and day to keep one from the door and the other from under the
10   windowsills. A Vulcan guarding the flames, he gives us instructions about which doors to keep closed or opened for proper distribution of heat, lays kindling by, discusses qualities of coal, and teaches us how to rake, feed, and bank the fire. And he will not unrazor his lips until spring.
15   Winter tightened our heads with a band of cold and melted our eyes. We put pepper in the feet of our stockings, Vaseline on our faces, and stared through dark icebox mornings at four stewed prunes, slippery lumps of oatmeal, and cocoa with a roof of skin.
20   But mostly we waited for spring, when there could be gardens.

By the time this winter had stiffened itself into a hateful knot that nothing could loosen, something did loosen it, or rather someone. A someone who splintered the

25   knot into silver threads that tangled us, netted us, made us
      long for the dull chafe of the previous boredom.

From The Bluest Eye, by Toni Morrison

87. It can be inferred from the opening paragraph that

     (A) the narrator's father was a cold and unloving man.

     (B) the house was besieged by wild animals in the winter.

     (C) the narrator's father was strange and alien to his children.

     (D) the narrator's father fought hunger and cold unceasingly.

     (E) the narrator's father was an accomplished hunter.

88. The sentence "My daddy's face is a study" (line 1) is best inter-
     preted to mean that his face

     (A) reflects the formal learning he has acquired.

     (B) reflects the quiet of a study room.

     (C) is an expressive landscape.

     (D) is expressive of his extensive experiences in life.

     (E) is worthy of attention.

89. The phrase "will not unrazor his lips until spring" (line 14) evokes his

     (A) determination to win the battle for survival.

     (B) refusal to shave.

     (C) decision not to shave until spring comes.

     (D) preoccupation with his appearance.

     (E) stern, hostile attitude toward the family.

90. The image of a "hateful knot" (line 23) is a reference to

     (A) the poverty of their home.

     (B) the unspent anger of their father.

     (C) the boredom of school.

     (D) the unyielding cold weather.

     (E) their cold, stiffened muscles.

CLEP ANALYZING AND INTERPRETING LITERATURE
TEST 1

ANSWER KEY

1.	(A)	31.	(C)	61.	(C)
2.	(C)	32.	(D)	62.	(A)
3.	(D)	33.	(C)	63.	(E)
4.	(E)	34.	(D)	64.	(A)
5.	(E)	35.	(A)	65.	(C)
6.	(B)	36.	(D)	66.	(B)
7.	(B)	37.	(C)	67.	(B)
8.	(C)	38.	(E)	68.	(B)
9.	(D)	39.	(A)	69.	(D)
10.	(E)	40.	(A)	70.	(C)
11.	(E)	41.	(D)	71.	(C)
12.	(D)	42.	(D)	72.	(D)
13.	(B)	43.	(D)	73.	(A)
14.	(B)	44.	(C)	74.	(E)
15.	(D)	45.	(E)	75.	(E)
16.	(C)	46.	(B)	76.	(D)
17.	(A)	47.	(D)	77.	(C)
18.	(E)	48.	(C)	78.	(C)
19.	(B)	49.	(D)	79.	(A)
20.	(C)	50.	(D)	80.	(C)
21.	(C)	51.	(E)	81.	(E)
22.	(D)	52.	(A)	82.	(E)
23.	(B)	53.	(B)	83.	(D)
24.	(D)	54.	(D)	84.	(C)
25.	(A)	55.	(B)	85.	(B)
26.	(D)	56.	(B)	86.	(A)
27.	(D)	57.	(A)	87.	(D)
28.	(A)	58.	(E)	88.	(C)
29.	(B)	59.	(C)	89.	(A)
30.	(D)	60.	(E)	90.	(D)

DETAILED EXPLANATIONS OF ANSWERS

TEST 1

1.   **(A)**   Throughout the poem, the narrator examines man's relationship with God and man's search for a close relationship with God. This search includes man's inadequate ability to communicate effectively with his "Deare Lord," choice (B), but the theme of the poem is not limited to the problem of communication because that would exclude the concept of the despair man feels when he no longer feels God's presence (stanzas 2 and 5). Although the poem certainly deals with (C), the main thrust is man's relationship with God. Choice (D) is a characteristic of God mentioned in many religious poems, and obliquely present in this poem, but (D) and (E) are not specifically mentioned by the narrator.

2.   **(C)**   The narrator knows "not what to say" (line 1) because his "Speech is too Course" (line 2) to express his love of God. The narrator feels nothing he can say will adequately describe his feelings. Although the narrator does say "Thy Love to mee's too great" (line 5), (B) includes the idea of love being too demanding, an idea not found in the poem. Partially implied is (E), but that idea is not developed as fully as the problem of communicating with God. God's distance from man (A) is not discussed in stanza 1. The "coarse web" in stanza 1 is not (D) but the crudeness of language to express sublime love.

3.   **(D)**   "Loath" means "dislike" or "hate." Although "web" is usually associated with snares or spiders, in this poem the speaker uses "web" to show that even the most gossamer filaments are too "Coarse" for the fine feelings he has. "To array" means "to clothe" and is used in the same context with "to make a mantle" (cloak) and "to shape/A Vesture" (covering or garment). The narrator holds his love for God in his heart, but he cannot find words beautiful enough to express this love. God knows this love is

there, but the narrator can only "clothe" his feelings in the coarse "garments" of the words in this poem as a means of communicating with God.

4.   **(E)**   A somewhat shocking metaphor is that of God as renting out his love to man and man as paying back interest but keeping the principal. Thus, God becomes a Usurer because man will never repay God his love. However, as the narrator points out, there is no "Extortion in such Usury" (line 16) and this "blessed Usury" (line 21) is profitable to both man and God because both exchange precious love; therefore, the loving relationship between man and Maker is extended indefinitely. In this loving harmony, man and God "shall not Jar" (line 20).

5.   **(E)**   The language is at first off-putting, but reading carefully through the passage's first few lines reveals clearly the author's viewpoint. He blames the devil but does not say poets write about him. He does not want poets to write about passion of loving women nor fantasies of any kind. In "lieu of" simply means "instead of"; "solemn and devout" can easily translate to serious matters pertaining to God — the answer is (E).

6.   **(B)**   Although the word "wedded" is in the area of criticism, the author does not criticize poets for their views on marriage; he does criticize that poets have wedded their wills to expressing themselves on "unworthy affections." Because he sets these up in direct contrast to the love of God, one translates such affections as passion for women. He suggests also, through the association with the "Divell," that such affections are beyond poets' control. The answer then is a combination of I and III: (B).

7.   **(B)**   You need to find the figure of speech (an extended metaphor of the weaver and weaving) and determine what it means in the context of the whole piece. He is not personifying, nor jaded, nor encouraging alliteration. He makes a plea that his poetry "a few coarse threads" will weave "a new webbe in their loom," so that better poets will carry on what he has started or begin an even better strain of poetry, "a finer peece," which will combine verse and goodness together in the implied sense of woven together. The answer is (B).

8.   **(C)**   You need to sort out all the mannered flattery of the concluding lines and understand the word "importune." The cousin in fact asked the author to write the book (C).

9. **(D)** The author's tone is lecturing to begin with, but does not change to praise. It is didactic but moves from that. He is not encouraging the cousin at the end but humbly setting out his reasons for writing poetry. Arrogant does not fully capture the tone at the beginning. It is too sincere for arrogance. The best couple is the simplest — harsh to gentle (D).

10. **(E)** Science fiction, also known as fantasy or escape fiction, does in fact lead us to a contrast between real and fantasy lives (statement I). In this passage, science fiction also connotes security and stability in lines 12–13 (statement II). Finally, since it can be fantasy and it is fiction that may help the characters deal with crises in their lives, it could also serve as a metaphor suggesting the need for lies to escape ugly moments in life (statement III). Having read the foregoing, it should become obvious that choice (E), inclusive of statements I, II, and III, is the correct one.

11. **(E)** Taking just this passage into consideration, we would be hard pressed once again to find irony, choice (A), in the use of the phrase. In the whole novel, the author uses the phrase more than a hundred times, about once every two pages; and it does accumulate to verbal irony, but not in this passage, which is all you have to use as a text. Both choices (B) and (C), however, miss the target as well. The phrases have the feel of insensitivity and lack of empathy rather than the opposite, as the choices state. Nor does the phrase strike us as excuses, so choice (D) is not the best one. We are left with the correct choice (E). "So it goes" does seem to describe a shrug of the shoulders, a sense that something may be unpleasant but unavoidable. The speaker using the phrase seems to be saying he is not responsible for unfortunate accidents or tragedies.

12. **(D)** Choice (A) is not correct because the text states directly the book is not science fiction. Inferences must be deduced from what is said and what is suggested, not what is stated without interpretation. For the same reason, we can eliminate choices (C) and (E), although the latter stands closer to the set of correct answers than does (C). Choice (B) sounds like a reasonable answer that contends with the correct or best choice (D). The reason (B) loses stems from the context: re-invention of self goes with science fiction; the book is not science fiction. Therefore, it is not necessarily about re-invention of self. The context of lines 14–18, does, however, support choice (D).

13. **(B)** The correct choice, (B), stands out here and even calls attention to itself by its clear difference from the other choices. The whole

passage seems to argue against (B), but particularly the last six lines. Choice (A) is supported particularly by lines 17–18, as are choices (C), (D), and (E), the latter also being reinforced by lines 19–22.

14. **(B)** Monologue is the best answer; the passage is a long speech given by a single person. (A) soliloquy is not the correct choice as a soliloquy expresses the character's private, intimate thoughts. (C) is not correct; a dramatic lyric is found within a lyric poem, not a play. (D) is not correct as a dialogue would require a second person to speak, and in this excerpt only Oedipus is speaking. (E) poetic drama is not the best choice, for the dialogue is not written in verse.

15. **(D)** Choice (D) is the correct answer as the indignance of the speaker's parents is modified by the word "this" as he is satisfied by their denial of the charge. "This" does not refer to (A) the satisfaction, (B) the drunken man, (C) the charge against the speaker, or (E) the anger of the speaker. These choices are incorrect.

16. **(C)** Choice (C) is the correct answer as the word infamies suggests that something is becoming well known. (A) is not correct; the infamy of the rumor may have caused Oedipus' anger, but it does not reaffirm the existence of the charge. (B) is incorrect, for his parents denial has nothing to do with its circulation. (D) is incorrect; the speaker's visit to Delphi was made secretly. (E) is also the wrong choice; the unanswered question remained an enigma to the speaker while the spread of the rumor became a reality.

17. **(A)** Choice (A) is the correct answer as Oedipus is ridden with guilt and horror upon realizing the implications of his actions. He is neither timid nor fearful, for he has already committed the acts and is willing to face punishment; (B) is an incorrect answer. Although Oedipus is sorrowful, (C) is not the correct answer as he realizes what has been done and is therefore not confused. (D) is incorrect; he is more horrified at his actions than enraged by them and he does not attempt to deny what has been done. Although he is filled with remorse, the speaker does not carry resentment; thus, (E) is incorrect.

18. **(E)** (E) is the correct answer as his sudden violence indicates that he can be easily provoked. (A) is incorrect as the "He" that Oedipus refers to is the man that brought the goad down upon his head, not the drunken man who originated the rumor. (B) is not the answer as it is

obvious that Oedipus did not heed the advice of the herald; the heavy price has nothing to do with the herald's warning. Although he conquered the men, his actions do not warrant an understanding of bravery; (C) is incorrect. (D) is not the best answer as a monetary fine is a literal interpretation of the figurative phrase "heavy price."

19.   **(B)**   Choice (B) is the correct answer as the rising action indicates that the dramatic complication has been introduced and now controls the course of events. (A) is not correct as the exposition is found at the opening of the story. (C) is incorrect as the falling action occurs after the climax, and this scene is building up to the climax. As the climax has not yet taken place, (D) is incorrect. (E) is incorrect as well, for the resolution is found at the end of the plot, after the rising action and the climax.

20.   **(C)**   (C) is the correct choice as he repeatedly suggests that he must be banished from the kingdom. (A) is incorrect for he contends that he cannot return to his adopted parents. Although he is distraught, Oedipus does not claim that he will kill himself; (B) is not the answer. (D) is not the correct answer, for he had already consulted Apollo at Delphi and his visit proved fruitless. (E) is not the answer, for it is not specific enough. Although he promises he will make restitution for his actions, this restitution is made specifically in the form of ostracization.

21.   **(C)**   Choice (C) diary is the best answer as it is a daily recording of the author's personal experiences and thoughts. While the speaker recounts his personal traumas to the audience in his first person narrative, the passage is not autobiographical. It does not concentrate upon describing events and establishing the character of the subject for the obvious purpose of publication; thus, (A) is not correct. (B) is not correct as a memoir solely focuses on recounting events, places, and people the author has known and not the developing self. (D) is an incorrect choice as the subject of a biography is not the author and this passage is written in first person narrative. This passage is also not (E) prose poetry as it lacks the compactness and rhythm of this form.

22.   **(D)**   Choice (D) is the correct answer as the author's tone is not one of determination but of acceptance. He is (A) introspective as he ponders his internal workings and psychology. He seems to be somewhat listless and confused as to what is causing his strange feelings; thus, (B) and (C) are not correct. Finally, the author presents his observations with a tone of languor; he realizes something has changed but remains uncertain

and apathetic regarding the understanding of the source. For this reason, (E) is also incorrect.

23.   **(B)**   The speaker's strange feeling is "blossoming" in line 7; thus, (B) is the best answer. The choice of figurative language the speaker uses throughout the text is analogous to such a description. (A) is incorrect as the speaker claims the feeling possesses the characteristics of an illness, but it is not to be literally taken as such. (C) is incorrect as the speaker decides that the feeling is a false alarm at once, it does not continually develop and grow. (D) is incorrect as the stagnant, quiet uncertainty modifies the feeling, but it does not do the blossoming. (E) is also not correct as the speaker's job as a historian is already established and static; blossoming suggests development.

24.   **(D)**   Choice (D) is the best answer as the speaker admits that his job does not require or allow the exercise of self-knowledge he wishes he possessed in order to determine the source of his strange feeling. While he admits that his job does not allow for introspection, he does not state that he is unhappy with his career choice (A), nor does he claim it to be entirely mindless; therefore, (B) and (D) are not the best choices. Although the speaker intimates that he does not relish the sentimental titles necessary to his work, this scorn is not the main focus of this paragraph; (E) is incorrect.

25.   **(A)**   Choice (A) is the correct answer as such a description holds a particular connotation of disgust and revulsion. Few people want to hold a "fat white worm." Although the worm is a lowly creature, the attitude of condescension is not the best description of tone as the speaker does not place himself in a superior position; (B) is not the best answer. The speaker seems to describe the hand with a certain amount of removal; however, the figurative language employed suggests that he is not entirely indifferent; (C) is incorrect. (D) and (E) are incorrect also as the narrator's tone is not one of utter disrespect or disclosure.

26.   **(D)**   Choice (D) is the correct answer as the entire passage focuses upon the narrator's newly emerging discovery of self and his surroundings. (A) is incorrect as a love of self suggests adoration, and the speaker does not vainly look upon his hands. (B) is incorrect as the speaker seems to lack familiarity with his own body, and hence views his hand as if seeing it for the first time. (C) is not the correct answer; narcissism is the infatuation with one's self, and the speaker does not exhibit

such a trait. (E) is not the correct answer; the narrator notices a change, but does not admit to consciously inventing one.

27.   **(D)**   Although the speaker repeatedly confirms that a change has taken place, he cannot prove such a belief; thus, (D) is the answer. The sudden changes well may be a product of his imagination, but the passage does not indicate such a fact; thus, (A) is not the best answer. The speaker admits that he is not at ease with the sounds and sights which surround him in the city, but it is not the only cause for confusion; (C) is incorrect. (E) is not the correct answer as the speaker's confusion has nothing to do with his choice of residence.

28.   **(A)**   We can relatively quickly eliminate choices (B) and (C) as either inappropriate or as misleading. The context suggests nothing about illness, and the notion of "accounts" should not mislead us into thinking the term has much to do with mathematics. Likewise, choice (E) fails the test of logic when substituted for "sinecure" in the passage. The phrase following "sinecure," i.e., "with a moderate allowance," negates the idea of choice (D). That leaves choice (A) as the correct answer, both in the context and from the definition of "sinecure" as an "office or position that requires little or no work."

29.   **(B)**   (E) A "simile" is essentially the same as a metaphor except that it usually requires a comparative word such as "like" or "as" to make the comparison. (C) An "image" is a broad term referring to anything that can be perceived through the senses (sight, sound, smell, taste, and touch). Clearly, the story serves as an example or an implied comparison between the Indian and the narrator; hence, it is a "metaphor," and choice (B) correctly identifies the function. The story is not a "simile" because the narrator does not use "like" or "as" to make the comparison; instead he simply says "I too" did what the Indian did, thereby equating the two.

30.   **(D)**   A couple of choices compete here. However, we can dismiss (B) because the narrator never mentions any "business partners," nor do the phrases imply such a possibility. Likewise, choice (E) does not directly relate to the use of the phrases. Choice (A) fails because the phrases have little to do with business success, except in the sense of keeping accounts, and because choices (C) and (D) could serve as better answers than (A). Choice (C) yields to (D) — the correct answer — because there is no "satire" present in the passage. The term means, in essence, the use of ridicule to try to change a situation. We could argue that ridicule can be

found in the passage and maybe even in the specific phrases, but they seem to exude, if anything along that line, mild parody or gentle humor applying business language to life. Nonetheless, choice (D) accurately describes the author's sense of ethics (upright behavior) and, to a lesser extent, humility ("without boasting"), which would be considered an appropriate stance to take.

31. **(C)** This question gives us a relative break because the choices differ so greatly. Choices (D) and (E) clearly miss the target. Likewise, choice (A) fails because the lines in question do not make a categorical statement about truth but, instead, question the idea that only one type of successful life exists. Thus, we can eliminate choice (B) and settle on choice (C) as the correct one. Arguably, a "truth" is stated about success, but not an absolute one upon which all readers would agree.

32. **(D)** We know the narrator rejects conventional definitions of success at the end of the passage, so we can eliminate choices (B), (C), and (E). They characterize him appropriately, and we are looking for exceptions. The phrase says, in effect, "I know they [his "baskets"] won't sell, but I'll make them anyway." That means his behavior is a (A) thoughtful or philosophical choice (rather than whim) which reflects ideals (idealism) because it is done without thought of immediate economic reward. Choice (D) wins because it incorrectly characterizes the narrator's attitude shown in the phrase in question.

33. **(C)** Mrs. Malaprop is a famous character in English literature, giving rise to the term "malapropism" (C). First analyze what she does to the language, then, if you are not familiar with the word, analyze the options: (A) homonym – words that sound the same but are spelled differently (there, their, they're); (B) altruism – doing good for the poor; synonym – words that have the same meaning (joyful, glad); (E) synecdoche – part is used for the whole or vice versa (ten sail – ten ships).

34. **(D)** The key here is to find out exactly what Mrs. Malaprop does. It is not just that she uses the wrong word but the one she uses is so close in sound but so ridiculous in meaning (D).

35. **(A)** You need not only to analyze what Mrs. Malaprop is doing to the language but also to appreciate the fact that some words that may sound wrong are in fact in their true use. (A) fluxions here is correct — a mathematical term to do with time. If you do not know the word, work

through the others which do tend to stand out in their misuse as long as your vocabulary can substitute the right meaning: (B) ironically; (C) ingenuousness; (D) contiguous; (E) orthography.

36.   **(D)**   Sir Anthony gives the metaphor of the circulating libraries being "evergreen trees of diabolical knowledge" (with a hint of the biblical tree of Knowledge in the Garden of Eden), not a simile because the words "like" or "as if" are not employed, but then Sir Anthony cannot seem to give the metaphor up and extends it (not mixes it — he still keeps to the tree with blossoms and fruit and leaves). The answer is (D).

37.   **(C)**   All of the options have something of truth in them except (E) which plays with another notion of books and their covers. Sir Anthony believes books should be for learned subjects. The books he condemns are the "new" novels full of fantasies and exciting adventures — very tempting to young women who had very little to do in those days. The answer is then (C).

38.   **(E)**   Sir Anthony obviously does enjoy an argument and knows what it should entail, but he realizes there that he has not in fact had one. Mrs. Malaprop is too kind an arguer because she has agreed with him on most points. (E) is the closest explanation of the man's polite but ironic statement.

39.   **(A)**   Droll (amusing in an odd way) and dry (an edge to what he says) sum up the tone (A). The man is (B) amused but he is not angry, nor (C) sarcastic. He is (D) whimsical (a tinge of fanciful humor to his words) but certainly not weary. He is accused of being (E) laconic (expressing much in a few words but Mrs. Malaprop has the wrong word), and sardonic (akin to sarcastic) is too harsh.

40.   **(A)**   Although magic and mystery (B) are mentioned as is the will of the crowd (D), the controlling metaphor hinges on the stage and acting (A) when the audience wills the leading actor of the piece. There is no mention of the hunt (C) itself nor a ventriloquist's dummy (E), simply an absurd puppet and a dummy not necessarily a ventriloquist's.

41.   **(D)**   Nowhere in this excerpt is the writer referred to as a policeman (D). You may know this from your reading but do not let knowledge outside the passage sway you. All the other reasons are clearly expressed in the passage.

42. **(D)**   The whole meaning of the piece suggests that the white man must not make a fool of himself in front of the crowd. He does not see the stupidity in his role but the emptiness of it (D). The tone of the piece here does not suggest a wish to play the fool nor any prejudice toward the natives.

43. **(D)**   This is a fun show for the rabble. At this point the reader knows the people do not like the narrator but has not yet learned the deeper meaning of the role of sahib not wanting to make a fool of himself, nor the fact that the people are waiting for that result. The closest answer is (D) — the people are not on a feast day but have turned it into a celebration of sorts by wanting to see the elephant killed, even by someone they dislike.

44. **(C)**   There is no scorn for the rabble but a personal analysis of what must be done. Hence, the "I" pronoun. But at the same time the narrator realizes he is engaged in a much larger situation, that he is a symbol or represents "the white man" the many in the colonial set-up (C). He stands alone in the sense that he must kill the animal alone but the killing represents something much bigger than just one man versus an animal. The personal pronoun use is not a distancing device but a personal involvement.

45. **(E)**   The tone of the passage involves elements of anger but furious (A) is too strong. There is no amusement (C) in the serious tone. There is a certain sad sarcasm in the passage, but again sardonic (D) is too strong, and although the narrator is expressing a philosophy of sorts, philosophic (B) suggests a depth that is not present. The best word is one that shows he has faced an awakening here and all illusions of his role disappear (E).

46. **(B)**   If you do not know the word "enjambment" — the running of one line of poetry into the next without a break for the rhyme or syntax — eliminate the options from words you do know. (A) Alliteration is the repeat of the consonants; in (C) onomatopoeia the words sound like the action; (D) personification is describing an inanimate object or season or virtue as a person, usually capitalized; and (E) bathos is extreme anticlimax. None of these applies here, so (B) must be the answer.

47.   **(D)**   Even without seeing the painting you should see the characters and things through the poem. The boy falls from the sky, the sun goes on shining, but the ship and the plowman turn away (D). The painter of course is not in the painting.

48.   **(C)**   All of the options are too strong except (C). The poet does not extol courage, the style alone reveals that, nor agonize over suffering. He calmly states and accepts that society could not care less about the suffering of others.

49.   **(D)**   The tone throughout is distanced, calm, and objective. What sets the scene is the conversational "for instance" at the beginning of this, the second verse, as if the poet is holding a pleasant after-dinner conversation with you, the reader (D). If this is not immediately apparent, work your way through the options: (A) didactic – too strong, no lecturing voice here; (B) ironic – straightforward "truths" here; (C) irregular scansion – the free verse form cannot be analyzed for scansion nor does it have regular rhythm (E).

50.   **(D)**   Lines 3 and 4 make it clear that his friends, seeing his advanced state of decline better than he can see it, may be tolling the bell for him without his knowing it.

51.   **(E)**   The imagery in lines 5–9 is that of a body of which the church is the head and all baptized individuals are members of the body (arms and legs).

52.   **(A)**   The imagery of lines 10–13 compare all men to a chapter in a book, each of which will be translated into a better language and find its place in a better book. Translating, then, is similar to going to one's reward, in a better life.

53.   **(B)**   In defining man's relationship to his fellow men, the poet is serious and straightforward. He is, in effect, making a point which is so important that no writer's "trick" would be appropriate.

54.   **(D)**   The prisoners are speedily sentenced because the judges and the jurymen are hungry and want to go home for supper as the day ends — the prisoners may be guilty, but the wrong reasons determine their sen-

tences (D). No doubt the people do believe in the system, but the sarcasm of the piece suggests that this society uses the system for personal selfish benefits — certainly not a humanitarian society.

55. **(B)** The society depicted is shallow and trivial, engaging in chatty conversations that everyone takes seriously. Serious as the discussions may be, they possibly involve extramarital affairs rather than affairs of state — such gossip ruins reputations (B). The gossiping involves the Queen but it is not revealed that she is slandered.

56. **(B)** The question wants you to analyze the clash or conflict of two very different concepts in conversation: the glory of the Queen in one breath and a fire screen (or room divider) in another. The juxtaposition is not so much to suggest trivia (A) or seriousness (E) (the Queen's glory is serious but the furniture is not), but that this society holds both in equal reverence (B). No real evidence is given that the people are Royalists (D) or Imperialists (C).

57. **(A)** There is a clever use of the language in this one adverb. It stands for the angle of the sun as it declines at a steep angle (B) but also for the hidden meanings (C) behind the word as it refers to this society: the deceit, the amorality (E). It certainly does not mean that the sun is at a perpendicular angle (A).

58. **(E)** The move is light to dark (A) in the physical movement of the day but not specifically in the voice. On analysis you will find the "coming down" of mood from amusement at the chat of the day — the trivia — to a sadness of the effect of the hunger of the court officials, a hunger which sends men to the gallows. The answer is (E).

59. **(C)** Choice (C) is correct. Through her illustration, Woolf intimates that women held an inferior position within society, and consequently not allowed the same creative expression as men. Woolf argues that Judith was not intellectually inferior to her brother, thus (A) is not

correct. Although women were responsible for household chores, these duties did not deny them creative expression, but merely occupied much of a woman's time, making (B) an incorrect choice. It is true that women were denied an education so that they did not know how to read Latin, but it was not the reason they were not allowed artistic expression, therefore (D) is incorrect. (E) is incorrect because obeying one's parents may not have always been creatively stifling.

60.   **(E)**   Choice (E) is correct as Ovid, Virgil, and Horace were famous Latin writers studied by the educated at this time. Their names directly follow the fact that Shakespeare studied Latin, allowing the reader to infer that these men were authors of Latin texts. The passage does not indicate that they were (A) Shakespeare's professors, (B) instructors of Latin, (C) instructors of grammar and logic, or (D) fellow classmates. These choices are incorrect.

61.   **(C)**   Choice (C) is the best choice as the speaker suggests that Shakespeare's marriage was premature due to the birth of a child that soon followed. Although his wife was said to be from the same town, this fact is not the primary focus of these lines; therefore, (A) is incorrect. (B) is not correct, as the child was not born prematurely, but rather, the birth took place prematurely in relation to the date of the marriage. (D) is not the best choice because the passage does not indicate Shakespeare's feelings about the marriage. Nowhere in the text does it mention his age, thus it cannot be stated that he was too young to marry. (E) is incorrect.

62.   **(A)**   Choice (A) is the best choice because it seems that Judith is equally as eager to venture into the world as her brother. (B) is not correct as she is not intimidated by the world, but intrigued by it. Although Judith may be expecting to leave home and begin her own life, such an emotion is not indicated by the word agog, making (C) an incorrect choice. (D) is not correct because she has not yet been disappointed by the denial of such a desire. It seems that she is as equally deserving of independence as her brother, however, such a fact is not indicated by the word agog. (E) is incorrect.

63.   **(E)**   Choice (E) is the correct answer as the speaker focuses on the difference of experience had by men and women solely due to their gender roles, regardless of talent or intelligence. Nowhere in the passage does the speaker crusade for women's rights; thus, (A) is incorrect. The main purpose of the speaker is not to complain; (B) is incorrect. (C) is not correct; the story in this passage is fictional. Although the speaker sug-

gests that Judith was equally as capable as her brother, the main purpose of the passage is not to demonstrate gender equality. (D) is incorrect.

64.   **(A)**   The author describes Mabel's actions in careful detail, stressing her pleasurable bond to death and her new found self-control. The author does not sound disparaging or repulsed; rather Mabel is presented in a sympathetic light, inviting emotional response from the reader.

65.   **(C)**   Mabel's self-questioning expresses her new-found defiance, and her growing independence from the onus of responding to the prejudices of the wider world. When Lawrence asks: "Why should she answer anybody?" we can hear the tragically directed Mabel saying: "I don't have to answer you or anybody," as she walks down the "dark main street of the small town."

66.   **(B)**   Lawrence presents us with a machine-gun procession of depressing images: "gray, wintry…saddened, dark green…blackened by the smoke." Along with this are the depressing images of foundries and graveyards.

67.   **(B)**   Mabel has already decided on the path she will take to eliminate her troubles. The brief description of Mabel and her bag seems almost medical. Perhaps she is gone to perform an operation — and in this sense it might be an omen. But Lawrence places this description next to the smoky and depressing landscape: Mabel will clean the headstone, Mabel will wipe her own slate clean.

68.   **(B)**   Lawrence states: "She felt reserved within the thick churchyard wall as in another country." It is a difficult concept for the reader to understand fully until he or she confronts the concept again in the last paragraph quoted in this passage.

69.   **(D)**   What is indicated here is a general and gradual separation from the living and a removal to the world of the dead. There is also specific movement discerned within the general: that is, a shift from all the ties (not just with the bothersome people of the town, but with the suffering members of her family) toward one original bond, not just with her mother, but with the world of death.

70.   **(C)**   Personification involves assigning human qualities to inanimate objects as is done by describing the dark green fields as "saddened." The correct answer is (C) personification.

71.   **(C)**   Thomas' message is perhaps unexpected. Acceptance of death is not the issue; rather, protest is encouraged. Maintaining the will to live is not enough; old people should rage against it in every possible way.

72.   **(D)**   While the image is used just before this and then later in the poem in conjunction with the passage of the sun across the sky, it is repeated throughout as a metaphor for dying and death. It is interesting to note that, like "winter," "sunset" is usually taken to mean this, at least since Shakespeare's time ("In me thou sees the setting of the sun..."). Yet Thomas uses the metaphor in a way that is both interesting and lyrically fresh.

73.   **(A)**   The repetition of "rage" serves many purposes, but its clearest purpose is to provide emotional intensity — and by an apt choice of a word which allows growing intensity with only slightly varied pronunciation of the heavy "r" which begins the word. Thomas' Welsh accent exaggerates this effect when recordings of his readings are reviewed.

74.   **(E)**   In an artful dance of words, Thomas uses a contradictory phrase like "blinding sight" and the simile "Blind eyes could blaze like meteors." In addition, these dying men can be "gay" (meaning happy), and dying blind men can see (that) being blind is not as powerless a state as death. These are statements that seem to contradict common sense and yet are true — the definition of paradox.

75.   **(E)**   (A) is a likely choice. The poet is saying, "Look, wise men feel this way, and good men, too." He could therefore be trying to say to the father, "You are all of these — so you should rage as well." However, in the last stanza, the poet tells us that the father is crying "fierce tears" — a terse restatement of raging against the prospect of imminent death. Thus, the poem becomes almost a "cheer" for his father to continue to face death with righteous indignation.

76.   **(D)**   The poet asks to be "cursed," as well as "blessed" by his father's tears — symbols of inevitable death and human rage against it. It should be clear, by now, that the poet is speaking to his father (and not heavenly father — who presumably does not have to face death). Thomas regularly emphasized the continuum of life and death — the cycles — the passage of the generations. He will face death soon enough, he implies — as his father is doing now. With horrible irony, Dylan Thomas died one year after this poem was published — at the age of 39.

77. **(C)** In each stanza the human effort involves introducing light onto the dark stage of death. Wise men try to throw lightning; good men need light to see their deeds; wild men try to save the sun's rays; grave men find that their blind eyes can blaze in the face of darkness. Darkness, however, and therefore, death, wins out (they are each going into that "good night" — though not gently). Thus, each is frustrated in his confrontation with death.

78. **(C)** While there is some apprehension about a future confrontation at the end of the passage, the passage begins with Macomber's desire to "clear away that lion business" (line 1) and then continues to dwell on Macomber's reflections about what went wrong just before. The Somali proverb underscores the indirect references to what must have been Macomber's cowardice when confronting the lion.

79. **(A)** Hemingway's passage is remarkable for its clear precise descriptions of time. This is reinforced by the proper and effective breakage of paragraphs at particular demarcations. The passage begins, evidently, with a conversation at dinner. A new paragraph is then begun with, "But that night…" and ends with the word "now." This ending is intentional and important, because the next paragraph begins with the time notation. "It had started the night before" and ends with another transition. "Then while they were eating…."

80. **(C)** Stream of consciousness is debatable here because it is the author's voice which is telling the reader what Macomber is thinking — not Macomber's voice. Excitement is created because the reader senses Macomber's emotional turmoil. The extent of the characters' formal education does not enter the picture, and few authors would advertise the inappropriateness of segments of their writing. The seemingly casual style here is in interesting contrast to much of Hemingway's writing — noted for short sentences and therefore little need for punctuation.

81. **(E)** Wilson knows that "any one could be upset by his first lion" experience, and he is not threatened by the lion's roar because he knows from its "cough" it is an "old-timer" (line 31). While Wilson may be less expressive than Macomber, most of this may be due to his having been a "veteran" of many years in East Africa. (C), then, is also a remote possibility, but clearly Wilson is a European.

82. **(E)** Macomber is not inexperienced in hunting or shooting. Indeed, Wilson tells him, "You shoot very well" (line 48). It is Macomber's knowledge that is limited, and Wilson's that seems complete. It is his knowledge that he offers to Macomber. Macomber's lack of knowledge as he approaches this dangerous situation is ominous.

83. **(D)** Although Mrs. Duval claims not to be "common," the fact that she says it betrays her lack of breeding; a true lady never would feel constrained to declare herself a "person of fashion" (line 7) or threaten to send another to prison for insulting her. The Captain's verbal abuse (A) is insufficient for a threat of prison, even if it is obvious he is not teasing (B). She might or might not be making an idle threat (E), but the chances are that Justice Fielding would take her demands with a grain of salt. The increasing hostilities (C) alarm the others, but only to the extent that Mrs. Mirvan feels constrained "to remonstrate with the Captain" (line 2), not physically interfere, so the conflict has not been terribly serious.

84. **(C)** It is likely Evelina is writing to her guardian. She refers to herself as "your Evelina" (line 14), and addresses the man as "my protector, my friend, and my refuge" (line 18). If Evelina were writing to Mrs. Mirvan's son, she would refer differently to Mrs. Mirvan (A) and probably include a phrase such as "you mother" somewhere in the narrative. Evelina's father (E) and grandfather (B) would be addressed in more familiar, familial terms, and likely some reference to the family connection to Mrs. Duval would be made. The least likely answer is (D), as there is no reference to the "closest friend"; also, Evelina would probably be writing the friend and not the father if this were a viable option.

85. **(B)** The lack of surprise on Madame Duval's part is the most telling piece of evidence for presuming the meeting had been planned. Another clue is the passionate argument she has with a supposed stranger, the Captain, and the fact that Evelina does not describe or even mention any apology of the Captain's (E) to Madame Duval, an apology certainly due a stranger. It is likely the Captain already despises Madame Duval. As a stranger in town, Madame Duval would certainly have rooms let (C).

86. **(A)** Because Evelina has such a severe reaction to the mention of the woman's name, it is obvious that the girl had known of Madame Duval's existence (A) but had not wanted to seek her out. It is true Madame Duval (B) is a "supposed foreigner" (line 13), but this is not the critical thrust of the scene. This scene may or may not be the worst one

Evelina has endured (C) and perhaps everyone would have been better off if it had never taken place (E), but there is no evidence for either of these answers. Evelina thinks her newly found relative is gross in expression, and the girl refuses to spend the night with her grandmother, so there is evidence to contradict (D).

87. **(D)** Choice (A) is wrong. Although he is described in wintery terms, he is never accused of harshness or indifference. His devotion to keeping them warm displays his love. Choices (B) and (E) are wrong because they stem from a misreading of the figurative expressions "wolf killer," and "hawk fighter," i.e., one who battles the wolf of hunger and the winds of winter. Choice (C) is wrong because it stems from a misreading of "Vulcan" to mean alien rather than the Roman god of fire and metalworking. Choice (D) is correct and is supported by lines 8–10.

88. **(C)** Choice (A) is wrong because it is based on a misreading of the word "study" to mean the acquisition of learning. Choice (B) is wrong because it interprets "study" to mean a room. Choice (C) is correct because "study" in this context means a description or portrait. Choice (D) is incorrect because the paragraph does not reveal anything about his experiences in life other than his actions to protect his family from the cold. Choice (E) is wrong because it arises from a misreading of the word "study" to mean "apply the mind," which it does not in this context.

89. **(A)** Choice (A) is correct because he will not relax or open up until the threat of winter disappears completely. Choices (B) and (C) are wrong because "unrazor" in this context does not have anything to do with shaving. Choice (D) is wrong because it implies that "unrazor" has a literal instead of a figurative meaning in this context, which it does not have. Choice (E) is wrong because it is unsupported by the paragraph. He does not scold, but instructs the family on how to keep the house warm.

90. **(D)** Choice (A) is wrong because the passage only implies their poverty and does not pass judgment on it. Choice (B) is wrong because nowhere in the passage is there any mention of the father's anger. Choice (C) is wrong because the passage makes no mention of being bored with school. They are bored with winter, not school. Choice (D) is the correct answer because the unyielding cold weather has tightened around them like a knot. Choice (E) is wrong because the passage states that the winter "stiffens," not their muscles.

PRACTICE
TEST 2

This test is also on CD-ROM in our special interactive CLEP Analyzing & Interpreting Literature TEST*ware*®. It is highly recommended that you first take this exam on computer. You will then have the additional study features and benefits of enforced timed conditions, individual diagnostic analysis, and instant scoring. See page 2 for guidance on how to get the most out of our CLEP Analyzing & Interpreting Literature book and software.

CLEP ANALYZING AND INTERPRETING LITERATURE
Test 2

(Answer sheets appear in the back of this book.)

TIME: 90 Minutes
80 Questions

DIRECTIONS: Each of the questions or incomplete statements below is followed by five possible answers or completions. Select the best choice in each case and fill in the corresponding oval on the answer sheet.

QUESTIONS 1–7

PRAXAGORA
     That's all we need.
Card your wool indeed. *No man must see*
the slightest bit of your body.
     We've got to hurry;
5   the littlest slip and we're undone. I can see it all:
The people assemble, Congressmen commences…and then
we arrive in a flap, some woman climbs over a bench,
flips up her cloak, and exposes to all and sundry,
some misplaced whiskers.
10   But if we get there first
and take our places, we can adjust our clothing
and no one'll be the wiser. And once we're there,
with proper beads tied on and arranged in place,
what casual observer will say that we're not men?

FIRST WOMAN

15   You're right. Agyrrhios started out as a woman,
but then he stole a flute player's beard, and pulled
the wool over everyone's eyes, and look at him now:
He runs the city.

PRAXAGORA

        And Agyrrhios, girls, is our model.
20   By the gods of daylight robbery, let's try to pull
a *coup* as big as his. Let's devise a device
to take command, take charge, take over. *We'll* run
the city, run it right and proper and well.
No more sitting and drifting in a ship of state
25   with empty oarlocks and barren masts!

From "The Congresswomen," by Aristophones

1. What words best describe the tone of the passage?

    (A) Serious and prudent   (D) Devious and diabolic

    (B) Foolhardy and mindless   (E) Silly and inane

    (C) Plotting and comical

2. What best defines the word "card" as used in line 2?

    (A) Share   (D) Remove

    (B) Fasten   (E) Comb

    (C) Disregard

3. Line 5 is best interpreted to mean

    I.   If you move too quickly your wool will fall off and our plan
         will be exposed.

    II. We must be careful not to expose our true identities.

    III. If you tell our secret, the news will circulate and everyone will
         know.

    (A) I only   (D) I and II only

    (B) II and III only   (E) II only

    (C) I and III only

4. The term "misplaced whiskers" (line 9) refers to

    (A) bawdy innuendo.

    (B) the fallen beards.

    (C) the scratchy wool capes.

    (D) the men at the meeting.

    (E) the long hair of the women.

5. From the plan discussed in the passage, a reader may infer that

    (A) women enjoy dressing like men.

    (B) men allowed women to attend congress.

    (C) if women were quiet and arrived early they could take part.

    (D) although they wanted to, women were not allowed to take part
         in politics.

    (E) the women only wanted to attend the meeting to listen to the
         current political agenda.

6. The word which LEAST describes Praxagora is

    (A) determined.   (D) boastful.

    (B) scheming.   (E) persuasive.

    (C) authoritative.

7. The metaphor on lines 24–25 is best interpreted as being

    (A) the corrupt political system run by men.

    (B) the powerlessness of women in their government.

    (C) the feeling of loneliness experienced by women.

    (D) a woman's inability to vote.

    (E) the restlessness of women's everyday lives.

QUESTIONS 8–14

Medea:

The man I loved, hath proved most evil,—Oh,
Of all things upon earth that bleed and grow,
A herb most bruised is woman. We must pay
Our store of gold, hoarded for that one day,
5   To buy us some man's love; and lo, they bring
A master of our flesh! There comes the sting
Of the whole shame. And then the jeopardy,
For good or ill, what shall that master be;
Reject she cannot: and if he but stays
10   His suit, 'tis shame on all that woman's days.
So thrown amid new laws, new places, why,
"Tis magic she must have, or prophesy—
Home never taught her that—how best to guide
Toward peace this thing that sleepeth at her side.
15   And she who, laboring long, shall find some way
Whereby her lord may bear with her, nor fray
His yoke too fiercely, blessed is the breath
That woman draws! Else pray for death.
Her lord, if he be wearied of the face
20   Withindoors, gets him forth; some merrier place
Will ease his heart: but she waits on, her whole
Vision enchained on a single soul.
And then, forsooth, 'tis they that face the call
Of war, while we sit sheltered, hid from all
25   Peril! False mocking! Sooner would I stand
Three times to face their battles, shield in hand,
Than bear one child.

From "Medea" by Euripedes

8.   The dramatic situation suggested by Medea's speech is that of a woman

   (A)   mocking the institution of marriage.

   (B)   worried about the future of her marriage.

   (C)   betrayed by a man; lamenting the plight of her gender.

   (D)   forsaken by her father.

   (E)   contemplating motherhood.

9. In the context of this passage, the word "yoke" (line 17) refers to

    (A) a device for constraining animals.

    (B) Medea's strong religious beliefs.

    (C) a husband's rule over his wife.

    (D) the anger of a woman's husband.

    (E) the rules which sanction women's labor in the fields.

10. In lines 3–6 Medea is critiquing the act of

    (A) females relinquishing savings to a man upon marriage.

    (B) bribery used by women to obtain desirable husbands.

    (C) the dowry system which provides the groom with a sum of money in exchange for the betrothal of a woman.

    (D) the selling of female slaves.

    (E) the use of money in matters of love.

11. The speaker's tone changes from

    (A) disapproving to enraged.

    (B) mournful to resentful.

    (C) proud to indignant.

    (D) detached to reflective.

    (E) regretful to chiding.

12. Lines 23–27 most imply that

    (A) Medea fears the prospect of war.

    (B) women's exclusion in battle is an example of gender inequality.

    (C) a shield is of little use to women during childbirth.

    (D) although men face the violence of war, women are not spared the greater threat of childbirth.

    (E) raising a child is a greater task than being a warrior in battle.

13. With minor variations, this passage is written in

(A) blank verse.   (D) free verse.

(B) verse paragraphs.   (E) spondaic hexameter.

(C) heroic couplets.

14. The prevailing message Medea wishes to explicate throughout her rhetorical speech is that

(A) women are treated ill by their husbands.

(B) men are scoundrels while women are virtuous.

(C) women have little freedom in choosing a marriage partner.

(D) through cultural sanctions, women are denied rights both in and out of marriage.

(E) childbirth endangers the lives of women.

QUESTIONS 15–19

The Prologue

1

To sing of wars, of captains, and of kings,
Of cities founded, commonwealths begun,
For my mean pen are too superior things;
Or how they all, or each, their dates have run;
5   Let poets and historians set these forth;
My obscure lines shall not so dim their worth.

2

But when my wond'ring eyes and envious heart
Great Bartas' sugared lines do but read o'er,
Fool, I do grudge the muses did not part
10   'Twixt him and me that overfluent store.
A Bartas can do what a Bartas will;
But simple I according to my skill.

3

From schoolboy's tongue no rhet'ric we expect,
Nor yet a sweet consort from broken strings,

15 Nor perfect beauty where's a main defect.
    My foolish, broken, blemished Muse so sings;
    And this to mend, alas, no art is able,
    'Cause nature made it so irreparable.

                        4
    Nor can I, like that fluent, sweet-tongued Greek
20 Who lisped at first, in future times speak plain.
    By art he gladly found what he did seek;
    A full requital of his striving pain.
    Art can do much, but this maxim's most sure:
    A weak or wounded brain admits no cure.

                        5
25 I am obnoxious to each carping tongue
    Who says my hand a needle better fits;
    A poet's pen all scorn I should thus wrong,
    For such despite they cast on female wits.
    If what I do prove well, it won't advance;
30 They'll say it's stol'n, or else it was by chance.

        By Anne Bradstreet

15. From the context the word "mean" (line 3) can be interpreted as

    (A) judgmental.   (D) unknown.

    (B) unimportant.   (E) angry.

    (C) aged.

16. The best paraphrase of stanza one is

    (A) the author is not interested in writing about ancient things.

    (B) the author thinks that wars, captains, kings, and dates are not
        worthy topics for poets.

    (C) events and people in history make superior subjects for poetic
        contemplation.

    (D) many little-known poets have chosen to write about significant
        events from the past.

    (E) the author feels unable to use important past events as subjects
        for verse.

17. Which of the following is NOT a contrast found in the poem?

    (A) "Bartas' sugared lines" (line 8) and "that overfluent store" (line 10)

    (B) "schoolboy's tongue" and "rhet'ric" (line 13)

    (C) "sweet consort" and "broken strings" (line 14)

    (D) "perfect beauty" and "main defect" (line 15)

    (E) "Muse so sings" (line 16) and "this to mend" (line 17)

18. What is the best meaning of stanza 4?

    (A) The author feels she, like the Greek poet, will find peace through poetry.

    (B) Through his writing, the Greek poet found an outlet for his suffering.

    (C) The early poetry of the Greek author was weaker than his later efforts.

    (D) If she continues to write, the author's poetry will become better.

    (E) The Greek poet, though unable to speak correctly, wrote beautiful poetry.

19. Which of the following is an observation the author makes about her own writing?

    I.   She will never be a good writer because men will not give her the opportunity.

    II. She will never be a good writer because she lacks the inspiration and noble subjects of her predecessors.

    III. She will never be a good writer because she lacks the skill.

    IV. She will never be a good writer because she does not have adequate knowledge of poetic forms.

    (A) I only   (D) III and IV only

    (B) III only   (E) I, II, III, and IV

    (C) I and II only

QUESTIONS 20–24

       The widow was as complete a contrast to her third bridegroom, in everything but age, as can well be conceived. Compelled to relinquish her first engagement, she had been united to a man of twice her own years, to whom
5   she had become an exemplary wife, and by whose death she was left in possession of a splendid fortune. A southern gentleman, considerably younger than herself, succeeded to her hand, and carried her to Charleston, where, after many uncomfortable years, she found herself again a widow. It
10   would have been singular if any uncommon delicacy of feeling had survived through such a life as Mrs. Dabney's; it could not be crushed and killed by her early disappointment, the cold duty of her first marriage, the dislocation of the heart's principles consequent on a second union, and
15   the unkindness of her southern husband, which had inevitably driven her to connect the idea of his death with that of her comfort. To be brief, she was the wisest, but unloveliest variety of women, a philosopher, bearing troubles of the heart with equanimity, dispensing with all that should have
20   been her happiness, and making the best of what remained. Sage in most matters, the widow was perhaps the more amiable for the one fraility that made her ridiculous. Being childless, she could not remain beautiful by proxy, in the person of a daughter; she therefore refused to grow old and
25   ugly, on any consideration; she struggled with Time, and held fast her roses in spite of him, till the venerable thief appeared to have relinquished the spoil, as not worth the trouble of acquiring it.

By Nathaniel Hawthorne

20. Her first marriage can best be described as

    (A) an exercise in duty but without love.

    (B) the one spot of romantic loveliness in an otherwise lackluster existence.

    (C) an intellectually challenging relationship.

    (D) an experience in poverty made bearable by mutual trust and understanding.

(E) a relationship marred by disloyalty and unchastity.

21. Her second marriage to the southern gentleman was different from the first in that it was

(A) based on mutual love and understanding.

(B) forced upon them by social pressures with which they could not cope.

(C) the result of her desire for status.

(D) founded upon greed and lack of tender feelings rather than upon love.

(E) an illegal arrangement unsanctioned by either civil or religious custom.

22. The "early disappointment" mentioned in line 12 refers to

(A) her first marriage.

(B) her second marriage.

(C) her contemplated third marriage.

(D) her first serious love.

(E) a combination of her romantic experiences up to this time.

23. The last part of the paragraph involves the use of an interesting personification. Who is personified?

(A) The bride   (D) Beauty

(B) Her third husband   (E) Time

(C) Marriage

24. In this context "roses" (line 26) represents

(A) contentment in marriage.

(B) beauty of youth.

(C) hope for happiness.

(D) troubles of the heart.

(E) kindness of the married state.

QUESTIONS 25–29

[Volpone in a large bed. Enter Mosca. Volpone awakes]
Volpone: Good morning to the day; and next, my gold!
Open the shrine, that I may see my saint.
[Mosca draws a curtain, revealing piles of gold]
Hail the world's gold, and mine! More glad than is
5   The teeming earth to see the longed-for sun
Peep through the horns of the celestial Ram,
Am I, to view thy splendour darkening his;
That lying here, amongst my other hoards,
Show'st like a flame by night, or like the day
10   Struck out of chaos, when all darkness fled
Unto the centre. O, thou son of Sol
(But brighter than thy father) let me kiss,
With adoration, thee, and every relic
Of sacred treasure in this blessed room.
15   Well did wise wise poets by thy glorious name
Title that age which they would have the best,
Thou being the best of things, and far transcending
All style of joy in children, parents, friends,
Or any other waking dream on earth.

From "Volpone, or the Fox," by Ben Jonson

25.   Volpone's greeting of the day and then his gold is a(n)

    (A)   satire.   (D)   aubade.

    (B)   ode.   (E)   parody of an aubade.

    (C)   parody of an ode.

26.   Which best explains the greeting "Hail the world's gold and mine!"?

    (A)   Money has become the center of both the world and Volpone.

    (B)   Like everyone else, Volpone loves money more than his soul.

    (C)   Volpone has replaced the goodness of his soul with worldly commodities like gold.

    (D)   Volpone worships worldly goods like gold.

    (E)   Volpone has sold his soul for the world's acclaim for his gold.

27. Which best explains the use of the word "relic"?

    (A) The playwright puns on the idea of religious antiques.

    (B) The playwright pokes fun at Volpone kissing the gold.

    (C) The playwright puns on the idea of people kissing religious relics.

    (D) The playwright satirizes people who kissed old bones thinking they were religious relics.

    (E) The playwright stresses the fact Volpone worships his treasures as if they were religious relics.

28. The age referred to in lines 15–16 is the

    (A) Age of Affluence.   (D) Age of the Poets.

    (B) Renaissance.   (E) Age of the Alchemists.

    (C) Golden Age.

29. Thou in line 17 refers to

    (A) Volpone's soul.   (D) the saint in the shrine.

    (B) Mosca.   (E) the Sun.

    (C) the shrine.

QUESTIONS 30–36

I went to the Garden of Love,
And saw what I never had seen:
A Chapel was built in the midst,
Where I used to play on the green

5   And the gates of this Chapel were shut,
And "Thou shalt not" writ over the door;
So I turned to the Garden of Love
That so many sweet flowers bore;

And I saw it was filled with graves,
10   And tomb-stones where flowers should be;
And Priests in black gowns were walking their rounds,
And binding with briars my joys and desires.

From "The Garden of Love," by William Blake

30. What best explains the Chapel?

   (A) The Chapel symbolizes pure love.

   (B) The Chapel represents rules that religion enforces over free love.

   (C) The Chapel symbolizes the power the Church holds over secular love.

   (D) The Chapel is an image of the strict love of God rather than of religious fervor.

   (E) The Chapel represents the strict rules of commitment in marriage.

31. The words "Thou shalt not" on the closed gates suggest

   (A) religion sets up a barrier to the human experience of love.

   (B) the poet rebels against the Ten Commandments.

   (C) religion has closed the gate on human happiness.

   (D) the poet has rejected religion.

   (E) the poet feels shut out by the Church.

32. The repetition of the conjunction in the last stanza suggests

   I.   the poet is building to a climax.

   II. the poet is growing more and more frustrated.

   III. the poet's hatred of the priests is about to erupt.

   (A) I and III only   (D) I, II, and III

   (B) I only   (E) I and II only

   (C) III only

33. The poem is a(n)

   (A) fable.   (D) fabliau.

   (B) parable.   (E) allegory.

   (C) dramatic monologue.

34. What best explains the verbs "play" (line 4) and "bore" (line 8)?

    (A) As a child the poet felt free in this garden with so many beautiful flowers that now simply bore him.

    (B) In his youth the poet felt no limits to the way he loved; now he feels hemmed in by the garden.

    (C) In his youth the poet revelled in free, untrammeled love which seemed to surround him like flowers.

    (D) As a child the poet was surrounded by people who loved him as if by flowers in the garden.

    (E) In the past the poet was able to give love freely which he did as if giving away flowers.

35. The Garden is now filled with graves and tombstones because

    (A) the Industrial Revolution has blighted the "garden," turning countryside into wasteland.

    (B) industry has turned gardens into factory sites — graveyards for the workers.

    (C) strict rules of society have turned free expression of poets and writers into dead things.

    (D) religious rules have turned the beautiful free expression of human love into something dead and ugly.

    (E) religion has taken away individuality and turned people into automatons, dead inside, incapable of loving.

36. What figure of speech is "binding with briars"?

    (A) Onomatopoeia   (D) Feminine rhyme

    (B) Alliteration   (E) Assonance

    (C) Internal rhyme

QUESTIONS 37–39

Ode on Indolence
John Keats [1795–1821]
They toil not, neither do they spin.

One morn before me were three figures seen,
    With bowed necks, and joined hands, side-fac'd;
And one behind the other stepp'd serene,
    In placid sandals, and in white robes grac'd;
5   They pass'd, like figures on a marble urn,
    When shifted round to see the other side;
        They came again; as when the urn once more
Is shifted round, the first seen shades return;
    And they were strange to me, as may betide
10   With vases, to one deep in Phidian lore.

How is it, shadows! that I knew ye not?
    How came ye muffled in so hush a mask?
Was it a silent deep-disguisèd plot
    To steal away, and leave without a task
15   My idle days? Ripe was the drowsy hour;
    The blissful cloud of summer-indolence
        Benumb'd my eyes; my pulse grew less and less;
Pain had no sting, and pleasure's wreath no flower:
    O, why did ye not melt, and leave my sense
20   Unhaunted quite of all but—nothingness?

A third time pass'd they by, and, passing, turn'd
    Each one the face a moment whiles to me;
Then faded, and to follow them I burn'd
And ach'd for wings because I knew the three;
25   The first was a fair maid, and Love her name;
    The second was Ambition, pale of cheek,
        And ever watchful with fatigued eye;
The last, whom I love more, the more of blame
    Is heap'd upon her, maiden most unmeek,—
30   I know to be my demon Poesy.

37. In line 8, the phrase "the first seen shades return" is best taken to mean which of the following?

    (A) Shadows cast by the vases

    (B) Greeks risen from the dead

    (C) Shadows made by the rising sun

    (D) Strange new shades of color

    (E) Ghostly visitors

38. The relationship between lines 1–10 and lines 25–30 is best described as which of the following?

    (A) Lines 1–10 establish a thesis; lines 25–30 refute it.

    (B) Lines 1–10 present a description; lines 25–30 enlarge upon it.

    (C) Lines 1–10 present a rule; lincs 25–30 propose an exception to it.

    (D) Lines 1–10 pose a question; lines 25–30 answer it.

    (E) Lines 1–10 begin a narrative; lines 25–30 conclude it.

39. The change referred to in lines 23–24 is described as one from

    (A) frivolity to exertion.

    (B) seriousness to lethargy.

    (C) restraint to freedom.

    (D) sinfulness to piety.

    (E) straightforwardness to subtlety.

QUESTIONS 40–45

At the Everglades Club after dark Paula and Lowell Thayer and Anson and a casual fourth played bridge with hot cards. It seemed to Anson that her kind, serious face was wan and tired—she had been around now for four,
5   five, years. He had known her for three.

"Two spades."

"Cigarette?...Oh, I beg your pardon, By me."

"By."

"I'll double three spaces."

10   There were a dozen tables of bridge in the room, which was filling up with smoke. Anson's eyes met Paula's, held them persistently even when Thayer's glance fell between them....

"What was bid?" he asked abstractedly.

15   *"Rose of Washington Square"*
sang the young people in the corners:
"I'm withering there
In basement air——"

The smoke banked like fog, and the opening of a
20 door filled the room with blown swirls of ectoplasm. Little Bright Eyes streaked past the tables seeking Mr. Conan Doyle among the Englishmen who were posing as Englishmen about the lobby.

"You could cut it with a knife."

25   "...cut it with a knife."

"...a knife."

At the end of the rubber Paula suddenly got up and spoke to Anson in a tense, low voice. With scarcely a glance at Lowell Thayer, they walked out the door and
30 descended a long flight of stone steps — in a moment they were walking hand in hand along the moonlit beach.

From "The Rich Boy," by F. Scott Fitzgerald

40. What is significant about the length of time Anson has known Paula?

(A) He is so infatuated with her that he cannot keep track of time.

(B) She has been around in his social circles for a few years before he met her.

(C) His relationship with her has become routine and a bit boring for him.

(D) Although he met her before, he has only been serious about her for three years.

(E) His friendship with Lowell Thayer is more important than his feelings for Paula.

41. All of the following are signs of intense passion in the passage EXCEPT the

    (A) cards.

    (B) smoke filling up the room.

    (C) players' glances.

    (D) tone in Paula's voice.

    (E) fourth player at the bridge table.

42. Which of these is the best explanation for "Thayer's glance fell between them"?

    (A) Thayer disapproves of the fact that Paula and Anson are smoking cigarettes.

    (B) Thayer has been courting Paula behind Anson's back and trying to win her love.

    (C) Thayer suspects that Paula has been having a secret affair with Anson.

    (D) Thayer is the only one who notices that Paula and Anson are in love.

    (E) Thayer is hoping to cue his bridge partner across the table.

43. How does the song the young people are singing reflect the action at the table?

    I.   Paula is suffering because Anson does not love her enough.

    II.   Anson is suffering because Paula cannot decide between the two men.

    III. Lowell is suffering because Paula obviously prefers Anson.

    (A) I only   (D) I and II only

    (B) II only   (E) I and III only

    (C) III only

44. The references to "blown swirls of ectoplasm" and "who were posing as Englishmen" are indicative of

    (A) local color of the seaside resort club.

(B) obstacles of society that Paula must overcome.

(C) the lack of clarity and honesty.

(D) the easy acceptance of wealthy foreigners into society.

(E) objects of amusement to the members of the club.

45. By the end of the passage it can be inferred that

(A) Lowell has proposed marriage to Paula several times.

(B) Paula would like for Anson to propose marriage to her.

(C) Paula is tired of the animosity Lowell feels for Anson.

(D) Anson is unaware of the problem Lowell creates.

(E) The friendship between Lowell and Anson is over.

QUESTIONS 46–50

MRS. PINCHWIFE.

O my dear, dear bud, welcome home! Why dost thou look so fropish? Who has nangered thee?

PINCHWIFE.

You're a fool.

(Mrs. Pinchwife *goes aside and cries*)

ALITHEA.

5   Faith, so she is, for crying for no fault, poor tender creature!

PINCHWIFE.

What, you would have her as impudent as yourself, as arrant a jill-flirt, a gadder, a magpie, and to say all, a mere, notorious town-woman?

ALITHEA.

Brother, you are my only censurer; and the honor of
10   your family shall sooner suffer in your wife there than in me, though I take the innocent liberty of the town.

PINCHWIFE.

Hark you, mistress, do not talk so before my wife. The innocent liberty of the town!

ALITHEA.

    Why, pray, who boasts of any intrigue with me? What
15   lampoon has made my name notorious? What ill
    women frequent my lodgings? I keep no company
    with any women of scandalous reputations.

PINCHWIFE.

    No, you keep the men of scandalous reputations com-
    pany.

ALITHEA.

20   Where? Would you not have me civil? answer 'em in
    a box at the plays, in the drawing room at Whitehall,
    in St. James's Park, Mulberry Garden, or—

PINCHWIFE.

    Hold, hold! Do not teach my wife where the men are to
    be found! I believe she's the worse for your town docu-
25   ments already. I bid you keep her in ignorance, as I do.

MRS. PINCHWIFE.

    Indeed, be not angry with her, bud; she will tell me
    nothing of the town, though I ask her a thousand times
    a day.

PINCHWIFE.

    Then you are very inquisitive to know, I find!

MRS. PINCHWIFE.

30   Not I, indeed dear; I hate London. Our place-house in
    the country is worth a thousand of 't; would I were
    there again!

PINCHWIFE.

    So you shall, I warrant, But were you not talking of
    plays and players when I came in? — [*To* Alithea.]
35   You are her encourager in such discourses.

MRS. PINCHWIFE.

    No, indeed, dear; she chid me just now for liking the
    playermen.

PINCHWIFE (*aside*).

    Nay, if she be so innocent as to own to me her liking
    them, there is no hurt in't. —Come, my poor rogue,
40   but thou lik'st none better than me?

MRS. PINCHWIFE.

    Yes, indeed, but I do; the playermen are finer folks.

PINCHWIFE.

    But you love none better than me?

MRS. PINCHWIFE.

You are mine own dear bud, and I know you; I hate a stranger.

PINCHWIFE.

45   Ay, my dear, you must love me only, and not be like the naughty town-women, who only hate their husbands and love every man else, love plays, visits, fine coaches, fine clothes, fiddles, balls, treats, and so lead a wicked town-life.

MRS. PINCHWIFE.

50   Nay, if to enjoy all these things be a town-life, London is not so bad a place, dear.

PINCHWIFE.

How! If you love me, you must hate London.

From "The Country Wife," by William Wycherly

46. In its context, "why dost thou look so fropish" suggests that the husband

(A) is concerned for his wife's health.

(B) enters the house in a bad mood.

(C) has heard people gossip about his sister.

(D) wants nothing more than to be left alone.

(E) frequents bars and play-houses.

47. It can be inferred from her lines that Mrs. Pinchwife is a(n)

(A) totally arrogant snob.

(B) somewhat naive young woman.

(C) immoral, adulterous wife.

(D) victim of idle social gossip.

(E) envied, beautiful socialite.

48. Because Alithea defends her honor so quickly, it can be inferred that

(A) she has actually been keeping company with men of dubious reputation.

(B)   her female friends have questionable reputations.

(C)   many wives suspect her of having an affair with their husbands.

(D)   this is a conversation she has had many times with her brother.

(E)   she is afraid her sister-in-law will get the wrong impression of her.

49.   The humor in this conversation is created by which of the following?

I.   Alithea has already shown her sister-in-law some of the pleasures of town life.

II.   The husband, while trying to explain what his wife should avoid, shows her what to look for.

III. It is obvious the wife does not want to be kept ignorant by her husband.

(A) I only   (D) I and II only

(B) II only   (E) I, II, and III

(C) III only

50.   Mr. Pinchwife does not want his wife to attend plays because he is afraid she will

(A)   become used to spending too much of her time away from home.

(B)   refuse to return to their home in the country.

(C)   have an affair with one of the actors.

(D)   spend more money than he can afford.

(E)   catch him having an affair with one of the actresses.

QUESTIONS 51–55

Well, children, where there was so much racket there must be something out of kilter. I think that 'twixt the negroes of the South and the women in the North, all talking about rights, the white men will be in a fix pretty soon.
5   But what's all this here talking about?

That man over there says that women need to be helped into carriages, and lifted over ditches, and to have the best place everywhere. Nobody ever helps me into carriages or over mudpuddles, or gives me any best place!
10 And ain't I a woman? Look at me! Look at my arm! I have ploughed and planted, and gathered into barns and no man could head me! And ain't I a woman? I could work as much and eat as much as a man—when I could get it—and bear the lash as well! And ain't I a woman? I have borne
15 thirteen children, and seen them most all sold off to slavery, and when I cried out with my mother's grief, none but Jesus heard me! And ain't I a woman?

Then they talk about this thing in the head; what's this they call it? [Intellect, someone whispers.] That's it,
20 honey. What's that got to do with women's rights or negro's rights? If my cup won't hold but a pint, and yours holds a quart, wouldn't you be mean to not to let me have my little half-measure full?

From "Ain't I a Woman?" by Sojourner Truth

51.   The question "Ain't I a woman?" repeatedly posed throughout this passage most suggests

(A)   that black women are not given respect by white men.

(B)   the different levels of patriarchal oppression.

(C)   the speaker seeks reaffirmation of her gender by the audience.

(D) the speaker wants the same rights as white women.

(E) the speaker is unhappy with her status as compared to white women.

52. The main purpose of this passage is to

(A) show the commonalities shared by abolitionists and the women's suffrage movement.

(B) argue against slavery.

(C) concede that slaves are intellectually inferior, yet are deserving of freedom.

(D) reveal the speaker's tortured existence.

(E) express resentment towards white women.

53. Lines 10–14 support the speaker's assertions that

(A) women can be exposed to male labor.

(B) slaves can lead a physically rigorous life.

(C) although treated as inferiors, women are as capable as men and therefore should be treated equally.

(D) the expectations for women are determined by their capabilities.

(E) the speaker does not regret her strenuous labor.

54. When the speaker refers to intellectual capacities in the last paragraph she

(A) wishes to present men as being superior.

(B) attempts to transcend the argument and instead focus on the issue of equal rights for blacks as well as women.

(C) inadvertently refutes her own argument.

(D)   reveals a hidden agenda: to prove that slaves are equally as intelligent.

(E)   shows the necessity for focusing on intellect.

55.   The "cup" in line 21 may best be interpreted to mean

(A)   the rights of women.

(B)   the desire for equality shared by slaves and women.

(C)   the lives of black women compared to black men.

(D)   the intelligence of slaves vs. free blacks.

(E)   the emptiness felt by black women.

QUESTIONS 56–64

RUBEK: Hate? You hated me?

IRENE (*Again vehemently*): Yes, you! I hated the artist who so completely, without grief, without any kind of concern, took a young human being and tore the soul

5   out of its warmblooded body because it was needed for a work of art!

RUBEK: How can you say that? You used to glow with desire as you posed. You had an almost holy passion to be with me in the midst of my work. Each morning

10   it brought us together as if for an act of devotion.

IRENE (*Coldly as before*): I will tell you one thing, Arnold.

RUBEK: Yes?

IRENE: I never loved your art before I met you—nor after.

15   RUBEK: But the artist Irene?
      IRENE: The artist I hated!
      RUBEK: The artist in me, too?
      IRENE: Most of all in you. When I undressed completely
             and stood there before you—then I hated you, Arnold.
20   RUBEK *(vehemently):* No you couldn't have. It isn't true!
      IRENE: I hated you because you stood there so unfeelingly.
      RUBEK *(laughing):* Unfeelingly? Did you think that?
      IRENE: At any rate, so intolerably self controlled! And
             then you were so thoroughly an artist—only an artist
25   and not a man.
             (Changing to a warm intimately concerned voice) But
             that statue in the wet, living clay—Oh how I loved it!
             Each day I watched it grow and finally emerge as a
             human being, alive and vital—casing its way out of
30   the raw, shapeless mass, full of soul. It was our cre-
             ation. I knew that it had come to life because of me,
             too. Our child—mine and yours.

      From "When We Dead Awaken," by Henrik Ibsen

56.   What literary device does Irene employ in lines 25–28?

      (A) Metaphor   (D) Hyperbole

      (B) Simile   (E) Chiasmus

      (C) Parody

57.   The phrase "holy passion" (line 8) in this passage suggests that

      (A) Irene was overcome with irreverent lust.

      (B) the model felt impassioned about posing.

      (C) Rubek's art was mostly religious.

      (D) Irene was dedicated and vehement to be included in Rubek's art.

      (E) Irene compared Rubek's work to divine splendor.

58.   According to Irene, in what temporal order did her malice develop?

      I.   Art

      II.   Rubek

      III. The artist in Rubek

(A) III, I, II   (D) II, III, I

(B) III, II, I   (E) II, I, III

(C) I, III, II

59. The underlying metaphors from this passage are drawn mostly from

(A) art.   (D) childbirth.

(B) religion.   (E) death.

(C) nature.

60. For Irene and Rubek the creation of the statue has become a metaphor for

(A) their solidifying relationship.

(B) their developing disgust with each other.

(C) the birth of a new style of art.

(D) marriage.

(E) their child together.

61. Irene's accusation against Rubek is interpreted to mean

(A) he has neglected his humanity with his sole concern for art.

(B) he stopped his romantic involvement with her.

(C) their relationship ended.

(D) Rubek was neglecting his duties as a father.

(E) in order to be an artist, Rubek had to relinquish his humanity.

62. What literary device is used in Irene's representation of the statue?

(A) Metonymy   (D) Allusion

(B) Realism   (E) Personification

(C) Dead metaphor

63. The attitude of Irene has changed from

(A) contemptful to menacing.

(B)   devoted to scornful.

(C)   sorrowful to vengeful.

(D)   accusatory to reminiscent.

(E)   melodramatic to realistic.

64.   It may be inferred that this passage is located in what area of the plot?

(A)   Resolution   (D)   Catastrophe

(B)   Climax   (E)   Falling action

(C)   Exposition

QUESTIONS 65–69

"Charlie, I haven't a cent!" answered Vandover, looking him squarely in the face. "Would I be here and trying to get work from you if I had? No; I gambled it all away. You know I had eighty-nine hundred in U.S. 4 per cents…For a
5   time I got along by work in the paint shop. But they have let me out now; said I was so irregular. I owe for nearly a month at my lodging-place." His eyes sought the floor, roll- ing about stupidly. "Nearly a month, and that's what makes me jump and tremble so. You ought to see me sometimes
10   —b-r-r-r-h!—and I get to barking! I'm a wolf mostly, you know, or some kind of animal, some kind of a brute. But I'd be all right if everything did not go around so slowly, and seem far off. But I'm a wolf….Ah! It's up four flights at the end of the hall, very dark, eight thousand dollars in a
15   green cloth sack, and lots of lights a-burning. See how long my finger nails are — regular claws; that's the wolf, the brute! Why can't I talk in my mouth instead of in my throat? That's the devil of it. When you paint on steel and iron your colours don't dry out true; all the yellows turn
20   green…And when all those eight thousand little lights be- gin to burn red, why, of course that makes you nervous! So I have to drink a great deal of water and chew butcher's paper. That fools him and he thinks he's eating. Just so I can lay quiet in the Plaza when the sun is out…."

From <u>Vandover and the Brute</u>, by Frank Norris

65. Which best explains what happened to the speaker?

    (A) He refused to get a job because of all his money; now he cannot get a job and is starving.

    (B) He could not do the work in the paint shop and now is homeless and ill.

    (C) He gambled all of Charlie's money away; now that he is out of work he wants Charlie to come to his rescue.

    (D) He gambled all his money away, lost his job, and is now suffering from malnutrition.

    (E) He lost his job and had to resort to gambling to pay his bills; now he is starving and ill.

66. Which best answers the speaker's question, "Why can't I talk in my mouth instead of in my throat?"

    (A) Because he is so hungry, his voice is getting deeper and deeper.

    (B) Because he is slipping into senility, his voice is losing its timbre.

    (C) Because he is growing into manhood (symbolized by the brute motif), his voice is growing gruffer.

    (D) Because gradually the brute inside him is trying to get out.

    (E) Because the brute, not the man, is expressing itself in growling tones.

67. The pronoun in "It's up four flights" refers to

    (A) the money at the end of the hall.

    (B) some sort of brute at the end of the hall.

    (C) the apartment at the end of the hall.

    (D) the painting of eight thousand eyes at the end of the hall.

    (E) the wolf at the end of the hall.

68. Which best explains the use of the third person pronouns in "That fools him and he think's he's eating"?

    (A) The speaker distances himself from the devil inside him.

(B)   The speaker considers the brute inside him a totally integrated part of his personality.

(C)   The speaker considers the butcher's dog a threat to his way of life.

(D)   The speaker considers Charlie as a threat to his way of life and distances himself from him.

(E)   The speaker considers the brute inside him as divorced from his true human self.

69.   The 8,000 little lights represent

(A)   all the guilt the speaker feels at gambling away his money.

(B)   all the U.S. bonds the speaker lost.

(C)   the bonds that the speaker gambled away.

(D)   the opportunities the speaker missed by gambling away the bonds.

(E)   all the missed opportunities in a futile life.

QUESTIONS 70–74

The great fault of a modern school of poetry is that it is an experiment to reduce poetry to a mere effusion of natural sensibility; or what is worse, to divest it both of imaginary splendor and human passion, to surround the
5   meanest objects with the morbid feelings and devouring egotism of the writers' own minds. Milton and Shakespeare did not so understand poetry. They gave a more liberal interpretation both to nature and art. They did not do all they could to get rid of the one and the other, to fill up the
10   dreary void with the Moods of their own Minds. They owe their power over the human mind to their having had a deeper sense than others of human life. But to the men I speak of there is nothing interesting, nothing heroical, but themselves. To them the fall of gods or of great men is the
15   same. They do not enter into the feeling. They cannot understand the terms. They are even debarred from the last poor, paltry consolation of an unmanly triumph over fallen greatness; for their minds reject, with a convulsive effort

20 and intolerable loathing, the very idea that there ever was, or was thought to be, anything superior to themselves. All that has ever excited the attention and admiration of the world, they look upon with the most perfect indifference; and they are surprised to find that the world repays their indifference with scorn. "With what measure they mete, it

25 has been meted to them again."

Shakespeare's imagination is of the same plastic kind as his conception of character or passion. "It glances from heaven to earth." Its movement is rapid and devious. It unites the most opposite extremes: or, as Puck says, in boasting of

30 his own feats, "puts a girdle round about the earth in forty minutes." He seems always hurrying from his subject, even while describing it; but the stroke, like the lightning's, is sure as it is sudden. He takes the widest possible range, but from that very range he has his choice of the greatest variety and

35 aptitude of materials. He brings together images the most alike, but placed at the greatest distance from each other; that is, found in circumstances of the greatest dissimilitude. From the remoteness of his combinations, and the celerity with which they are effected, they coalesce the more indissolubly

40 together.

From "On Shakespeare and Milton," by William Hazlitt

70. In context, the sentence "They gave a more liberal interpretation both to nature and art" (lines 7–8) suggests which of the following?

  (A) Shakespeare and Milton did not espouse the political conservatism of the modernists.

  (B) Shakespeare and Milton were tolerant in matters concerning nature and art.

  (C) Shakespeare and Milton did not understand poetry in the same way as the modernists.

  (D) The modernists had a greater right to their viewpoints than the Romantics.

  (E) The modern age is one of egotism.

71. The passage suggests that Classical Tragedy would not be of interest to the "modern school" because they

(A) pay too much attention to their superiors and not enough to themselves.

(B) do not see any difference between "the fall of gods or of great men."

(C) they hate anything that holds the "admiration of the world."

(D) they cannot deal with the scorn the critical world has for them.

(E) they feel compelled to substitute their own "dreary world" for the real thing.

72. The "girdle round about the earth" (line 30) is best understood as

(A) Shakespeare's universal appeal.

(B) Shakespeare's ability to give form to indiscriminate images.

(C) Shakespeare's ability to discuss all topics.

(D) Shakespeare's capacity to bring together extremes.

(E) Shakespeare's ability to communicate quickly using appropriate symbols.

73. At the end of the second paragraph, the critic distinguishes between similar images and

(A) dissimilar meanings.   (D) indissoluble combinations.

(B) indissoluble materials.   (E) dissimilar circumstances.

(C) dissimilar ranges.

74. The use of the words "dissimilitude" and "indissolubly" has the effect of

(A) providing closure with the opening contention in the first sentence of the second paragraph.

(B) providing poetic consonance that is appropriate to the discussion of Shakespeare's works.

(C) providing a point of contrast to concepts of similarity as advanced in the preceding sentences.

(D) providing parallelism between the ideas contained in the two sentences.

(E) providing a further description of the range of Shakespeare's writing.

QUESTIONS 75–79

> After great pain a formal feeling comes
> The nerves sit ceremonious like tombs;
> The stiff Heart questions — was it He that bore?
> And yesterday — or centuries before?
>
> 5   The feet mechanical
> Go round a wooden way
> Of ground or air or Ought, regardless grown,
> A quartz contentment like a stone.
>
> This is the hour of lead
> 10 Remembered if outlived,
> As freezing persons recollect the snow —
> First chill, then stupor, then the letting go.

"After Great Pain," by Emily Dickinson

75. The "He" (line 3) is

   (A) the one who is instrumental in inflicting the pain.

   (B) the pain itself which has been personified.

   (C) the person who is inflicted with the pain.

   (D) a disinterested observer trying to understand the cause of the pain.

   (E) the poet himself.

76. Which other word is LEAST analogous to the word "ceremonious"?

   (A) Stiff   (D) Remembered

   (B) Mechanical   (E) Regardless

   (C) Formal

77. The phrase "recollect the snow" (line 11) means

   I.   think of the formal whiteness of the snow.

   II.   recall the quiet precision of the snowfall.

   III. remember the experience of freezing.

(A) I and III only   (D) I only

(B) II only   (E) III only

(C) II and III only

78. The word "regardless" (line 7) is best read as a synonym for

(A) careless.   (D) unwary.

(B) unmindful.   (E) reckless.

(C) unthoughtful.

79. "Ought" is an archaic word which the poet here uses to mean

(A) nothing at all.

(B) everything which can be imagined.

(C) that which cannot be known.

(D) anything else.

(E) what may be misunderstood.

QUESTIONS 80–82

The points that I particularly wish to make about
Yeats' development are two. The first, on which I have
already touched, is that to have accomplished what Yeats
did in the middle and later years is a great and permanent
5   example — which poets-to-come should study with reverence — of what I have called Character of the Artist: a kind
of moral, as well as intellectual, excellence. The second
point, which follows naturally after what I have said in
criticism of the lack of complete emotional expression in
10   his early work, is that Yeats is preeminently the poet of
middle age. By this I am far from meaning that he is a poet
only for middle-aged readers: the attitude towards him to
younger poets who write in English, the world over, is
enough evidence to the contrary. Now, in theory, there is
15   no reason why a poet's inspiration or material should fail,
in middle age or at any time before senility. For a man who
is capable of experience finds himself in a different world
in every decade of his life; as he sees it with different eyes,

the material of his art is continually renewed. But in fact,
20 very few poets have shown this capacity of adaptation to
the years. It requires, indeed, an exceptional honesty and
courage to face the change. Most men either cling to the
experiences of youth, so that their writing becomes an in-
sincere mimicry of their earlier work, or they leave their
25 passing behind, and write only from the head, with a hollow and wasted virtuosity. There is another and even worse
temptation: that of becoming dignified, or becoming public
figures with only a public existence — coatracks hung
with decorations and distinctions, doing, saying, and even
30 thinking and feeling only what they believe the public expects of them. Yeats was not that kind of poet: and it is,
perhaps, a reason why young men should find his later
poetry more acceptable than older men easily can. For the
young men can see him as a poet who in his work remained
35 in the best sense always young, who even in one sense
became young as he aged. But the old, unless they are
stirred to something of the honesty with oneself expressed
in the poetry, will be shocked by such a revelation of what
a man really is and remains. They will refuse to believe that
40 they are like that.

From "On Poetry and Poets," by T.S. Eliot

80. In context, the statement "Now, in theory, there is no reason why a
poet's inspiration or material should fail, in middle age or at any
time before senility" (lines 14–16) suggests which of the following?

(A) Yeats and other poets used this theory as a defense against
criticism.

(B) Yeats used this theory as an excuse.

(C) Eliot is praising Yeats for not having "failed."

(D) Many poets' inspiration and material blossom in middle age.

(E) Many poets' inspiration and material fail in middle age, and
these poets use this observation to excuse their failure.

> **Please Note: This is where the actual CLEP exam would end.
> We provide 10 extra questions for practice purposes.**

81. "Public figures" (lines 27–28) are often "coatracks" (line 28) because they

    (A) are public "skeletons" of their previous selves.

    (B) are sensitive to contemporary poetic and public "fashion."

    (C) are dignified, rigid, and uninspired.

    (D) are only fit to remain in the "back rooms" of poetry's "house."

    (E) are content to behave according to public whim.

82. Eliot determines that young men find Yeats' later poetry more acceptable than older men do because

    (A) younger men have not yet achieved Yeats' level of emotional maturity.

    (B) younger men see the older Yeats as a contemporary.

    (C) Yeats was too far ahead of his time for his own generation to understand him.

    (D) Yeats was emotionally immature.

    (E) younger men relate to Yeats' disdain for the older writer.

QUESTIONS 83–85

DREAM DEFERRED

What happens to a dream deferred?
Does it dry up
like a raisin in the sun?
Or fester like a sore —
5 And then run?
Does it stink like rotten meat?
Or crust and sugar over —
like a syrupy sweet?

Maybe it just sags
10 like a heavy load.

Or does it explode?

By Langston Hughes

83. The effect of such phrases as "dry up" (line 2), "fester like a sore" (line 4), "stink like rotten meat" (line 6), "crust and sugar over" (line 7), "sags like a heavy load" (lines 9–10), and "explode" (line 11) is to

(A)   catalog the many negative possibilities of deferred dreams.

(B)   stress the speaker's dissatisfaction with reality.

(C)   satirize those who defer dreams.

(D)   underscore the necessity to dream.

(E)   suggest the fruits of dreaming.

84.   The effective meaning of the simile in lines 7–8 is to

(A)   parody children's visions at Christmas.

(B)   suggest sweetness allays the burden of dreams.

(C)   suggest the speaker's craving for sweets.

(D)   satirize those who refuse to dream.

(E)   suggest that sweet on the outside might mean sour on the inside.

85.   Which of the following changes is introduced in line 11?

(A)   The deferred dream could lead to violence.

(B)   The deferral of dreams is accepted.

(C)   The deferral of dreams is rejected.

(D)   The question in line 1 is answered.

(E)   The deferred dream is defined.

QUESTIONS 86–90

Two paper tendrils, also accordian-pleated, hung down from the clapper of the bell. Miss Faust pulled one. It unfolded stickily and became a long banner with a message written on it. "Here," said Miss Faust, handing the free end
5   to Dr. Breed, "pull it the rest of the way and tack the end to the bulletin board."

Dr. Breed obeyed, stepping back to read the banner's message. "Peace on Earth!" he read out loud heartily.

Miss Faust stepped down from her desk with the
10   other tendril, unfolding it, "Good Will Toward Men!" the other tendril said.

"By golly," chuckled Dr. Breed, "they've dehydrated Christmas! The place looks festive, very festive."

15   "And I remembered the chocolate bars for the Girl Pool, too," she said. "Aren't you proud of me?"

Dr. Breed touched his forehead, dismayed by his forgetfulness. "Thank God for that! It slipped my mind."

"We musn't ever forget that," said Miss Faust. "It's tradition now—Dr. Breed and his chocolate bars for the
20   Girl Pool at Christmas." She explained to me that the Girl Pool was the typing bureau in the Laboratory's basement. "The girls belong to anybody with access to a dictaphone."

All year long, she said, the girls of the Girl Pool listened to the faceless voices of scientists on dictaphone
25   records—records brought in by the mail girls. Once a year the girls left their cloister of cement block to go a-caroling—to get their chocolate bars from Dr. Asa Breed.

"They serve science too," Dr. Breed testified, "even though they may not understand a word of it. God bless
30   thcm everyone!"

From Cat's Cradle, by Kurt Vonnegut

86.   "they've dehydrated Christmas" means all of the following EXCEPT

    (A)   they've fossilized it.

    (B)   they've concentrated it.

    (C)   they've decimated it.

    (D)   they've dessicated it.

    (E)   they've condensed it.

87.   Dr. Breed is a nuclear warfare scientist. What is the closest explanation for this name?

    (A)   An oxymoron, because of his job

    (B)   A pun on his job

    (C)   Pathetic fallacy, because he destroys nature

    (D)   Ironic, because of his potential for destroying life

    (E)   A paradox on what his job entails

88. When Dr. Breed reads the banner's messages, what literary technique is at work?

    (A) Homile   (D) Symbolism

    (B) Irony   (E) Parable

    (C) Emblemism

89. The use of the words "cloister of cement block" suggests the girls are like

    (A) nuns trained to work silently in modern surroundings.

    (B) nuns sequestered in peaceful surroundings.

    (C) prisoners in a modern efficient facility.

    (D) prisoners who prefer austere surroundings.

    (E) nuns immured in modern-day harshness.

90. Miss Faust is talking to

    I.   herself and Dr. Breed.

    II.   the Girl Pool and the scientists.

    III. Dr. Breed and the narrator.

    (A) I and II only   (D) III only

    (B) I only   (E) II only

    (C) II and III only

CLEP ANALYZING AND INTERPRETING LITERATURE
TEST 2

ANSWER KEY

1.	(C)	31.	(A)	61.	(A)
2.	(B)	32.	(E)	62.	(E)
3.	(D)	33.	(E)	63.	(D)
4.	(A)	34.	(C)	64.	(B)
5.	(D)	35.	(D)	65.	(D)
6.	(D)	36.	(B)	66.	(E)
7.	(B)	37.	(E)	67.	(C)
8.	(C)	38.	(B)	68.	(E)
9.	(C)	39.	(A)	69.	(C)
10.	(C)	40.	(C)	70.	(B)
11.	(B)	41.	(E)	71.	(B)
12.	(D)	42.	(B)	72.	(D)
13.	(C)	43.	(E)	73.	(E)
14.	(D)	44.	(C)	74.	(D)
15.	(B)	45.	(B)	75.	(C)
16.	(E)	46.	(B)	76.	(D)
17.	(A)	47.	(B)	77.	(E)
18.	(E)	48.	(A)	78.	(B)
19.	(B)	49.	(E)	79.	(D)
20.	(A)	50.	(C)	80.	(E)
21.	(D)	51.	(B)	81.	(E)
22.	(D)	52.	(A)	82.	(B)
23.	(E)	53.	(C)	83.	(A)
24.	(B)	54.	(B)	84.	(E)
25.	(E)	55.	(B)	85.	(A)
26.	(A)	56.	(A)	86.	(C)
27.	(E)	57.	(D)	87.	(D)
28.	(C)	58.	(C)	88.	(B)
29.	(D)	59.	(B)	89.	(E)
30.	(B)	60.	(E)	90.	(D)

DETAILED EXPLANATIONS
OF ANSWERS

TEST 2

1.   **(C)**   Choice (C) is the best answer as the women of this play are plotting their entrance into Congress with a great deal of hilarity and burlesque. (A) is incorrect as the tone is not grave, nor does it seem to be one of caution or discretion. Instead, it is rather lighthearted. (B) is not correct as foolhardy and mindless suggest carelessness and stupidity: two characteristics not present in the tone of the passage. (D) is also wrong as devious and diabolic intimate the intention of committing wrongs or evil. (E) is not the best choice as the women are seeking to take part in their government; the terms silly and inane suggest that their actions are pointless.

2.   **(B)**   Attempting to conceal their genders by covering themselves with wool robes, the term "card" is defined as meaning (B) fasten in the context of the passage. Although all of the women are attempting to conceal themselves in a similar costume (A) share is not the correct answer. (C) and (D) are not correct as Praxagora instructs them to cover themselves throughout the passage, not to disregard or remove their costumes. (E) is not the correct answer, for the women are not concerned with the neatness of their appearance; combing their wool is not necessary.

3.   **(D)**   Choice (D) is the best answer as line 5 is most concerned with the securing of their costumes in order not to reveal their true gender. (A) is not the correct choice as the removal of the wool is not their only concern. (B) and (C) are incorrect choices as the women are not concerned with the circulating of their plan through word-of-mouth. (E) is incorrect; exposing their true identities is not the only concern of the plotting women; they are also worried about the men discovering their plan.

4.   **(A)**   Typical of Aristophanes' humor, the "misplaced whiskers" refers to a woman's pubic area; (A) bawdy innuendo is the correct answer. While the whiskers described refer to hair, the hair does not belong to the fake beards; (B) is incorrect. (C) is not the correct answer as the wool costumes are the objects which must fall to reveal the hair that the speaker describes. (D) is not correct, as the whiskers dwell beneath the robes; the men are outside of the robes. (E) is not correct as whiskers implies short, shaggy strands; the women probably have long, smooth hair.

5.   **(D)**   Choice (D) is the correct answer as the whole premise of the women's plot lies in attending the Congress so that they may take part in the political system; this is a freedom denied them. (A) is not correct as the women do not express a desire to dress like men for the love of masculine clothing, but rather, to obtain the power associated with this style of dress. (B) is not correct; obviously women are not allowed to attend Congress as they must construct this elaborate plan in order to gain admittance. (C) is not correct; although the women plan to arrive early, they still must disguise themselves as men in order to take part. (E) is incorrect as the women admit that they not only plan to attend the meeting, but they also plan on taking over the entire political system.

6.   **(D)**   Choice (D) is the correct answer; although she is confident about her plan, Praxagora is not boastful. Her scheming and determination are revealed in her carefully constructed plan as well as her desire to execute this plan; thus, (A) and (B) are incorrect. (C) is not the correct answer, for she proves her authoritative skills by organizing and directing the women to carry out the plot. (E) is incorrect, as she quickly incites eager followers with her persuasive rhetoric and passion.

7.   **(B)**   Choice (B) is the correct answer as the metaphor suggests a feeling of frustration and powerlessness; the same feeling the women experience when they are denied their political rights. While the speaker complains about the political system run by men, she does not accuse it of being corrupt; thus, (A) is incorrect. (C) is incorrect as the metaphor does not suggest loneliness in the context of the passage, but rather, unfulfilled desires. (D) is not the correct answer for the women do not specifically state that they wish to vote. (E) is not correct as the restlessness of the everyday lives of women does not correspond with the theme of this passage.

8.   **(C)**   Choice (C) is the best answer to the question. Medea laments

in the first few lines that she has been betrayed by her husband and later goes on to criticize the treatment of women in her society. (A) is incorrect because she is not mocking the institution of marriage, she is critiquing it. (B) is not the correct answer as it seems she is not worried about the marriage; it may be inferred that the marriage is over. Although she claims to be betrayed by a man, it is obvious that this man is a lover, and not her father; thus, (D) is incorrect. (E) is also not the best answer, for although she discusses motherhood, it is not the main focus in this passage.

9. **(C)** Choice (C) is the correct answer; Medea's entire speech is based upon the imprisoning of a woman in marriage and this figurative language serves to further emphasize her point. (A) is incorrect, for although a yoke is literally a device to constrain a farm animal, she means this word to function as a metaphor for a husband's rule. (B) is not correct as Medea does not make reference to her religious beliefs in the context of this passage. The yoke represents a husband's harnessing of a wife, but this action is not fueled by anger, but by convention; (D) is incorrect. (E) is also not correct; this passage refers to the labor of women, but not as horticulturists.

10. **(C)** Choice (C) is the best answer as Medea is critiquing the dowry system. She views it as tantamount to female slavery. Although women were expected to give all of their money (if indeed they had any) to their husbands upon marriage, lines 3–6 do not refer to this expectation; (A) is incorrect. Although there is an exchange of money, this exchange is not a bribe, but more like a business transaction and it was not used by women, but by their families; (B) is also incorrect. Medea views the dowry system to be figuratively equivalent to the selling of female slaves, but this act is not literal and therefore (D) is incorrect. Medea does not suggest that she is against the use of money in matters of love; (E) is incorrect.

11. **(B)** Choice (B) is the best answer as Medea's tone begins mournfully as she laments her betrayal. This tone changes to resentment as she catalogues the wrongs done to women by both patriarchy and men. Medea may be disapproving and enraged; however, these feelings remain subtle so that (A) is incorrect. While Medea may be viewed as being proud and indignant overall, these characteristics are not prevalent throughout the passage; (C) is incorrect. Although perhaps reflective about her situation, Medea is not detached, but very emotional; (D) is incorrect. Medea merely complains but does not scold. She does not regret her specific

situation, but instead laments that it is common to her gender. For this reason, (E) is not the best choice.

12. **(D)** Choice (D) is the best answer. Medea suggests that more women risk their lives in childbirth than men in war. (A) is not correct as she does not fear the prospect of war, but merely uses it as an example. Although she claims that women are excluded from war, she does not express any desire to participate in one, nor does she feel discriminated against because she is excluded; thus, (B) is not correct. While Medea addresses the issue of childbirth, she does not suggest that a woman would be better equipped with armor or a shield; (C) is not correct. (E) is also incorrect, for women risk their lives giving birth to children, not raising them.

13. **(C)** Heroic couplets is the correct answer as this passage is written in rhyming pairs of iambic pentameter. (A) is incorrect as blank verse is composed of unrhymed iambic pentameter lines. (B) is also incorrect as verse paragraphs are a further division of blank verse and this passage is written in heroic couplets. (D) is not the correct answer as free verse is written in an open form with short lines and a controlled rhythm. The passage is not written in successive stressed syllables of six, thus it is not (E) spondaic hexameter.

14. **(D)** Medea's prevailing message is that (D) women are denied rights due to cultural sanctions. She continually refers to the unfair laws of her society governing married and unmarried women. Despite the fact that she has been betrayed, Medea does not claim that all women are treated ill by their husbands; thus, (A) is incorrect. Nor does she suggest that all men are scoundrels and all women are virtuous; (B) is incorrect. While she does mention the dangers of childbirth (E), this argument is not the prevalent message within the passage.

15. **(B)** The word "mean" is in contrast to "superior" in line 3; the opposite of superior is inferior or unimportant. Although the subjects of the poetry are historical events or figures, "aged" (C) does not modify the author's pen. The author is making a judgment, but "judgmental" (A) or "angry" (E) is not the intended meaning. The author's lines of verse are "obscure" (line 6) or unknown (D), not the pen that produces them.

16. **(E)** The meaning of the first stanza is that poems about wars, leaders, and beginnings of cities are better left to better writers. Choice (C)

is certainly true, but not the main thrust of meaning for the stanza. Choice (B) is directly contradicted by the phrase "superior things" (line 3). There is no mention of little-known poets (D), nor does the poet indicate disinterest (A) in historical subjects.

17. **(A)**   Both items listed in choice (A) refer to the same thing— Bartas' beautiful poems and his talent in poetry. All other choices contrast the author's inadequacies with the abilities or products of better writers. The author contrasts her childish verse with rhetoric (polished language) in choice (B); her "broken strings" will not produce beautiful music ("sweet consort") in choice (C); her defect prohibits "perfect beauty" in choice (D); and her Muse of poetry is "foolish, broken, blemished" (line 16) so that nothing can "mend" it in choice (E).

18. **(E)**   The Greek poet "spoke" through his verse, so choice (E) is the correct choice. At first the Greek poet "lisped" or had trouble "speaking plainly," but in later times he spoke "plain"; the logical conclusion is that the author considers the Greek's (C) later poetry better and worth "his striving pain" (line 22). The phrase "striving pain" does not necessarily mean suffering (B). Because the poet views her abilities as weak, she is not saying her poetry will become better (D) or peace will be hers (A) as a writer.

19. **(B)**   The poet has obviously created her own opportunity to write poetry, so (A), (C), and (E) can be eliminated. Choices (C) and (E) can also be eliminated because the author lists several subjects inspiring to poets. Twice the poet makes reference to skills or "art" of poetry that "can do much" (line 23), but "no art is able" (line 17) to mend lack of talent portrayed by the "blemished Muse" (line 16) and "weak or wounded brain" (line 24). This line of reasoning eliminates choices (D) and (E).

20. **(A)**   Mrs. Dabney was during her first marriage an "exemplary" wife to a man twice as old as she was. The marriage was a "cold duty" (line 13) and, therefore, it is presumed, was without love.

21. **(D)**   We have to read between the lines for this one. We know he was an unkind husband (lines 9, 10, and 15) and that she had even considered suicide or at least wished for his death during this marriage (line 16). We also know that her first husband had left her well off financially (line 6). From these facts we must assume the nature of the relationship.

22.   **(D)**   Line 12 introduces a catalog of Mrs. Dabney's experiences, the first of which is the disappointment spoken of. It can only refer to the first engagement which she was compelled to relinquish (line 3).

23.   **(E)**   Personification involves giving human qualities to a non-human or abstract object, so the first two answers could not be correct. Of the three abstractions which make up the last three answers, the last, time, is the one being personified. Time is the "venerable thief" (line 26) who at first tries to steal the "rose" of her beauty and finally gives up.

24.   **(B)**   Mrs. Dabney is attempting to hold on to her youthful beauty despite the attempts of time to remove it from her. The author here uses "roses" to describe the beauty of youth.

25.   **(E)**   An aubade is usually a beautiful greeting of the day. Here Volpone spends one line on the day and the rest on his gold. The passage is a parody of what was a tradition in Renaissance poetry and drama (E).

26.   **(A)**   We do not know the rest of this world well enough to judge, nor the goodness of Volpone's soul, but we do learn that Volpone puts his gold before the world…the gold has not just replaced the soul, it is his center (A).

27.   **(E)**   The entire description makes fun of religion and the worshipping of saints in shrines. Relics were often sold as remains of saints or Christ (found to be totally bogus pieces of cloth or old pig bones as Chaucer describes in "The Pardoner's Tale"). The choices all have some element of truth but the best explanation is the stressing of Volpone's worshipping of his treasures as if they were actual relics (E).

28.   **(C)**   Go back to the opening of the previous sentence where Volpone addresses his gold. Trace the Latinate sentence along (verbal part rather than the object at the end) then you will understand that the title must have gold in it somewhere…The Golden Age (C).

29.   **(D)**   Volpone refers to his gold as "Thou" but that is not one of the options. Go back then to the opening when Volpone refers to his gold as "my saint" in the shrine. The answer is (D).

30.   **(B)**   Deceptively simple because of its meter and rhyme, Blake's poem says a great deal about love and freedom of love from religious laws. The best explanation of the Chapel is (B)…the other alternatives are

too specific — Blake is not criticizing commitment in marriage — or too far from the point — pure love is not symbolized but curtailed by the Church in Blake's view.

31.   **(A)**   The answer here is (A) as the most rational of the choices. The others are too extreme for what the poet is saying.

32.   **(E)**   The answer is (E) — the poet builds to a climax and expresses his increasing frustration with the priests as the representatives of the Church…not hatred which is too strong.

33.   **(E)**   The answer is (E). Make sure you know the terms for various pieces of poetry: allegory is the figurative treatment of one subject disguised under another subject. Blake describes the Garden of Love but really describes the state of free love. (A) A fable uses animals to explain a human failing or state of mind (the Fox and the Hen is a good example); (B) a parable is a simple story used by teachers (such as Christ in the Christian tradition) to explain a complex issue (the Prodigal Son is a good example); (C) a dramatic monologue is usually longer and gives one side of a conversation in poetic form ("My Last Duchess" by Browning is a good example); and (D) a fabliau is a coarse country tale to amuse yet give a moral (Chaucer's "Miller's Tale" is a good example).

34.   **(C)**   Certainly the poet is not bored by flowers; the verb refers of course to the flowers blooming in the garden when he was young, when he "played"; in other words, when he felt love as a free emotion. The answer is (C). The others go too far in the interpretation of how he feels now in the garden, or give information about the poet and other people, information not substantiated in the text.

35.   **(D)**   In other poems Blake did condemn the Industrial Revolution and made strong pleas for the workers, especially child laborers, but here his theme is the curtailing of free love, not art or poetry, or individuality. The answer is (D).

36.   **(B)**   Make sure you know the various figures of speech: (B) onomatopoeia: the sound is like the action — oozing, buzzing; (C) internal rhyme: when the rhyme comes not in the usual position at the end of the line but within the line; (D) feminine rhyme: two or three syllables where the second or third is unstressed, e.g., motion/notion, fortunate/importunate; (E) assonance is the opposite to alliteration: a stressed vowel sounds

alike but the consonant sound is unalike, e.g., late/make. The answer here is alliteration: the repeated consonant sound, e.g., binding/briars, often used to give a slowing effect to the rhythm (B).

37. **(E)** Choice (A) is incorrect because there is no actual urn. The speaker merely likens them to the figures on an urn. Choice (B) is incorrect because there is no mention of Greek dead in the poem. Choice (C) is incorrect because there is no sun mentioned or implied in the opening stanza. Choice (D) is incorrect because "shades" in this context means ghosts from his past. Choice (E) is correct because it accurately depicts the ghostly aspect the three figures convey.

38. **(B)** Choice (A) is incorrect because the first stanza is entirely descriptive. Choice (B) is correct because the first stanza describes them and lines 25–30 specify who they are. Choice (C) is incorrect because no rule is presented in the first stanza. Choice (D) is incorrect because no question is posed in the first stanza. Choice (E) is incorrect because although the opening stanza does begin a story, it is not concluded in lines 25–30.

39. **(A)** Choice (A) is correct and is supported by lines 16–18. Choice (B) is incorrect because the change described is closer to the opposite of this movement. Choice (C) is incorrect because the demands of the three figures all imply a loss of freedom and the undertaking of pursuits which are very demanding. Choice (D) is incorrect. Although the speaker "ach'd for wings," they were not wings of an angel but wings of poetic inspiration. There was nothing pious or holy about them. Choice (E) is incorrect because nothing in the poem supports this movement.

40. **(C)** Anson and Paula have known each other for three years, and it can be inferred that they have been dating for that time. That they know each other well can be seen by the close observation he makes of her face, the persistent looks, and the naturalness with which he goes outside with her. However, Anson's evaluation of Paula's face is not one of an infatuated man, for the details he notices are not those of beauty. To him, "her kind, serious face was wan and tired" — hardly those of (A). They have known each other for three years, so (D) is not accurate. Choice (B) is a logical answer, but not as significant a factor as (C). There is no indication in the passage of his feelings for Lowell Thayer (E).

41. **(E)** The fourth player is described as a "casual fourth" and is not mentioned again in the passage. This player is needed to make the game,

forcing the players to sit at the same table and deal with all their emotional undercurrents. The cards are "hot." The glance Anson gives Paula "persistently" holds her eyes, even when "Thayer's glance fell between them." Paula's voice is "tense, low." The smoke in the room, although from cigarettes, is probably symbolic of smouldering emotions, as in the cliche "smoke gets in your eyes."

42. **(B)** Because Thayer's glances come between Paula and Anson, and because Thayer figures so prominently in this passage, it can be assumed that Thayer has secretly been courting Paula. Choices (C) and (D) are unlikely because Paula and Anson have probably been dating for three years. Because they are playing bridge, choice (E) might be possible but it is not probable. There is no evidence to give credence to (A).

43. **(E)** Paula seems to be "withering" due to the lack of a marriage proposal. Lowell is "withering" due to lack of a commitment from Paula and through being an obvious second choice. There is no indication Anson is suffering, or that he is contemplating marriage.

44. **(C)** Ectoplasm is the vaporous substance emanating from a spiritualist medium's body during a trance. "Blown swirls of ectoplasm" would provide cloudy vision, and there is a further unspoken suggestion that people deceive themselves, or allow themselves to be deceived, when they attend a seance. The "Englishmen posing as Englishmen" are obviously exaggerating their habits in order to impress others, a deception on the part of the Englishmen and those who believe their posing. Therefore, what is portrayed in this portion of the passage is illusion and deception, or lack of clarity and honesty. Paula is not sure what to do about her problems in love. She is deceived in thinking Anson's jealousy of Lowell will spur Anson into a proposal. All three characters are involved in an elaborate but unspoken tension at the card table.

45. **(B)** By the end of the passage, Paula suddenly gets up and speaks to Anson; then, the two leave to walk hand in hand along the moonlit beach. Since Paula initiates the movement, it can be assumed she hopes Anson will now be "forced" by his jealousy into proposing marriage. There is no indication Lowell has proposed marriage (A), even though he seems interested in Paula. Anson is certainly aware (D) of the problem Lowell creates. The two men do not seem to be particular friends, nor is there apparent animosity emanating from Lowell, so choices (C) and (E) are incorrect.

46. **(B)**   The husband enters in a bad mood reflected by his sour facial expression. He might be in a bad mood because he has heard idle gossip (C) or wishes to be left alone (D), but neither of these come out in the dialogue. Choice (A) is not a consideration here. Choice (E) is probably true of the husband but is not the immediate cause of his poor frame of mind.

47. **(B)**   Mrs. Pinchwife, although longing to be more educated in the ways of the world, is probably a bit naive at this point. She confesses to her husband that Alithea has been scolding her for liking the actors, and she tells her husband she likes the players better than her husband because they are more refined. She may be a snob (A), but her naivete is the outstanding character trait. She knows little of society and so is probably not (E). Although there is no evidence in this scene of (C) or (D), she may yet attain those traits.

48. **(A)**   Alithea denies she has kept company with women of scandalous reputation (B). However, when Pinchwife accuses Alithea of keeping the company of men of scandalous reputation, she replies, "Where? Would you not have me civil?" Thus, she admits to having entertained men of dubious reputation (A). Although (C) and (D) may be possible, or even probable given the circumstances, there is not enough evidence in this passage to prove either one. Choice (E) is a likely answer because Alithea is protective of her reputation and says quickly that her brother is her only censurer; however, the main drift of the argument leads to choice (A).

49. **(E)**   Alithea has already taken Mrs. Pinchwife to the theater, at least, and perhaps to more places. Although Mr. Pinchwife would prefer to keep his wife ignorant of the town's pleasures, it is too late for that. In addition, Mr. Pinchwife leads his wife into more possibilities for misbehavior in his speech about the vices of the naughty town-women, "who only hate their husbands and love every man else, love plays, visits, fine coaches, fine clothes, fiddles, balls, treats, and so lead a wicked town-life." Mrs. Pinchwife, innocent as she is at this time, is only too eager to have fun in the city, for she states that these things her husband has listed make London "not so bad a place." The understatement of Mrs. Pinchwife and the exaggeration of the husband, combined with the cosmopolitan protestations of Alithea, create a humorous scene.

50.   **(C)**   Although Mr. Pinchwife is obviously familiar with the pleasures of town life, (E) is an answer that cannot be determined from this passage. Of the remaining possibilities, all are somewhat likely and can be supported. Fine clothes and coaches cost a great deal (D), and all that time spent in entertainment would keep Mrs. Pinchwife away from home (A) more than her husband would prefer. Once used to a faster-paced life, Mrs. Pinchwife might not be coaxed back to the much duller country life (B). However, most of Pinchwife's conversation with his wife concerns his wife's being attracted to the playermen (C); he does not want her to become one of the "notorious town-women" he accuses his sister of being.

51.   **(B)**   The correct answer is (B). The speaker wishes to reveal the hypocritical nature of patriarchal oppression with her repeated question. She seems to be asking, "If women are only capable of certain things and to be treated in a certain way, is that different for me, a black woman?" Although it seems evident that black women are not granted rights by white men, neither are white women, therefore, such an agenda is not the main focus of this passage and (A) is incorrect. The speaker seems proud of her gender, wanting no affirmation from the audience; thus, (C) is not the right answer. The speaker wants to be treated equally with men and women, not just white women; therefore, (D) is not the preferred answer. While seemingly unhappy with her status as a black woman, she does not truly envy that of a white woman, making (E) incorrect.

52.   **(A)**   Choice (A) is the best answer as the speaker unites the concerns of the abolitionists with those of the suffragists in an effort to overcome white male domination as both an African-American and a woman. While it is implicit in her argument, the speaker does not directly argue against slavery; (B) is incorrect. The main focus of this passage is not intelligence, but equal rights, making (C) incorrect. Although the speaker does speak of the horrors endured, she does not dwell on them; (D) is not correct. Choice (E) is not the best answer as the speaker does not express resentment towards white women, but instead seeks to fight alongside them for equality.

53.   **(C)**   The lines discussed in this question reveal the speaker's belief that women are just as capable as men, although treated differently; thus, (C) is correct. While it is evident that the speaker has endured male labor, this assertion is not central to this portion of the passage; (A) is not the correct choice. The speaker presents experiences which support the fact that slaves lead a physically rigorous life, however, this fact is obvi-

ous and not the main purpose of these lines. In consequence, (B) is incorrect. (D) is also incorrect, for the speaker intimates that women, in fact, are capable of more than what is expected from them. (E) is not the best choice, for the speaker does not express regret or pleasure in having completed her difficult labors.

54. **(B)**   Choice (B) is the best answer for the speaker does not wish to dwell upon the issue of intellect; her agenda lies in achieving equality. (A) is incorrect, as the speaker does not name any gender as being inferior or superior. (C) and (D) are incorrect, for the speaker does not wish to detract from her argument by addressing the debate over intelligence. Instead, she argues that intelligence is not the issue. (E) is not the correct answer because the speaker does not claim intelligence to be a necessity in order to deserve freedom.

55. **(B)**   The cup may best be interpreted to mean (B) the desire for equality shared by both slaves and women as the figurative language suggests that they both suffer from unfulfilled desires presented in the form of an empty cup. (A) is incorrect, for solely speaking about the rights of women in her speech would overlook the needs of the black population. (C) is incorrect, for the speaker does not directly allude to the lives of black men in her speech. (D) is incorrect; the speaker does not address free blacks in her speech, but rather, concentrates upon the plight of those in slavery. (E) is not the correct choice because the speaker does not delve into the emotions or the psyche of black women.

56. **(A)**   Choice (A) is the best answer as the speaker is creating a metaphoric child through the description of the creation of the work of art. (B) is not the correct answer as the speaker does not draw similarities with the word "like." (C) is incorrect because the lines do not perform the function of a parody, to imitate the seriousness of another literary work. (D) is also incorrect, for the passage is neither a bold overstatement nor an exaggeration of the truth. Chiasmus is the reversal of the corresponding words in two phrases; (E) is incorrect as no such occurrence is found in the lines named.

57. **(D)**   The phrase "holy passion" suggests Irene's dedication and worship of Rubek's art; (D) is the correct answer. (A) is incorrect as the word passion does not mean lustful in the context of this phrase. (B) is incorrect as it is stated that Irene felt impassioned wholly about Rubek's art, not necessarily only about posing. (C) is not correct; the word holy in

this phrase refers to a religious reverence, but not one of a particular denomination. (E) is incorrect as again, the term holy does not imply divinity in the context of this passage.

58. **(C)** Choice (C) is the correct answer as Irene states that she first began to despise the art, then the artist in Rubek, and then finally Rubek himself. (A), (B), (D), and (E) are incorrect as they do not follow the temporal order as suggested in the passage.

59. **(B)** The metaphors in this passage are mostly religious; (B) is the correct answer. It is implied that Irene once worshipped Rubek and his art as a god; Rubek has abandoned his humanity for art, making him a higher being; and Rubek's creation of the statue is similar to a creation myth. (A) is not correct as art is literally mentioned throughout the passage; metaphors are figurative. (C) is not the correct answer, for nature is not alluded to in the passage. Although Rubek and Irene figuratively give birth to the statue, this metaphor is not found throughout the rest of the passage; (D) is incorrect. (E) is not the correct choice as death is not referred to by the speakers.

60. **(E)** Choice (E) is the correct answer as the statue is thought of as being the child that they never had. In fact, Irene refers to this birth in very literal terms towards the end of the passage. (A) is not correct, for after the creation of the statue, their relationship seemingly dissipated. Although they eventually develop a distaste for each other (B), this change takes place after the construction of the statue, not during the creation. (C) is incorrect as the speakers do not allude to a new style of art developed in the statue. (D) is not the best answer; the creation of the statue does not bond them closer together—it is thought of as a combination of both Irene and Rubek.

61. **(A)** Choice (A) is the best choice as Irene suggests that Rubek had become too concerned with the perfecting of his art and his role as an artist that he had forgotten his human qualities in the process. (B) is not correct as Irene does not state specifically if he lost his romantic interest for her in the passage. (C) is not correct; their relationship seems to be ending in this passage, not before. (D) is not correct; it may be inferred that Rubek and Irene do not have a child together. Rubek cannot be neglecting his duties as a father if he doesn't have a child. It seems that Rubek chose to cease his human qualities in order to concentrate upon his art; it is not necessary to relinquish one's humanity when deciding to be an artist. Thus, (E) is incorrect.

62.   **(E)**   Choice (E) is the correct answer as Irene endows the inanimate statue with human characteristics. She does not practice (A) metonymy, for a literal term has not been substituted for something else associated with that term. (B) is not the answer as the statue is not a child, and therefore it cannot be considered to be realistic. (C) is not the correct answer; a dead metaphor is something so commonly stated that it is readily accepted and understood, such as the phrase "leg of a table." (D) is not correct; the statue is not used as reference to a well-known person, place, event, or work of literature.

63.   **(D)**   Choice (D) is the best choice; Irene begins the passage accusing Rubek of losing his humanity and ends with recalling the beauty of the work they created together. (B) is not the correct answer as Irene does not initially express devotion to Rubek; her scorn is felt in the beginning of the passage. (C) is not correct, for Irene hints that she is sorrowful at the end; not initially, and nowhere in the passage is he vengeful. (E) is not the correct choice, for Irene reveals neither melodrama nor realism in her attitude.

64.   **(B)**   This scene seems to be located in the climax as Irene reveals her hatred and anger for Rubek, and the story will soon enter into the falling action; (B) is the correct answer. (A) is not the correct answer; the conflict has not been resolved and the play does not seem to be drawing to a close. (C) is not the correct answer as it seems obvious that this scene is not found in the beginning of the play, and little necessary background information has been provided. (D) is not the best answer as the catastrophe is a dramatic situation usually located in the falling action of a plot that involves an outcome; the outcome has not yet been decided in this passage. (E) is not correct; the falling action occurs after the climactic point in the plot, and this scene is one of intense drama and climactic emotions.

65.   **(D)**   By reading carefully, you gather Vandover's downfall from what he says. He did have money; he did have a job but no longer has it; and the detail of how things go around and seem far off suggest extreme hunger. The answer is (D).

66.   **(E)**   Once you have grasped the fact of the lycanthropy, all the details of the brute become clearer. None of the first three options is viable. The brute is not trying to get out — witness Vandover's passivity — but is there nevertheless, first heard in the guttural nature of words from the throat, not the mouth (E).

67. **(C)** Because of the hunger and "brutedom," Vandover is not expressing himself coherently or sequentially. He darts from one subject to the next. Trace back what possibly might be at the end of the hall. "It" then logically refers back to his lodging place, interpreted here as an apartment (C).

68. **(E)** A change from first person pronoun to third should always signal a distancing. He mentions the devil in connection with his voice but to say the devil is in him is too strong. The brute is not integrated yet but still developing. The butcher's dog is not even mentioned, only the butcher's paper which would have a taste of meat to satisfy the "brute." Charlie at this point is simply listening to Vandover. The answer is (E).

69. **(C)** Mentally, Vandover rounds off his bonds into an even number of dollars which then return to haunt him. The money was not just "lost" but gambled away — herein lies the problem (C).

70. **(B)** According to the critic, Shakespeare and Milton were not determined "to get rid of" nature and art, introducing as much of their own personal views into their art as did the "modern school." Instead, they have a "deeper," and, by inference, "wider" understanding of human life — a greater tolerance in general.

71. **(B)** The key to tragedy, especially Classical Tragedy (the principles of which Shakespeare followed closely), is that a being of great or lofty station is brought down to a much lower level. A lesser personage — an "average" person — would not be a candidate for tragedy because he or she has less distance to fall. The modernists, says Hazlitt, are indifferent to the various distances different stations in life entail, and therefore, they would not be interested in Classical Tragedy.

72. **(D)** Hazlitt wants to emphasize the point that Shakespeare is able to embrace and unite even "opposite extremes": "He brings together images ... placed at the greatest distance from each other."

73. **(E)** Hazlitt finds it remarkable that Shakespeare can so easily bring together similar images "found in circumstances of the greatest dissimilitude." It is this that provides the "coalescence" that is the genius of Shakespeare's writing, according to the author.

74.   **(D)**   The words are almost opposite in meaning; the first refers to dissimilarity, and the second refers to a lack of distinction — close to a fusing of various elements. Hazlitt contends that Shakespeare was able to "coalesce" images of the first description into the material of the second. His use of similar-sounding words provides a bridge between sentences with seemingly opposite thrusts.

75.   **(C)**   One might say also that the heart itself is a bearer of the pain for it is the heart that questions the pain's reality. The reference of the poem is general and it describes a feeling experienced by anyone who goes through great pain.

76.   **(D)**   The words stiff, mechanical, formal, and regardless all describe the character of the defenses raised by the heart to protect itself against the pain. The remembering of that feeling, if it comes at all, is done later and is not a defensive measure.

77.   **(E)**   The word "snow" is here a poetic shorthand for the remembered experience. The meeting of the last stanza of the poem is that the formal feeling numbs or deadens one against the pain, just as a person who is freezing to death first becomes numb against the cold.

78.   **(B)**   The "stiff" heart and the "mechanical" feet of the one in great pain insulate themselves from that pain by becoming unmindful of it like the quartz is unmindful of blows which might be delivered to it.

79.   **(D)**   Line 7 is an inversion, a common practice of poets, with the phrases reversed. The poet's meaning is that the feet have grown regardless of ground or air or of anything else.

80.   **(E)**   Eliot is implying not just that middle-aged poets often do "fail," but that they often use this common observation as an excuse, as if to say, "Of course I'm not as inspired as when I was younger. No one is." Eliot believes the opposite is true of Yeats.

81.   **(E)**   Eliot criticizes poetry's public figures not because they are sensitive to contemporary fashion, but because they are sensitive to it ONLY, and, in addition, are more than content to behave this way and to let this govern their writing, statements, acts, and thoughts as well.

82. **(B)** Eliot contends that younger men "can see him as a poet who in his work remained in the best sense always young." Young, as defined here, relates to honesty about oneself expressed in the poetry.

83. **(A)** Perhaps this question could challenge you a bit more than it does. Looking at the cumulative effect leaves us with several tantalizing possibilities which do not hold up to scrutiny. For example, (E) looms large as a choice, but the speaker does not imply that dreams should cease because the fruits of dreams are rotten or otherwise forbidden. Neither does (D) hold up well. If anything, the results of dreams deferred might lead one to quit dreaming instead of reinforcing the necessity of dreaming. Choice (C) also falls out of contention because, rather than satirize, the speaker seems to empathize with those whose dreams are deferred. Choice (B) comes closer to a possibility of truth about the poem. Yes, the speaker does seem dissatisfied with a reality that forces people to defer their dreams, but is that the effect of the phrases? No. In fact, the phrases suggest what the best choice, (A), states: deferred dreams lead to negative consequences of different sorts (possibilities).

84. **(E)** Choice (A) can be easily dismissed. Likewise, choices (C) and (D) seem not germane to the meaning of the simile. Sweetness does not allay the burden of dreams (B); it further defers them. The best choice, (E), specifies the exact meaning of sugar-coating a problem.

85. **(A)** The meaning of the question in line 11 most certainly negates choices (B) and (E). That it remains a question negates to a certain extent choice (D). Between choices (C) and (A), we must discriminate carefully. The question does, in fact, reject the deferral of dreams by exploding the pent up frustration into violence. That is exactly and specifically what the best choice, (A), tells us, albeit with ambivalence: it could explode, but the phrasing in question form leaves other possibilities as well.

86. **(C)** The point of the banner is that it has compressed and preserved the meaning of Christmas into two sides of paper, so all the words that have to do with shrinking or drying are appropriate. Decimated means destroyed in great numbers; this is the odd one out (C).

87. **(D)** The name is ironic because of the lack of potential for breeding that such a scientist brings to the world (D). To check on the validity of your answer make sure that you know the other terms: oxymoron is

usually used in poetry for two paradoxical words in close proximity: "pleasant pain" for example; a pun is a play on words which is what Vonnegut is doing but the answer is not full enough to show how the pun operates; pathetic fallacy is a term used for the empathy often shown for the human race from nature and human characteristics given to nature; and paradox is a seemingly self-contradictory phrase which turns out to be true.

88. **(B)**   The fact that a nuclear warfare scientist reads out the message of peace and love is irony, because it reverses the truth in an amusing yet sobering way (B). Homile (A) is a simple story used to illustrate a point using folk or country images, similar to a parable which has now taken on more religious connotations. Emblemism (C) was used to give an image a "concrete" reality: a gold-edged love poem for example—whereas symbolism (D) endows the image with greater hidden meanings beyond reality.

89. **(E)**   The words need to be clearly analyzed to interpret the meaning — "cloister" connotes "nunnery"; "cement block" conjures up the modern prison. You need to know the word "immured" as imprisoned and imagine the harshness of the Girl Pool environment. The answer then is (E).

90. **(D)**   In amongst all the banter, the narrator does in fact use the "me" pronoun. The answer is (D). You know that the Girl Pool is not there as they leave their cloisters only once a year. The scientists remain "faceless," certainly not there in the office.

PRACTICE
TEST 3

CLEP ANALYZING AND INTERPRETING LITERATURE
Test 3

(Answer sheets appear in the back of this book.)

TIME: 90 Minutes
          80 Questions

> **DIRECTIONS**: Each of the questions or incomplete statements below is followed by five possible answers or completions. Select the best choice in each case and fill in the corresponding oval on the answer sheet.

QUESTIONS 1–5

On a highway, behind the gate of a vast garden, at the end of which could be discerned the white hues of a pretty manor house bathed in sunlight, was a beautiful, fresh child, clad in those country clothes that are so coquettish.

5   Luxury, freedom from cares, the habitual sight of riches make such children so pretty that one is tempted to consider them moulded of a different substance from the children of mediocrity and poverty.

Beside him, lying on the grass, was a splendid toy,
10   as fresh as its owner, varnished, gilded, clad in a crimson cloak and covered with plumes and glass beads. But the child was taking no notice of his favourite toy, and this is what he was looking at:

On the other side of the gate, out on the roadway,
15   among the nettles and thistles, was another child, dirty, sickly, soiled with soot, one of those pariah-kids in whom an impartial eye would discover beauty, as the eye of a

connoisseur can divine an ideal painting underneath a layer
of carriage varnish, if only the repugnant patina of poverty
were washed away.

Through those symbolic bars separating the two
worlds, the highroad and the manor house, the poor child
showed the rich child his own toy, which the latter exam-
ined avidly, as a rare and unknowing object. Now this toy,
which the little slattern was teasing, shaking, and waving
about in a barred box was a live rat! The parents, no doubt
as a means of saving money, had found the toy in life itself.

And the two children laughed at one another frater-
nally, with teeth that were *equally* white.

From "The Poor Child's Toy," by Charles Baudelaire

1. What does "fresh" mean in the context of this passage?

    (A) Clean   (D) Ill-behaved

    (B) Well-fed   (E) Disrespectful

    (C) Rich

2. What is the best interpretation of the second paragraph?

    (A) Careless children act differently than those who must struggle
         for food.

    (B) Rich children are more attractive than underprivileged youth.

    (C) Children in poverty are not as clean as wealthy children.

    (D) Poverty breeds contempt in the eyes of children.

    (E) Although the children are fundamentally equal, the impover-
         ished child may be viewed as being inferior.

3. The phrase "impartial eye" (line 17) refers to

    (A) a blind observer.

    (B) one who lacks judgment.

    (C) one who is fooled by wealth.

    (D) one who looks beyond exterior attributes.

    (E) one who cannot bear to view children in poverty.

4. The bars which separate the children are "symbolic" because

    (A) they are from different homes.

    (B) the wealthy clean child is not allowed to associate with the poor, soiled child.

    (C) the disadvantaged child is mentally inferior to the affluent youth.

    (D) the pauper may have an adverse effect upon the prosperous counterpart.

    (E) the experience and lifestyle of the indigent children are vastly different from those of the rich children.

5. The literary device this passage exemplifies is

    (A) realism   (D) allusion

    (B) allegory   (E) tragic irony

    (C) anecdote

QUESTIONS 6–8

As time went by our need to fight for the ideal increased to an unquestioning possession, riding with spur and rein over our doubts. Willy-nilly it became a faith. We had sold ourselves into its slavery, manacled ourselves to-
5   gether in its chain-gang, bowed ourselves to serve its holiness with all our good and ill content. The mentality of ordinary human slaves is terrible — they have lost the world — and we had surrendered, not body alone, but soul to the overmastering greed of victory. By our own act we
10 were drained of morality, of volition, of responsibility, like dead leaves in the wind.

The everlasting battle stripped from us care of our own lives or of others'. We had ropes about our necks, and on our heads prices which showed that the enemy intended
15 hideous tortures for us if we were caught. Each day some of us passed; and the living knew themselves just sentient puppets on God's stage: indeed, our taskmaster was merciless, merciless, so long as our bruised feet could stagger forward on the road. The weak envied those tired enough to

20   die; for success looked so remote, and failure a near and certain, if sharp, release from toil. We lived always in the stretch or sag of nerves, either on the crest or in the trough of waves of feeling. This impotency was bitter to us, and made us live only for the seen horizon, reckless what spite

25   we inflicted or endured, since physical sensation showed itself meanly transient. Gusts of cruelty, perversions, lusts ran lightly over the surface without troubling us; for the moral laws which had seemed to hedge about these silly accidents must be yet fainter words. We had learned that

30   there were pangs too sharp, griefs too deep, ecstasies too high for our finite selves to register. When emotion reached this pitch the mind choked; and memory went white till circumstances were humdrum once more.

    From The Seven Pillars of Wisdom, by T.E. Lawrence

6.   Which is NOT an image which develops the author's perception of his own actions?

    (A)   "riding with spur and rein" (lines 2–3)

    (B)   "manacled ourselves together in its chain-gang" (lines 4–5)

    (C)   "puppets on God's stage" (line 17)

    (D)   "either on the crest or in the trough of waves of feeling" (line 23)

    (E)   "reckless what spite we inflicted or endured" (lines 24–25)

7.   As used by the narrator, the phrase "meanly" (line 26) can be construed to mean which of the following?

    I.   Halfway between extremes, moderate

    II.   Low in value

    III.   Malicious

    IV.   Ignoble

    (A)   I only   (D)   I and II only

    (B)   II only   (E)   III and IV only

    (C)   IV only

8. Which of the following best presents the central paradox of the author's argument?

    (A) "Willy-nilly it became a faith." (line 3)

    (B) "The mentality of ordinary human slaves is terrible." (lines 6–7)

    (C) "By our own act we were drained of morality, of volition, of responsibility." (lines 9–10)

    (D) "We lived always in the stretch or sag of nerves." (lines 21–22)

    (E) "When emotion reached this pitch the mind choked; and memory went white till circumstances were humdrum once more." (lines 31–33)

QUESTIONS 9–15

      Such as the sweet-apple
      Reddening on a high branch
      Right at the very top
      And the fruit-pickers
5   Have overlooked it
      Not that they have really forgotten
      Rather that they could not reach so high

      Just as the hyacinth
      Is trampled underfoot in the mountains
10   By men who are shepherds
      And her purple flower
      Is flung to the earth

      By Sappho

9. The phrase "sweet-apple" (line 1) of this poem is an example of

    (A) simile.   (D) paradox.

    (B) description.   (E) euphemism.

    (C) metaphor.

10. The symbols and references of this poem are drawn from

    (A) religion.   (D) nature.

    (B) literature.   (E) dreams.

    (C) foods.

11. The best interpretation of lines 2–5 is

    (A) when left unadulterated, the results are enhanced.

    (B) high altitudes and a warm climate produce ripe fruit.

    (C) when one is at the top, others cannot easily corrupt him/her.

    (D) even the apple will eventually rot because it has not been attended.

    (E) there are few and precious at the top.

12. What does "it" refer to in line 5?

    (A) the high branch.

    (B) the reach of the fruit-pickers.

    (C) the top of the tree.

    (D) the sweet-apple.

    (E) the memory of the fruit-pickers.

13. Which of the following seem most compatible with the speaker's understanding of purity and corrosion?

    I.   The more virtuous the person, the more one distinguishes him/herself from others.

    II. The most desirable state is one of uninterrupted purity.

    III. Inferiors often attempt to cause the downfall of their moral superiors.

    (A) I and II only   (D) I only

    (B) II and III only   (E) III only

    (C) I and III only

14. The first two words in each stanza (lines 1 and 8) suggest

    (A) the fruit and the flower lead similar existences.

    (B) both the fruit and the flower are metaphors for something un-named in the poem.

    (C) human actions are similar to occurrences in nature.

    (D)   humans cannot exist without nature, yet we often affect it in negative ways.

    (E)   the apple-pickers are more careful than the rough shepherds.

15.   The rhyme and meter of line 8 is

    (A)   phyrric tetrameter.   (D)   trochaic trimeter.

    (B)   trochaic tetrameter.   (E)   iambic pentameter.

    (C)   dactylic trimeter.

QUESTIONS 16–19

He entered the tavern, and was guided by the murmer of voices and the fumes of tobacco to the public-room. It was a long and low apartment, with oaken walls, grown dark in the continual smoke, and a floor which was
5 thickly sanded, but of no immaculate purity. A number of persons — the larger part of whom appeared to be mariners, or in some way connected with the sea — occupied the wooden benches, or leather-bottomed chairs, conversing on various matters, and occasionally lending their atten-
10 tion to some topic of general interest. Three or four little groups were draining as many bowls of punch, which the West India trade had long since made a familiar drink in the colony. Others, who had the appearance of men who lived by regular and laborious handicraft, preferred the in-
15 sulated bliss of an unshared potation, and became more taciturn under its influence. Nearly all, in short, evinced a predilection for the Good Creature in some of its various shapes, for this is a vice to which, as Fast Day sermons of a hundred years ago will testify, we have a long hereditary
20 claim. The only guests to whom Robin's sympathies inclined him were two or three sheepish countrymen, who were using the inn somewhat after the fashion of a Turkish caravansary; they had gotten themselves into the darkest corner of the room, and heedless of the Nicotian atmo-
25 sphere, were supping on the bread of their own ovens, and the bacon cured in their own chimney-smoke. But though Robin felt a sort of brotherhood with these strangers, his eyes were attracted from them to a person who stood near

the door, holding whispered conversation with a group of
30 ill-dressed associates. His features were separately striking
almost to grotesqueness, and the whole face left a deep
impression on the memory.

From "My Kinsman Major Molineaux," by Nathaniel Hawthorne

16. Of all the people in the room, Robin would be most inclined to
strike up a conversation with the

(A) tavern-keeper.

(B) mariners.

(C) day laborers.

(D) countrymen.

(E) person standing near the door.

17. From all indications, which of the following is probably true of the
men eating their home-cooked food?

I. They are from the countryside.

II. They are uncomfortable being in the tavern.

III. They are resented by the rest of the men in the tavern.

(A) I only   (D) I and II only

(B) II only   (E) II and III only

(C) III only

18. Taken in context of the passage, the best interpretation of "Nearly
all, in short, evinced a predilection for the Good Creature" (lines
16–17) is best interpreted to mean that nearly all the

(A) mariners looked as if they might be pirates.

(B) mariners are celebrating a successful voyage to the West
Indies.

(C) people in the tavern are drinking an alcoholic beverage.

(D) people in the tavern had been reformed by turning to religion.

(E) men in the tavern were known for seeking out the enjoyable
things of life.

19. To what does the author say "we have a long hereditary claim" (lines 19–20)?

(A) Seafaring

(D) Gossiping

(B) Drinking

(E) Fasting

(C) Smoking

QUESTIONS 20–27

But his Honour, out of Curiosity, and perhaps (if I may speak it without Vanity) partly out of Kindness, was determined to see me in my Canoo; and got several of his neighboring Friends to accompany him. I was forced to
5 wait above an Hour for the Tide, and then observing the Wind very fortunately bearing towards the Island, to which I intended to steer my Course, I took a second Leave of my Master: But as I was going to prostrate myself to kiss his Hoof, he did me the Honour to raise it gently to my mouth.
10 I am not ignorant how much I have been censured for mentioning this last Particular. Detractors are pleased to think it improbable, that so illustrious a Person should descend to give so great a Mark of Distinction to a Creature so inferior as I. Neither have I forgot, how apt some travellers are to
15 boast of extraordinary Favours they have received. But, if these Censurers were better acquainted with the noble and courteous Disposition of the Houyhnhnms, they would soon change their Opinion.

From Gulliver's Travels, by Jonathan Swift

20. His Honor is

(A) the mayor.

(D) a chief.

(B) a mare.

(E) a captain.

(C) a horse.

21. The narrator is a

(A) native of the island.

(D) horse.

(B) journalist.

(E) canoeist.

(C) travel writer.

22. Which best describes why the *narrator* thinks he has been censured for "this last particular"?

    I.   He is lying about the favour bestowed upon him.

    II.   Travellers very often lie about the way they treat inferiors.

    III.   He is making up the entire story.

    (A) I and III only   (D) III only

    (B) I only   (E) II and III only

    (C) II only

23. Which best describes why *readers* censure the narrator?

    I.   He should not be so sycophantic to an animal.

    II.   He is not a reliable narrator.

    III.   Such a narrator always has tall tales to tell.

    (A) I only   (D) II and III only

    (B) I and II only   (E) I and III only

    (C) II only

24. Which pair best describes the narrator's attitude toward the Houyhnhnms?

    (A) Supercilious and arrogant

    (B) Humble and demeaning

    (C) Humble and demanding

    (D) Vain yet kind

    (E) Respectful yet equal

25. Which best explains the narrator's tone?

    (A) Frustrated at the wait for the tide

    (B) Sad at having to leave his Honour

    (C) Eager to set sail and leave such a place

    (D) Prostrate at having to leave the Islands

    (E) Regretful at having to leave such a beautiful place

26.   "so illustrious a Person" refers to

(A)   a Houyhnhnm.

(B)   a fellow traveller.

(C)   the chief of the Islands.

(D)   the owner of the canoo.

(E)   a detractor.

27.   The use of the word Master suggests

(A)   the narrator has been a slave.

(B)   the narrator has worked with love for the Houyhnhnms.

(C)   the narrator admires and respects His Honour.

(D)   the narrator is being satirical.

(E)   His Honour does not want to let the narrator go.

QUESTIONS 28–34

　　　　By the door of the station-keeper's den, outside,
was a tin washbasin, on the ground. Near it was a pail and a
piece of yellow bar soap, and from the eaves hung a hoary
blue woolen shirt, significantly — but this latter was the
5   station-keeper's private towel, and only two persons in all
the party might venture to use it — the stage-driver and the
conductor. The latter would not, from a sense of decency;
the former would not, because he did not choose to encourage the advances of the station-keeper. We had towels — in
10   the valise; they might as well have been in Sodom and
Gomorrah. We (and the conductor) used our handkerchiefs,
and the driver his pantaloons and sleeves. By the door,
inside, was fastened a small old-fashioned looking-glass
frame, with two little fragments of the original mirror
15   lodged down in one corner of it. This arrangement afforded
a pleasant double-barreled portrait of you when you looked
into it, with one half of your head set up a couple of inches
above the other half. From the glass frame hung the half of
a comb by a string — but if I had to describe the partiarch

20   or die, I believe I would order some sample coffins. It had come down from Esau and Samson, and has been accumulating hair ever since — along with certain impurities.... The table was a greasy board on stilts, and the tablecloth and napkins had not come — and they are not looking for

25   them, either. A battered tin platter, a knife and fork, and a pint tin cup, were at each man's place, and the driver had a queen's-ware saucer that had seen better days. Of course, this duke sat at the head of the table. There was one isolated piece of table furniture that bore about it a touching

30   air of grandeur in misfortune. This was the caster. It was German silver, and crippled and rusty, but it was so preposterously out of place that it was suggestive of a tattered exile king among barbarians, and the majesty of its native position compelled respect even in its degradation. There

35   was only one cruet left, and that was a stopperless, fly-specked, broken-necked thing, with two inches of vinegar in it, and a dozen preserved flies with their heels up and looking sorry they had invested there.

From "Roughing It," by Mark Twain

28.   The attitude of the author toward the place he describes is one of

(A) disgust.   (D) deference.

(B) condescension.   (E) sympathy.

(C) amusement.

29.   The humor of the description of the "towel" in lines 5–12 depends primarily on the fact that

(A) the shirt had once been blue but has become bleached with time.

(B) the woolen fabric will not absorb water well enough to make a good towel.

(C) the shirt is so old that it is probably full of holes.

(D) the driver and the conductor do not want to soil the only towel available.

(E) the shirt is probably so filthy that it would get clean hands dirty again.

30. The stage-driver will not use the station-keeper's towel because he is afraid

    (A) the station-keeper will consider it a sign of special friendship, and the driver hates the station-keeper.

    (B) he will have to share his own personal toilet articles with the station-keeper.

    (C) not to follow the good example of the stage conductor.

    (D) the station-keeper will strike him for being so presumptuous as to use that personal an object.

    (E) it will make the station-keeper think he has to offer unusual courtesies to all the travelers.

31. Which of the following does NOT contribute to the description of the age of the comb?

    (A) "the half of a comb" (lines 18–19)

    (B) "patriarch" (line 19)

    (C) "sample coffins" (line 20)

    (D) "Esau and Samson" (line 21)

    (E) "accumulating hair" (lines 21–22)

32. Which of the following creates humor through the greatest contrast of elegant language used to describe something quite disgusting?

    (A) "the driver his pantaloons and sleeves" (line 12)

    (B) "pleasant double-barreled portrait of you" (line 16)

    (C) "along with certain impurities" (line 22)

    (D) "a greasy board on stilts" (line 23)

    (E) "the tablecloth and napkins had not come" (lines 23–24)

33. As it is used in the passage (last line), "invested" can be understood in all of the following senses EXCEPT

    (A) to search into systematically and carefully.

    (B) to spend time or effort with the expectation of receiving pleasure or satisfaction.

(C) to install in office with ceremony.

(D) to cover.

(E) to hem in or besiege.

34. The device the author uses to create humor in such phrases as "in the valise" (lines 9–10), "along with certain impurities" (line 22), and "they are not looking for them, either" (lines 24–25) is

(A) exaggeration.   (D) imagery.

(B) afterthought.   (E) anticipation.

(C) simile.

QUESTIONS 35–42

"What is he, then?"

"Why, I'll tell you what he is," said Mr. Jonas, apart to the young ladies, "he's precious old, for one thing; and I an't best pleased with him for that, for I think my father

5   must have caught it of him. He's a strange old chap, for another," he added in a louder voice, "and don't understand any one hardly, but him!" He pointed to his honoured parent with the carving-fork, in order that they might know whom he meant.

10   "How very strange!" cried the sisters.

"Why, you see," said Mr. Jonas, "he's been addling his old brains with figures and book-keeping all his life; and twenty years ago or so he went and took a fever. All the time he was out of his head (which was three weeks) he

15   never left off casting up; and he got to so many million at last that I don't believe he's ever been quite right since. We don't do much business now though, and he an't a bad clerk."

"A very good one," said Anthony.

20   "Well! He an't a dear one at all events," observed Jonas; "and he earns his salt, which is enough for our lookout. I was telling you that he hardly understands any one except my father; he always understands him, though, and wakes up quite wonderful. He's been used to his ways so

25   long, you see! Why, I've seen him play whist, with my father for a partner; and a good rubber too; when he had no

more notion what sort of people he was playing against, than you have."

From Martin Chuzzlewit, by Charles Dickens

35. From this passage it can be inferred that Mr. Jonas is all of the following EXCEPT

(A) irritated that the old clerk understands hardly anyone except the father.

(B) unconcerned about hurting the old clerk's feelings.

(C) worried that the old clerk might make a serious error.

(D) intent upon impressing the sisters.

(E) terribly rude for saying the things he does about his father and the clerk.

36. If the old clerk is not "quite right" in the head, then why is he kept on as an employee?

(A) Mr. Jonas will not go against his father's wishes.

(B) Mr. Jonas does not want to offend the ladies.

(C) Mr. Jonas reveres people of the older generation.

(D) Mr. Jonas is somewhat afraid of the "strange old chap."

(E) Mr. Jonas knows the clerk is the best one in the business.

37. As used in the passage, the word "precious" means

(A) expensive.

(B) of high value.

(C) beloved.

(D) very overrefined in behavior.

(E) very great.

38. What has made the old clerk not "quite right" in the head?

(A) Going a bit deaf in his old age

(B) Working with numbers and bookkeeping all his life

(C)   Working sums and figures in his fever

(D)   Having to put up with Mr. Jonas' abuse

(E)   Having too much to do in the business now

39.   The sentence "He an't a dear one at all events" can best be interpreted to mean which of the following?

(A)   Mr. Jonas does not like the old clerk.

(B)   The customers of the business do not like the old clerk.

(C)   Sometimes the clerk creates serious problems.

(D)   He is only a good clerk with some things in the business.

(E)   His wages do not cost the company very much money.

40.   All of the following are things Mr. Jonas dislikes about the clerk EXCEPT that he is

(A)   old.

(B)   a bit strange.

(C)   a good whist player.

(D)   not always aware of who is around him.

(E)   not able to hear well.

41.   What is the meaning of "he got to so many million at last"?

(A)   He irritated countless customers.

(B)   He had trouble keeping up with the high figures.

(C)   He became quite advanced in years.

(D) He thought the three weeks was a million days.

(E) He lost the company too much money in revenues.

42. A reasonable description of the old man is that he

(A) knows what he is doing when it is something he has been accustomed to doing.

(B) only pretends to be deaf and addled in order to irritate Mr. Jonas.

(C) can do only the simplest of tasks, although he would like to be able to do more.

(D) can do anything he wants to do, but only chooses to do what pleases him.

(E) will only perform such tasks as please Mr. Jonas' father.

QUESTIONS 43–45

Dark house, by which once more I stand
    ·Here in the long unlovely street,
    Doors where my heart was used to beat
So quickly, waiting for a hand,

5 A hand that can be clasped no more —
    Behold me for I cannot sleep,
    And like a guilty thing I creep
At earliest morning to the door.

He is not here; but far away
10   The noise of life begins again,
    And ghastly thro, the drizzling rain
On the bald street breaks the blank day.

"In Memoriam A.H.H.," by Alfred Lord Tennyson

43. The attitude of the speaker, the "I" of line 1, toward the "he" of the poem represented by the hand is one of

    (A) loathing based upon a past misunderstanding of a bitter experience.

    (B) terror as a result of "ghastly" experiences with which they have been associated.

    (C) uncertainty, since he does not know how "he" will accept him when they eventually do meet.

    (D) guilt since "I" has been at least to some extent responsible for the fact that "he" is dead.

    (E) unqualified love, represented by his desire to clasp a hand that can no longer respond to him.

44. The word "ghastly" in line 11 conveys which of the following ideas?

    I. The empty (bald) street in the rain seems pale and ghostly.

    II. The individual who is dead haunts him in a spectral form.

    III. It seems to him horrible that the day should come to life again when the one he is writing of cannot do so.

    IV. The idea of a hand unconnected to a body causes terror.

    (A) I and IV only   (D) I and III only

    (B) III only   (E) I only

    (C) II and III only

45. The general tone of the poem could best be described as

    (A) ironic.   (D) condescending.

    (B) gloomy.   (E) satirical.

    (C) playful.

QUESTIONS 46–50

The world is too much with us; late and soon,
Getting and spending, we lay waste our powers:
Little we see in Nature that is ours;
We have given our hearts away, a sordid boon!
5   This Sea that bares her bosom to the moon;
The winds that will be howling at all hours,
And are up-gathered now like sleeping flowers;
For this, for every thing, we are out of tune;
It moves us not. — — Great God! I'd rather be
10 A Pagan suckled in a creed outworn;
So might I, standing on this pleasant lea,
Have glimpses that would make me less forlorn;
Have sight of Proteus rising from the sea;
Or hear old Triton blow his wreathed horn.

From "The World is too Much With Us," by William Wordsworth

46. Which of the following ideas best describes the meaning(s) of this poem?

I.   The purpose of life is to work hard in order to accumulate wealth.

II. We have lost our ability to appreciate and be uplifted by nature.

III. The pursuit of materialism has weakened us.

(A) I only   (D) I and II only

(B) II only   (E) II and III only

(C) III only

47. What is the effect of the change from first person plural voice (lines 1–9) to first person singular voice (lines 9–14)?

(A) To suggest that we are all alike

(B) To emphasize the similarity between Pagans and Christians

(C) To contrast the speaker's appreciation of nature to the lack of appreciation of nature by most people

(D) To emphasize the difference between Pagans and Christians

(E) To suggest that each person is different from other people

48. The speaker's tone in this poem can best be described as

(A) admonitory.   (D) appreciative.

(B) indifferent.   (E) kind and gentle.

(C) mocking.

49. What is the function of the phrases "to the moon" (line 5) and "sleeping flowers" (line 7)?

(A) They suggest the nature of the "Sea" (line 5).

(B) They suggest that "Nature" (line 3) is asleep.

(C) They suggest that we are asleep.

(D) They suggest that the time setting of the poem is night.

(E) They suggest that the speaker mourns our wasted powers.

50. In its context, the phrase "I'd rather be/A Pagan suckled in a creed outworn" (lines 9–10) suggests which of the following beliefs of the speaker?

(A) A "Pagan" was closer emotionally to "Nature" (line 3) than the speaker's contemporaries.

(B) "Pagan" beliefs are no longer valid.

(C) A "Pagan" has no specific beliefs.

(D) The speaker wishes to fantasize about life.

(E) Contemporary religions bring people close to "Nature" (line 3).

QUESTIONS 51–55

I think I see my father's sister stand
Upon the hall-step of her country house
To give me welcome. She stood straight and calm,
Her somewhat narrow forehead braided tight
5   As if for taming accidental thoughts
From possible pulses; brown hair pricked with gray
By frigid use of life (she was not old,
Although my father's elder by a year).
A nose drawn sharply, yet in delicate lines;
10   A close mild mouth, a little soured about
The ends, through speaking unrequited loves
Or peradventure niggardly half-truths;
Eyes of no color,—once they might have smiled,
But never, never forgot themselves
15   In smiling; cheeks, in which was a rose
Of perished summers, like a rose in a book,
Kept more for ruth than pleasure,—if past bloom,
Past fading also.
                She had lived, we'll say,
20   A harmless life, she called a virtuous life,
A quiet life, which was not a life at all
(But that, she had not lived enough to know),
Between the vicar and the county squires,
The lord-lieutenant looking down sometimes
25   From the empyrean to assure their souls
Against chance vulgarisms, and, in the abyss,
The apothecary, looked on once a year
To prove their soundness of humility.
The poor-club exercised her Christian gifts
30   Of knitting stockings, stitching petticoats,
Because we are of one flesh, after all,
And need one flannel (with a proper sense
Of difference in the quality)—and still
The book club, guarded from your modern trick
35   Of shaking dangerous questions from the crease,
Preserved her intellectual. She had lived
A sort of caged-bird life, born in a cage,
Accounting that to leap from perch to perch
Was an act and joy for any bird.

40   Dear heaven, how silly are the things that live
      In thickets, and eat berries!

From "Aurora Leigh," by Elizabeth Barrett Browning

51.   It can be inferred from the speaker's description of her father's sister in the first stanza that the aunt

    (A)   is stern and serious minded.

    (B)   is an old woman.

    (C)   has undergone great hardships.

    (D)   is a devout Christian.

    (E)   is a rude and arrogant person.

52.   Lines 14–16 are best interpreted to mean that the aunt

    (A)   rarely smiled.

    (B)   had difficulty expressing emotions.

    (C)   expressed controlled happiness long ago.

    (D)   had forgotten about happier times.

    (E)   refuses to share her feelings with the speaker.

53.   The phrase "like a rose in a book" (line 16) is an example of

    (A)   irony.   (D)   metaphor.

    (B)   simile.   (E)   tenor.

    (C)   personification.

54.   The first two lines of the second stanza mostly suggest that the aunt

    (A)   interprets her self-denial to be pious while the speaker views it as being guarded.

    (B)   never harmed anyone intentionally.

    (C)   is worthy of imitation.

    (D)   cannot practice the frivolity she desires.

    (E)   should be respected for her faithfulness.

55. The tone of the speaker is best described as being

    (A) absolutely scornful.

    (B) obstinate and bitter.

    (C) mildly condescending.

    (D) humanely sympathetic.

    (E) removed and apathetic.

QUESTIONS 56–60

I leant upon a coppice gate
    When Frost was spectre-gray,
And Winter's dregs made desolate
    The weakening eye of day.
5 The tangled bine-stems scored the sky
    Like strings of broken lyres,
And all mankind that haunted nigh
    Had sought their household fires.

The land's sharp features seemed to be
10   The Century's corpse outleant,
His crypt the cloudy canopy,
    The wind his death-lament.
The ancient pulse of germ and birth
    Was shrunken hard and dry,
15 And every spirit upon earth
    Seemed fervourless as I.

At once a voice arose among
    The bleak twigs overhead
In a full-hearted evensong
20   Of joy illimited;
An aged thrush, frail, gaunt, and small,
    In blast beruffled plume,
Had chosen thus to fling his soul
    Upon the growing gloom.

25 So little cause for carolings
    Of such ecstatic sound
Was written on terrestrial things
    Afar or nigh around,

That I could think there trembled through
30   His happy good-night air
Some blessed Hope, whereof he knew
          And I was unaware.

"The Darkling Thrush," by Thomas Hardy

56.   The attitude of the speaker toward the thrush could be described as

(A) puzzled admiration.   (D) fearful dismay.

(B) contemptuous indifference.   (E) unbounded love.

(C) hostile repugnance.

57.   There is a marked change in the poet's mood during the course of the poem. Where does this change begin?

(A) Line 29 with "I could think…"

(B) Line 17 with "At once a voice arose…"

(C) Line 9 with "The land's sharp features…"

(D) Line 5 with "The tangled bine-stems…"

(E) Line 13 with "The ancient pulse…"

58.   Which of the following images is NOT used in describing the day?

(A) A tea cup   (D) A grave

(B) A harp   (E) The sun

(C) A fence

59.   Which of the following could be used to describe the thrush?

I.   Intimidating

II.   Courageous

III. Timorous

IV.   Insightful

(A) I and III only   (D) I only

(B) II only   (E) II and III only

(C) II and IV only

60. The poem is full of good imagery. Which of the following is NOT included?

   (A) The sun looking upon the earth

   (B) The heavens as scratched

   (C) The world with blood vessels

   (D) Roots clutching the soil

   (E) The clouds covering a tomb

QUESTIONS 61–65

We know that there was an older play by Thomas Kyd, that extraordinary dramatic (if not poetic) genius who was in all probability the author of two plays so dissimilar as *The Spanish Tragedy* and *The Arden of Feversham*; and
5 what this play was like we can guess from three clues: from *The Spanish Tragedy* itself, from the tale of Belleforest upon which Kyd's *Hamlet* must have been based, and from a version acted in Germany in Shakespeare's lifetime which bears strong evidence of having been adapted from
10 the earlier, not the later, play. From these three sources it is clear that in the earlier play the motive was simply a revenge motive; that the action or delay is caused, as in *The Spanish Tragedy*, solely by the difficulty of assassinating a monarch surrounded by guards; and that the "madness" of
15 Hamlet was feigned in order to escape suspicion, and successfully. In the final play of Shakespeare, on the other hand, there is a motive which is more important than that of revenge, and which explicitly "blunts" the latter; the delay is unexplained on grounds of necessity or expediency; and
20 the effect of "madness" is not to lull but arouse the king's suspicion. The alteration is not complete enough, however, to be convincing. Furthermore, there are verbal parallels so close to *The Spanish Tragedy* as to leave no doubt that in places Shakespeare was merely *revising* the text of Kyd.
25 And finally there are unexplained scenes — the Polonius-Reynaldo scenes — for which there is little excuse; these scenes are not in the verse style of Kyd and not beyond doubt in the style of Shakespeare. These Mr. Robertson believes to be scenes in the original play of Kyd reworked

30   by a third hand, perhaps Chapman, before Shakespeare
       touched the play.

       From "Hamlet and His Problems," by T. S. Eliot

61.   The author suggests that Kyd's older play was called

       (A)   *The Spanish Tragedy.*   (D)   *A German Tragedy.*

       (B)   *Belleforest.*   (E)   *Hamlet.*

       (C)   *The Arden of Feversham.*

62.   The author suggests that Shakespeare's play is a revision of

       (A)   a German version of Kyd's.   (D)   the tale of Belleforest.

       (B)   *The Arden of Feversham.*   (E)   his own earlier play.

       (C)   *The Spanish Tragedy.*

63.   We can guess what the Kyd play was like through clues in

       I.   *The Arden of Feversham.*

       II.   a German version in Shakespeare's time.

       III. *The Spanish Tragedy* and the tale of Belleforest.

       (A)   I and III only   (D)   III only

       (B)   I only   (E)   II and III only

       (C)   II only

64.   Kyd's earlier play was a(n)

       (A)   historical saga.   (D)   chronicle.

       (B)   miracle play.   (E)   morality play.

       (C)   revenge play.

65.   Which of the following words best describe the author's tone?

       (A)   Calm and objective

       (B)   Erudite and pompous

       (C)   Pedagogical and dull

       (D)   Condescending and lecturing

       (E)   Learned and high-brow

QUESTIONS 66–69

Shall I compare thee to a summer's day?
Thou art more lovely and more temperate:
Rough winds do shake the darling buds of May,
And summer's lease hath all too short a date:
5   Sometimes too hot the eye of heaven shines
And often is his gold complexion dimmed;
And every fair from fair sometimes declines,
By chance or nature's changing course untrimmed;
But thy eternal summer shall not fade,
10   Nor lose possession of that fair thou ow'st;
Nor shall death brag thou wander'st in his shade,
When in eternal lines to time thou grow'st:
So long as men can breathe, or eyes can see,
So long live this, and this gives life to thee.

"Sonnet 18," by William Shakespeare

66. The poem is concerned primarily with the

    (A) eternal nature of love.

    (B) idea that nature never changes.

    (C) transient nature of flowers.

    (D) idea that humanity creates eternal objects.

    (E) eternal nature of summer.

67. The metaphoric use of "a summer's day" (lines 1–2) suggests all of
    the following EXCEPT

    (A) how much like a summer's day is the person addressed.

    (B) the shortness of life.

    (C) the contrast between the fleeting days of summer and the eternal quality of love.

    (D) the ugliness of life.

    (E) continuous, but ever-changing nature.

68.   Lines 13 and 14 of the poem can best be described as

(A)   blank verse.   (D)   pastoral elegy.

(B)   rhymed triplet.   (E)   rhymed couplet.

(C)   free verse.

69.   Lines 5–6 employ the figure of speech called

(A)   personification.   (D)   apostrophe.

(B)   allusion.   (E)   allegory.

(C)   alliteration.

QUESTIONS 70–74

The high-tech world of clocks and schedules, computers and programs was supposed to free us from a life of
toil and deprivation, yet with each passing day the human
race becomes more enslaved, exploited and victimized.
5   Millions starve while a few live in splendor. The human
race remains divided from itself and severed from the natural world that is its primordial community.
    We now orchestrate an artificial time world, zipping
along the electronic circuits of silicon chips, a time world
10   utterly alien from the time a fruit takes to ripen, or a tide
takes to recede. We have sped ourselves out of the time
world of nature and into a fabricated time world where
experience can only be simulated but no longer savored.
Our weekly routines and work lives are punctuated with
15   artificial rhythms, the unholy union of perspective and
power. And with each new electric dawn and dusk, we
grow further apart from each other, more isolated and
alone, more in control and less self-assured.

From Time Wars, by Jeremy Rifkin

70.   Which of the following most closely explains the use of "fruit" and
"tide"?

(A)   To compare natural processes in the world of time

(B)   To emphasize the uncontrollable natural processes in the
world of time

(C) To contrast well-known natural processes with the modern world

(D) To contrast the fast high-tech world with the slow world of nature

(E) To contrast the time processes of the natural world with the time of the modern world

71. The expression "electric dawn and dusk" functions as a(n)

(A) symbol of humanity's tampering with nature.

(B) image of humanity's power over nature.

(C) symbol of the computerized world of time.

(D) personification of light.

(E) symbol of the elongated day in the modern world.

72. What differentiates the two worlds of time?

(A) People are deprived in one, fulfilled in the other.

(B) People enjoy life in one but play at life in the other.

(C) People experience power in one but fantasize over power in the other.

(D) People move speedily in one and at leisure in the other.

(E) People experience full life in one but copy life in the other.

73. The author uses the adjectives in the comparative in the last sentence in order to

(A) show the balance and rhythm in the computerized world.

(B) emphasize the regret he feels at the loss of rhythm and balance.

(C) highlight the orchestration of the new world of time.

(D) draw attention to the "artificial rhythms" of our lives.

(E) build to a satisfying climax expressing the loss in our lives.

74. Which expression best describes the notion that we have become automatons in the new time world?

    (A) "severed from the natural world that is its primordial community"

    (B) "zipping along the electronic circuits of silicon chips"

    (C) "sped ourselves out of the time world of nature"

    (D) "unholy union of perspective and power"

    (E) "more in control and less self-assured"

QUESTIONS 75–79

Was I sleeping while the others suffered? Am I sleeping now? To-morrow, when I wake, or think I do, what shall I say of to-day? That with Estragon my friend, at this place, until the fall of night, I waited for Godot? That Pozzo
5 passed, with his carrier, and that he spoke to us? Probably. But in all that what truth will there be? (*Estragon, having struggled with his boots in vain, is dozing off again. Vladimir looks at him.*) He'll know nothing. He'll tell me about the blows he received and I'll give him a carrot.
10 (*Pause.*) Astride of a grave and a difficult birth. Down in the hole, lingeringly, the grave-digger puts on the forceps. We have time to grow old. The air is full of our cries. (*He listens.*) But habit is a great deadener. (*He looks again at Estragon.*) At me too someone is looking, of me too some-
15 one is saying, He is sleeping, he knows nothing, let him sleep on. (*Pause.*) I can't go on! (*Pause.*) What have I said?

From Waiting for Godot, by Samuel Beckett

75. The best paraphrase of "sleeping" (lines 1, 15) is

    (A) deliberately ignoring reality.

    (B) peacefully slumbering.

    (C) dreaming.

    (D) closing one's eyes.

    (E) opening up a dream world.

76. The tone of both the speaker and the passage is best described as

    (A) cheery.   (D) sinister.

    (B) bleak.   (E) comic.

    (C) sober.

77. In this passage the metaphor in "Astride of a grave and a difficult birth." (line 10) suggests which of the following?

    I.   Birth is the beginning of death.

    II. Birth is the beginning of life.

    III. Life is a struggle which ends in death.

    (A) I only   (D) I and II only

    (B) II only   (E) I and III only

    (C) III only

78. The speaker's attitude at the end of the speech can be described as all of the following EXCEPT

    (A) pessimistic.   (D) desperate.

    (B) optimistic.   (E) ambivalent.

    (C) confused.

79. The meaning of the phrase "…habit is a great deadener" (line 13) is that habitual behavior

    (A) kills us.   (D) keeps us going.

    (B) sensitizes us.   (E) slows us down.

    (C) makes life fun.

QUESTIONS 80–85

The Lovers of the Poor

> arrive The Ladies from the Ladies' Betterment
> League
> Arrive in the afternoon, the late light slanting
> In diluted gold bars across the boulevard brag
> 5   Of proud, seamed faces with mercy and murder hinting
> Here, there, interrupting, all deep and debonair,

The pink paint on the innocence of fear;
Walk in a gingerly manner up the hall.
Cutting with knives served by their softest care,
10   Served by their love, so barbarously fair.
Whose mothers taught: You'd better not be cruel!
You had better not throw stones upon the wrens!
Herein they kiss and coddle and assault
Anew and dearly in the innocence
15   With which they baffle nature. Who are full,
Sleek, tender-clad, fit, fiftyish, a-glow, all
Sweetly abortive, hinting at fat fruit,
Judge it high time that fiftyish fingers felt
Beneath the lovelier planes on enterprise.
20   To resurrect. To moisten with milky chill.
To be a random hitching-post or plush.
To be, for wet eyes, random and handy hem.
                    Their guild is giving money to the poor.

By Gwendolyn Brooks

80.   What does the phrase "pink paint" (line 7) reveal about the ladies
       from the Ladies' Betterment League?

       I.   They are flushed with embarrassment.

       II.   They are afraid of being harmed.

       III.   They are not showing their true feelings.

       (A)   I only   (D)   II and III only

       (B)   II only   (E)   I, II, and III

       (C)   III only

Please Note: This is where the actual CLEP exam would end.
We provide 10 extra questions for practice purposes.

---

81.   The paradox of "mercy and murder" (line 5) can be best understood
       as which of the following?

       (A)   The ladies must be cruel in order to be kind.

       (B)   The ladies are afraid of being murdered in spite of their charity.

       (C)   The ladies' lack of honesty in their kindness is cruel.

(D) The ladies make kind remarks while not giving very much to the poor they have come to serve.

(E) The ladies' chill reserve is cruel.

82. The narrator's tone can be identified as one of

(A) self-serving pity.

(B) patronizing understanding.

(C) bitter derision.

(D) incredulous disappointment.

(E) shocked amusement.

83. Which of the following pairs of words or phrases does NOT illustrate the contrast of intention and reality of the ladies' actions?

(A) "deep" and "debonair" (line 6)

(B) "barbarously" and "fair" (line 10)

(C) "coddle" and "assault" (line 13)

(D) "Anew" and "dearly" (line 14)

(E) "Sweetly" and "abortive" (line 17)

84. What is significant about the age of the ladies?

(A) Women that old have no business traipsing about town in late afternoon.

(B) Before that age, women are not mature enough to deal with such a different lifestyle.

(C) At that age, women have accumulated enough wealth to be able to help others.

(D) The women are ashamed of themselves for not having become concerned sooner in their lives.

(E) The women should have been concerned with the plight of others long before that age.

85. The meaning of the word "random" in line 22 is best understood as which of the following?

I. The ladies' periodic inspections of their work to make sure nothing goes astray

II. The picture the ladies have in their minds of themselves helping a deserving, grateful person or two

III. The inability of anyone to achieve an organized plan of action for assistance

(A) I only

(D) I and II only

(B) II only

(E) II and III only

(C) III only

QUESTIONS 86–90

It was there that, several years ago, I saw him for the first time; and the sight pulled me up sharp. Even then he was the most striking figure in Starkfield, though he was but the ruin of a man. It was not so much his great height

5 that marked him, for the "natives" were easily singled out by their lank longitude from the stockier foreign breed: it was the careless powerful look he had, in spite of a lameness checking each step like the jerk of a chain. There was something bleak and unapproachable in his face, and he

10 was so stiffened and grizzled that I took him for an old man and was surprised to hear that he was not more than fifty-two. I had this from Harmon Gow, who had driven the stage from Bettsbridge to Starkfield in pre-trolley days and knew the chronicle of all the families on his line.

15 Harmon drew a slab of tobacco from his pocket, cut off a wedge and pressed it into the leather pouch of his cheek. "Guess he's been in Starkfield too many winters. Most of the smart ones get away."

Though Harmon Gow developed the tale as far as his

20 mental and moral reach permitted there were perceptible gaps between his facts, and I had the sense that the deeper meaning of the story was in the gaps. But one phrase stuck in my memory and served as the nucleus about which I grouped my subsequent inferences: "Guess he's been in Starkfield

25 too many winters."

Before my own time there was up I had learned to know what that meant. Yet I had come in the degenerate day of trolley, bicycle and rural delivery, when communication was easy between the scattered mountain villages, and the

30 bigger towns in the valleys, such as Bettsbridge and Shadd's Falls, had libraries, theatres and Y. M. C. A. halls to which the youth of the hills could descend for recreation. But when

winter shut down on Starkfield, and the village lay under a
sheet of snow perpetually renewed from the pale skies, I
35 began to see what life there—or rather its negation—must
have been in Ethan Frome's young manhood.

From Ethan Frome, by Edith Wharton

86. The phrase "checking each step like the jerk of a chain" (line 8) is
     best interpreted to mean that Ethan

     (A) had served time on a chain gang.

     (B) moved about with uncertainty and timidity.

     (C) dragged along the dead weight of his injured leg.

     (D) was obviously one of the "stockier" breed.

     (E) bore the characteristics of a corrupt and criminal past.

87. The phrase "singled out by their lank longitude" (lines 5–6) evokes
     the

     (A) tall stature of the town "natives."

     (B) sailing history of the townfolk.

     (C) prejudice "natives" had for their own kind.

     (D) animosity shown toward the "natives" by the foreigners in
          town.

     (E) "natives'" superiority over the foreign breed.

88. In context, which of the following supports Harmon Gow's observa-
     tion "Guess he's been in Starkfield too many winters" (line 17)?

     (A) Ethan's being the town's most striking figure

     (B) Ethan's great height

     (C) Ethan's careless, powerful look

     (D) Ethan's bleak and unapproachable face

     (E) Ethan's awareness of Gow's opinion of him

89. In context, the phrase "degenerate day" (line 27) is best interpreted
     to mean

(A)   a time when winters were more severe.

(B)   a time of inferior trolley and mail service.

(C)   an earlier time of restricted communication between villages.

(D)   the time when winter clamped down on the village.

(E)   a time of modern worldly influence on the village.

90.   The tone of the first paragraph is best described as

(A)   cynical glee.   (D)   feigned sympathy.

(B)   sympathetic curiosity.   (E)   worshipful awe.

(C)   mild sarcasm.

CLEP ANALYZING AND INTERPRETING LITERATURE
TEST 3

ANSWER KEY

1.	(A)	31.	(C)	61.	(E)
2.	(E)	32.	(C)	62.	(C)
3.	(D)	33.	(A)	63.	(E)
4.	(E)	34.	(B)	64.	(C)
5.	(B)	35.	(C)	65.	(A)
6.	(E)	36.	(A)	66.	(A)
7.	(B)	37.	(E)	67.	(D)
8.	(C)	38.	(C)	68.	(E)
9.	(C)	39.	(E)	69.	(A)
10.	(D)	40.	(C)	70.	(C)
11.	(A)	41.	(B)	71.	(C)
12.	(D)	42.	(A)	72.	(E)
13.	(A)	43.	(E)	73.	(D)
14.	(B)	44.	(D)	74.	(B)
15.	(C)	45.	(B)	75.	(A)
16.	(D)	46.	(E)	76.	(B)
17.	(D)	47.	(C)	77.	(E)
18.	(C)	48.	(A)	78.	(B)
19.	(B)	49.	(D)	79.	(D)
20.	(C)	50.	(A)	80.	(D)
21.	(C)	51.	(A)	81.	(C)
22.	(B)	52.	(C)	82.	(C)
23.	(A)	53.	(B)	83.	(A)
24.	(B)	54.	(A)	84.	(E)
25.	(B)	55.	(C)	85.	(B)
26.	(A)	56.	(A)	86.	(C)
27.	(C)	57.	(B)	87.	(A)
28.	(C)	58.	(C)	88.	(D)
29.	(E)	59.	(C)	89.	(E)
30.	(D)	60.	(D)	90.	(B)

DETAILED EXPLANATIONS OF ANSWERS

TEST 3

1. **(A)** Choice (A) is the best answer; clean is the best understanding of the word "fresh" in the context of the passage. Although the child may be well-fed due to his privilege, such a fact is not stated; thus, (B) well-fed is not the correct answer. (C) is an incorrect choice; fresh is describing his appearance and it has already been previously established that the child is wealthy. In the context of the passage, "fresh" is not meant to be understood in its slang form; thus, (D) and (E) are incorrect.

2. **(E)** Choice (E) is the best answer; the paragraph discusses how poverty may breed contempt in the eye of the viewer although the children are fundamentally equal. (A) is incorrect; although rich children may act differently than poor children, the paragraph instead focuses upon the treatment of the children by others. (B) is not correct; the speaker is explaining that the children are not truly more or less attractive than one another; their surface appearance causes others to establish such a difference. (C) is not correct, for it seems obvious that the indigent child is not as clean as the wealthy boy. Such a point is not the main purpose of the paragraph. (D) is not correct; it is the prejudice of adults that judge the child in poverty and establish the notion of difference. The children do not even notice that they are dissimilar.

3. **(D)** Choice (D) is the correct answer; an impartial eye in this case would be one who is neither influenced by the sight of wealth or poverty. (A) is incorrect; the speaker does not state that such an observer would best judge the merits of both children fairly. (B) is not the answer as one without any judgment would not be able to decide that the boys were equal. Although one who is not fooled by wealth would constitute an impartial eye, one who is also equally not fooled by poverty is needed; (C)

is incorrect. (E) is not correct; there is nothing impartial about a person who cannot bear to see a child in poverty.

4. **(E)**   Choice (E) is the best answer for the symbolic fence both separates their homes as well as their lives. It seems that such a physical barrier symbolizes the difference in lifestyle and experience. (A) is not the answer, for it is a literal understanding that the fence separates the properties of the children. (B) is incorrect; while the fence is a barrier between them, nowhere is it stated that they are not allowed to come in contact with each other. (C) is incorrect as the mental inferiority or superiority of either child has not been established in the passage. (D) is not correct; the corruption of the wealthy child by the poor boy is not a concern of the author.

5. **(B)**   Choice (B) is the correct answer as the story of the children contains a social commentary; they are the personification of poverty and wealth presented in a fictional scenario in order to address and compare these two modes of life. (A) is not correct, as realism seeks to create an absolutely accurate representation of life, and this passage is obviously contrived in the mind of the narrator in order to prove a point. (C) anecdote is not correct, for an anecdote is the simple, unelaborated description of an incident; this incident is elaborated upon with interjections of the author's subjectivity. (D) is incorrect as this passage does not make reference to any other person, place, event, or literary work. (E) is also incorrect; there is no tragedy or dramatic reversal that occurs in this passage.

6. **(E)**   Choice (E) is the only one listed that is not an image, a verbal picture of something visual. Choice (A) is an image of a horse and rider; choice (B), a chain-gang; choice (C), puppets on a stage; and choice (D), a ship on rough waters. All of the first four, then, are things which can be visualized as specific pictures in the mind of the reader.

7. **(B)**   All the definitions listed could be viable options for "meanly" in different contexts. In this passage, however, the author intends that physical sensation was low in value (B) because it did not last long. All highs and lows of ecstasy and suffering were fleeting sensations and not to be trusted as the true measure of the men's existence.

8. **(C)**   A paradox represents two opposite but equally true things. The central paradox of the passage is that in choosing to fight the war wholeheartedly, the author gives up a sense of volition and control over

his own life. He refers to the fighters in the cause as "dead leaves in the wind" (line 11) something without a life of their own and totally at the mercy of something larger than themselves. All the other statements show how the soldiers felt, and most are contrasts, but they do not express paradox.

9.   **(C)**   (C) is the correct answer, for the "sweet-apple" is substituted in this poem to refer to something else. The speaker draws an analogy between the fruit and the actual referent. (A) is not the best choice because a simile suggests that two distinct objects are compared using the word like. Although "sweet" describes the apple, (B) is not the best answer choice because this phrase is to be interpreted figuratively, not literally. (D) is also incorrect as the phrase is not contradictory. (E) is not the correct answer; a euphemism is a more agreeable description or explanation substituted for something offensive or unflattering.

10.   **(D)**   (D) is the best choice as the symbols and references are drawn from nature. (A) is not the best choice as religious references may be inferred, but the concentration upon nature is more obvious. (B) is not the correct choice, for there are no references to literature found in this poem. Although an apple is a food, it is the only allusion to a food item; (C) is incorrect. (E) is not the correct answer as there are no fantastic, dream-like elements present in the poem. Instead, the allusions are drawn from realistic occurrences in nature.

11.   **(A)**   Choice (A) is the best choice as the poem compares two scenarios which end in different results. The apple that is left alone thrives while the flower which comes into human contact is destroyed. (B) is not the best choice, for it is too literal; this poem is not about producing fruit. (C) is not the correct choice; the poem does not address the issue of literal location, but rather, the figurative location. (D) is not correct; again, the poem should not be interpreted literally. The main focus of the poem is not on the quantity of those at the top (E).

12.   **(D)**   Choice (D) is the correct choice as the sweet apple is the referent of "it." (A) is incorrect; although the apple is growing on the high branch, the apple is the main focus of this stanza. (B) is incorrect, for the fruit-pickers have not overlooked their own reach, but what they were reaching for. (C) is not the answer, for they have not overlooked the top of the tree, but what is growing on the top of that tree. (E) is incorrect as the "it" does not refer to their memory, but what they have forgotten.

13.   **(A)**   Choice (A) is the correct answer; this poem is about the distinguishing of the virtuous as well as the beauty and goodness achieved when one is left unadulterated. (B) is incorrect; although statement II is compatible with the speakers understanding of purity and corrosion, the poem does not dwell upon the issue of others attempting to cause the downfall of superiors. Additionally, (C) is incorrect as it once again refers to statement III. (D) is incorrect; the poem does not only discuss the distinguishing of the virtuous, but also why and how that virtue is achieved. (E) is incorrect; again, the poem does not solely focus on the inferior others.

14.   **(B)**   Choice (B) is the correct choice; "Such as" and "Just as" intimate that the succeeding objects will stand for something else. (A) is incorrect; although the first two words of the stanzas are comparative, this analogy is not literal, but metaphoric. (C) is not the best choice, for the analogy of human actions and natural occurrences is not the main focus of this poem. (D) is incorrect; although interpreted literally, the shepherds do destroy the hyacinths, this poem is not about man's relationship to nature. Although the apple-pickers do not adversely affect the apple by picking it, the purpose of this poem is not to reveal the delicacy of those who pick fruit; therefore, (E) is incorrect.

15.   **(C)**   Choice (C) is the correct answer, for the line is composed of a stressed syllable followed by two light syllables and has three metric feet. (A) is not the best choice; a phyrric foot has two equally light stresses and a tetrameter is composed of four metric feet. (B) is not the correct answer as a trochaic foot is made up of a stressed syllable followed by an unstressed and a tetrameter has four feet. Although this line is a trimeter, it is not trochaic because it is a stressed syllable followed by two unstressed; thus, (D) is wrong. (E) is incorrect, for the line does not begin with a stressed followed by an unstressed syllable and it also does not contain five metric feet.

16.   **(D)**   Most of the guests are men who seem older and rougher (B) and (C), "mariners" (line 6) and "men who lived by regular and laborious handicraft" (13–14). Robin does not feel attracted to these, and the narrator states that the "two or three sheepish countrymen" (line 21) are the "only guests to whom Robin's sympathies inclined him" (lines 20–21). The tavern-keeper (A) is not mentioned. Although the man at the door (E) draws Robin's attention, he does not seem to be the kind of person with whom Robin would feel comfortable striking up a conversation.

17. **(D)** The author states these men are "countrymen" (line 21). That they feel uncomfortable is apparent by their position in the "darkest corner of the room" (lines 22–23), a place where they can hope to escape the notice of anyone else in the tavern. The other men in the tavern are not portrayed as hostile, but mariners and day laborers might not be the gentlest folk in dealing with outsiders, so one can assume the countrymen hope to avoid undue attention.

18. **(C)** Almost everyone in the tavern is drinking (C) an alcoholic beverage of some kind: "Nearly all, in short, evinced a predilection for the Good Creature in some of its various shapes" (lines 16–18). The "Good Creature" is the punch "long since made a familiar drink in the colony" (lines 12–13). Also, some men prefer the "insulated bliss of an unshared potation" (lines 14–15); a "potation" is an alcoholic beverage. The author does not indicate where the mariners might have traveled (B), nor that they look as if they might be pirates (A). That the men have not been reformed by religion is apparent (D) because they are still drinking alcohol. Although it can be assumed the men enjoy drinking, smoking, and talking, these things are not referred to as the "enjoyable things of life" (E).

19. **(B)** "We have a long hereditary claim" (lines 19–20) to the "vice" (line 18) of drinking. Seafaring (A) is hardly a vice. The men are smoking (C) and talking (D), but the author does not describe these activities as vices. Fasting (E) is associated with religious activities and a partner to alcoholic temperance, something these men are not exhibiting.

20. **(C)** The key here is to ponder over the use of the word "Hoof." His Honour, the Master behaves like a human being but has a hoof… so the human words cannot provide the answer…as the pronoun used is masculine the answer cannot be a mare but a horse (C)!

21. **(C)** The narrator puts himself in the category of travellers receiving favors and as he has written about his exploits the answer is (C).

22. **(B)** Of course he is making up the story but that is not the narrator's interpretation of the censure. Travellers did not lie about the way they treated *inferiors*…the answer is clearly (B).

23. **(A)** We do not have enough to go on to determine if the narrator is reliable (although we are skeptical of him talking to horses). We do not censure tall tales, we tend to enjoy them. What we do censure is a human

being prostrating himself before an animal, behaving in an overly flattering way (A).

24. **(B)** A man who prostrates himself before a horse and then is overwhelmed by the "honour" of the horse raising his hoof to be kissed is not supercilious, nor vain, nor equal. He is certainly not demanding. He is humble and puts himself down in this company...the answer is (B).

25. **(B)** The overwhelming feeling here is the regret at leaving his Honour (B). He is going *to* the islands; his frustration at waiting is very controlled; he never mentions the beauty of the place...the answer can be found through elimination of the facts.

26. **(A)** The illustrious person is still his Honour but as this option is not here, look for a class in which to place "his Honour the horse." The concluding sentence gives you that class as an answer to the detractors who might censure the narrator. The answer then is (A).

27. **(C)** Because of the love expressed for his Honour, the ideas of slavery or satire do not fit here. The narrator has not worked for the Houyhnhnms but respects the Master who does not express here unwillingness at letting him go. The answer then is (C).

28. **(C)** The author is deliberately trying to create a humorous scene. This effect is accomplished through exaggeration of the filth and rusticity of the stagecoach station. Although certain aspects of the place are disgusting — the "private towel," the comb, and the vinegar cruet — the author's tone is gentle. A sly humor is evidenced in such phrases as "sense of decency" (line 7) and "encourage the advances" (lines 8–9), and it is apparent through these that the author has a keen eye in observing human nature. There is no evidence that the author is deferential, condescending, or sympathetic.

29. **(E)** The word "hoary" means "white" and "old." Choice (A) might be a possibility, therefore, but given the conditions in the rest of the station-house, the towel is probably as filthy as everything else. The conductor and the narrator obviously think their handkerchiefs are cleaner than the towel. Choice (B) is illogical. Choice (C) may be true but there is no evidence in the passage to support it, and the shirt's being full of holes would not prevent it from absorbing what little water would be on the men's hands or faces.

30. **(D)** "Advances" in this context is certainly meant to refer to physical violence. This is a rustic location, and it is implied that the only person familiar enough with the station-keeper to use his towel is the conductor. The conductor refuses to use the shirt because of sanitary reasons, so (C) is not correct. There is no sign of friendship or animosity between the station-keeper and the driver. No indication is offered that the station-keeper feels moved to offer special considerations to anyone or expect special sharing from anyone (E).

31. **(C)** "Sample coffins" is a phrase the narrator uses to refer to his preference for death over describing the comb in more detail. Since the comb is old, it is broken (as the mirror is) and has "accumulated hair" because it has been used much. "Patriarch" indicates an aged object or person, and Esau and Samson are two people who lived during the times of Old Testament history.

32. **(C)** The "certain impurities" are almost certainly lice, among other equally noxious possibilities. As the phrase "certain impurities" is a delicate euphemism for the possibilities, humor is created. The language in (A) is ordinary. Choice (B) does create humor through the contrast of "pleasant" and "double-barreled," but the contrast is not as exaggerated as in choice (C). Ordinary word choice in (D) describe the filthy table, and although choice (E) contains humorous phrasing, there is nothing disgusting about it.

33. **(A)** Choice (A) is the definition for "to investigate." Although the flies obviously did investigate the cruet before they died there, all of the remaining choices are proper definitions of the word "invested." Each of the definitions can be used to describe the flies at various stages of their landing upon and entering the bottle. Choice (C) humorously echoes the pattern of royalty come to a fallen state, and the irony of (B) is particularly effective.

34. **(B)** All of these phrases come at the end of sentences in which the author has built in an expectation of a surprise or exaggeration at the end. This surprise or exaggeration creates humor by contrast with the rest of the sentence. The anticipation is built into the first part of the sentence, not the phrases in question. Rather than (A), these phrases are more understated than exaggerated.

35. **(C)** Evidence in the passage indicates the old clerk is still a good records keeper. Mr. Jonas observes that he "an't a bad clerk," to which Anthony adds, "A very good one." Mr. Jonas is obviously unconcerned about hurting the old clerk's feelings (B) as he says terribly rude things

(E) in front of his father and the old clerk. Mr. Jonas says the clerk is "old" and he is not "pleased with him for that." Mr. Jonas' irritation with the old man shows through when he points out the clerk's inability (A) to hear no one but Mr. Jonas' father. Perhaps Mr. Jonas is trying to impress the young ladies (D) as he addresses them "apart."

36. **(A)** Mr. Jonas' father is described in the passage as "honored parent." This wording might be taken ironically, and perhaps is humorous given the way he speaks in front of his parent, but Mr. Jonas goes on to say how the two old men are used to each other. As it would probably upset Mr. Jonas' father to do without his longtime companion, (A) is the logical conclusion. Choice (C) is a possible option, but "revere" is too strong a word given the tone Mr. Jonas uses. Choice (E) might be a possibility, but the highest praise the clerk receives is "very good one." Mr. Jonas is more concerned with impressing than offending the young ladies (B), and there is no evidence to support (D).

37. **(E)** Although "precious" can mean all of the definitions listed as possible answers, "very old" is the best meaning for "precious old" because the rest of the passage details the old clerk's eccentricities brought on by the passing of time. Choice (A) is directly refuted by "He an't a dear one." Choices (B) and (C) may apply to the way Mr. Jonas' father feels about the clerk, but they do not fit Mr. Jonas' feelings. Nowhere in the passage is (D) discussed.

38. **(C)** When the old clerk took a fever "twenty years ago or so," he was delirious for three weeks. The entire time he had fever, he "never left off" running figures in his head, and the figures eventually became so high that his brain became addled. Choice (B) may have contributed to the clerk's problem, but it is not the immediate cause. Choice (A) is incorrect as the fever happened many years before he grew deaf. Choice (D) may have contributed, but there is no evidence in the passage to indicate it. Choice (E) is contradicted in the passage.

39. **(E)** During the conversation between Mr. Jonas and Anthony about the clerk's worth as a worker, Mr. Jonas comments, "He an't a dear one" and then explains how he "earns his salt." The idiom "earns his salt" means he "earns his wages," so "dear" can be taken to mean "expensive" in this context: the old clerk does not have to be paid much but he earns his pay. Although (A) may be true, it is not the meaning in this context. There is no evidence to support (B), (C), or (D).

40. **(C)** The clerk's being a good whist player seems to strike a bit of admiration in Mr. Jonas because the old man can play well even when he "had no more notion what sort of people he was playing against, than you have." Even though he seems to be amazed at the old clerk's whist game, Mr. Jonas seems irritated the old man is unaware of anyone else but the "honored parent" (D). Mr. Jonas speaks disparagingly of the clerk's age (A), strangeness (B), and deafness (E).

41. **(B)** During his fever, the old clerk added numbers for three weeks. The numbers mounted steadily into "so many million at last." Choice (D) is a possibility, but evidence in the passage does not indicate this probability. The fever happened before (C) became a factor. Choice (E) is refuted by the passage, and choice (A) has no evidence to support it.

42. **(A)** The old clerk seems sharp enough dealing with accustomed things — clerking, whist, responding to Mr. Jonas' father — but he has difficulties with responding to new people and situations. There is no evidence (B) is correct, although he could hardly be blamed for getting a little of his own back. Keeping books and playing whist are not "the simplest of tasks" (C). What the old clerk "would like" (C) to do or is pleased (D) and (E) to do is not a consideration in this passage. It seems as if the old man's mind is permanently afflicted; Mr. Jonas says of him after the fever, "I don't believe he's ever been quite right since."

43. **(E)** Be careful not to read into the poem what is not there. Loathing, terror, uncertainty, and guilt are not part of Tennyson's message.

44. **(D)** The word "ghastly" may seem to you too strong for the feeling the poet is trying to achieve, but we can only deal with the poem in front of us, realizing that words take on new connotations as the years go by. There is nothing in the thought of his friend that causes terror. It is only in the real world and the contrast he feels between that world and the thought of his friend that he finds horror. He finds both the physical street itself and the incongruity between a living world and a friend who cannot live to be ghastly.

45. **(B)** The tone of the poem could be described as gloomy, though a number of other terms such as formal, sombre, and serious might also do. There is irony (A) involved in the poet's description of his feelings, but irony is not the overall tone of the poem. Neither (C) nor (D) have anything to do with this poem.

46. **(E)**   The first two lines of the poem eliminate the possibility that the purpose of life is to work to accumulate wealth. They state the exact opposite view. Having said that, we can throw out choices (A) and (D). Choices (B) and (C) characterize two complementary ideas: distance from nature and spirits weakened by materialism. The latter may be said to have caused the former as the poem suggests. So neither stands by itself as correct. Choice (E) includes both and identifies the major themes of the poem.

47. **(C)**   The speaker indicts all of humanity as he knew it when he wrote the poem, thus the use of first person plural in the first nine lines to characterize the dismal spiritual state of humanity. The very act of recognition sets the speaker apart from the rest, and he shows it beginning in line 9 by using first person singular in the rest of the poem. Choice (C) then is the best answer. The foregoing eliminates (A) as a choice; it also weakens (E) as a possibility. Only those who respond to nature and reject the cult of materialism stand out here. The last six lines of the poem suggest a strong difference between the ancients (Greeks and Romans, i.e., Pagans) and the contemporaries of the speaker, presumed to be Christians, eliminating choice (B). The change to "I" does suggest that difference, but choice (D) pales in comparison to (C) as the best one.

48. **(A)**   The exclamations in lines 4 and 9 suggest that the speaker is anything but gentle, so choice (E) stands far afield, as does choice (B). The speaker may be accused of many things, but not indifference. He also does not appreciate what he sees, as evidenced by his preference for paganism so as to be closer to nature than we readers. At the same time, he does not really mock us readers, but rather he admonishes (reproves or warns) us to veer off our foolish path of materialism. The current cliché is "stop to smell the roses." Thus, choices (C) and (D) do not pass muster; (A) correctly identifies the speaker's tone.

49. **(D)**   How does a poet suggest the setting of a poem? This question is addressed by test question 49. We can picture the poet standing by the sea one evening and reflecting on his culture's materialistic bent, to the exclusion of the appreciation of nature's splendor. He then transforms that time into poetic language of the sea baring her bosom to the moon (not the sun) and of the flowers sleeping (not awake and "catching some rays"). Choice

(D), then, is correct. None of the other choices makes sense except (C), possibly. But we are told that we are busy, active, not sleeping. Our intense pursuit of the materialistic blinds us to nature, not our eyes closed in sleep.

50. **(A)**   For most of the poet's audience, "Pagan" beliefs were not only invalid but also sinful. However, the poet/speaker chooses them. So choice (B) does not really work. Choice (C) also proves false by the language of the poem: a creed is a set of specific beliefs (even if "outworn"). Choice (E) is negated by the first four lines and lines 8–9; the speaker's preference for a "Pagan" creed also suggests the inadequacy of contemporary religions to bring people close to "Nature." Even though the speaker has a rich imagination, he recognizes and wishes to live in reality. Indeed, he wishes for us to re-think our reality, so choice (D) misses the mark. Choice (A) correctly defines both "Pagan" and the speaker's beliefs.

51. **(A)**   The speaker's description of the aunt indicates that she is (A) stern and serious minded, the correct choice. The solemnity of the aunt's greeting as well as her physical description support this choice. The speaker contends that the aunt is not old; thus, (B) is incorrect. Although the aunt does not smile easily and her brow is furrowed, the speaker says nothing of her hardships, making (C) an incorrect choice. (D) is also incorrect, as the aunt's faith is not spoken of until the following stanza. Despite the aunt's seriousness, it has not been established in this stanza that she is either rude or arrogant; thus, (E) is not correct.

52. **(C)**   Choice (C) is the correct answer. Lines 14–16 suggest that the aunt did enjoy happier times long ago, but her emotions were always controlled. Although seemingly stern, the speaker does not allude to the fact that the aunt rarely smiled in these lines; (A) is incorrect. The lines indicate that the aunt controlled her feelings, but not that she had difficulty expressing them; therefore, (B) is not the best choice. It is impossible to say what she has remembered or forgotten as the aunt does not speak for herself in this poem; (D) is incorrect. There is not enough information given in these two lines to determine whether or not the aunt shares her emotions with the speaker. This fact renders (E) incorrect.

53. **(B)**   Choice (B) simile is the correct answer, for this phrase compares two distinctly different things using the word "like." (A) is not correct as the phrase does not obscure the truth in an effort to produce the opposite meaning. (C) is incorrect as the phrase does not attribute human characteristics to an inhuman object. (D) is also not correct, for the object,

the rose, is not used in the place of the word book to indicate a likeness between them. (E) Tenor is incorrect because a tenor refers to the subject of a metaphor.

54. **(A)** Choice (A) is the correct answer as it is obvious that the aunt interprets her actions differently from the speaker's understanding of them. (B) is incorrect, as the word harmless is defined as being inoffensive and without excitement in the context of these lines. (C) is incorrect as it is clear that the speaker does not look favorably upon her aunt's existence. It is unknown whether or not the aunt wishes to practice frivolity; thus, (D) is incorrect. The speaker is not commending or demanding respect for her aunt. Instead, the speaker is doubting the purity of this faith; (E) is not correct.

55. **(C)** The speaker is mildly condescending in this passage; there-fore, (C) is the correct answer. It seems as if she feels that both her perspectives and her aspirations are better than her aunt's stilted existence. The speaker is neither (A) absolutely scornful nor (B) obstinate and bitter, as her observations and conclusions are drawn without malice. Her great care in describing both the aunt and the life of this aunt as well as the analysis involved render (E) to be incorrect.

56. **(A)** The poet confesses that he does not understand why the bird is singing, since it seems to have so little to sing about, but he certainly feels a sense of respect toward the bird for doing it.

57. **(B)** As the poem begins, the poet experiences a lethargic stupor while viewing the dead winter world. It is not until line 17 that his spirits are revived by the singing of the old, dying thrush.

58. **(C)** The dregs in line 3 refer to the grounds in the bottom of the tea cup, the broken lyre in line 6 is a harp, the crypt in line 11 is a grave, and the weakening eye of day (line 4) is the winter sun.

59. **(C)** The poet first sees the bird as merely courageous as it braves the cold winter blast, but he then proceeds to question the bird's prophetic powers as it seemingly has so little to hope for and yet seems to see the world and its future prospects in such a hopeful light.

60. **(D)** This image has been used before, but not here. The others are all present in lines 4, 5, 13, and 11, respectively.

61.　**(E)**　The key word here is "suggests." The author does not clearly say that Kyd's play was called *Hamlet* but refers to it as Kyd's *Hamlet* from the tale of Belleforest (E). Do not be confused by the many plays mentioned nor by the terms "earlier" and "older." Work your way systematically through the passage and the meaning is clear.

62.　**(C)**　The answer comes toward the end of the passage. The author clearly states that there are close "verbal parallels" to Kyd's *Spanish Tragedy* (C). Again, systematically eradicate the other options by close reading of the text.

63.　**(E)**　In the opening sentence, the author's vague "this play" with the antecedent in the previous clause refers to the older play by Kyd. He then suggests that clues to this play lie in *The Spanish Tragedy*, the tale of Belleforest, and a version acted in Germany (E).

64.　**(C)**　The author does not directly refer to the play as a revenge play but clearly states that the motive was simply revenge (C). To back up your choice, eliminate the other options by learning what they entail: a historical saga (A) would be longer and entrenched in historical fact (Shakespeare's *Henry* plays for example); a miracle play (B) is a medieval religious drama based on the life of Christ; a chronicle (D) would again be more historical and chronologically based; and a morality play (E) is again medieval, showing the vices opposed to good virtues, as in *Everyman*.

65.　**(A)**　The author's tone throughout is consistent in its calm objectivity (A), even when he is criticizing Shakespeare's play for incompleteness. The tone is erudite in that what is being said is learned and well researched, but the tone is professional rather than pompous, for the educated reader rather than for the highbrow.

66.　**(A)**　The poem leaves us with no basis for choosing (D) since it neither alludes to nor mentions human artifacts at all. Choices (B) and (E) echo each other and contradict what the poem tells us. In the poem "summer's lease hath all too short a date" (line 4); the only "eternal summer" (line 9) belongs to the female love addressed by the speaker. The idea that nature indeed changes rather quickly pops up often in the poem (for example, lines 5–8). Choice (C) could serve as a subject for a poem, but this one uses the "transient nature of flowers" — "Rough winds do shake the darling buds of May" (line 3) — as a contrast to the "eternal nature of love" embodied in the lover's description of his object of desire in line 9 (and lines 10–14). Thus, choice (A) correctly identifies the main idea of the poem.

67. **(D)** Nothing about summer mentioned in the poem suggests "ugliness of life," nor can we infer such a concept from it; thus, choice (D) is the correct answer. Choice (A) comes close because the poem shows how different "thee" is from a summer's day. However, an initial possibility exists, or the comparison would appear ludicrous. "Thee" addressed obviously has some of the loveliness of a summer's day, but far exceeds it, according to the speaker. Summer's connotation, in fact, brims over with the idea of the transient; the fleeting days of summer quickly fade. Choices (B) and (C) echo that connotation. And since summer, all too quickly departing, stands as part of the continuity of nature, choice (E) likewise reinforces the metaphor.

68. **(E)** If one has even a nodding acquaintance with the terms used as choices, (E) stands out as the obvious correct one. This particular sonnet form conventionally ends with a rhymed couplet. Neither (A) nor (C) applies as neither blank nor free verse rhymes. A triplet by definition is three lines, so choice (B) is incorrect. And even though the poem praises nature, perhaps engendering a pastoral atmosphere, it does not meet the definition of an elegy (D); nor does it fulfill its particular requirements, including the most common one: the death of an admired person.

69. **(A)** An allegory uses abstract ideas in the form of characters, so it would not apply and would negate choice (E). Similarly, apostrophe, a speaker's address to an inanimate object or concept (usually) does not appear in lines 5–6. Choice (D) fails the test. An allusion refers to another literary or historical work; and these lines, although they may vaguely suggest biblical definitions, hardly allude to any single identifiable passage. Choice (B) falls out. Alliteration, the repetition of similar sounds, admittedly appears in line 6 ("is his"), but not in line 5; so choice (C) must yield to choice (A) as the correct one. Both the "eye of heaven" and "his gold complexion" ascribe human characteristics to a concept or place, which defines personification.

70. **(C)** The key word here is contrast. Rifkin chooses two natural processes that we are all familiar with, then contrasts such processes with the fast artificial world we have created. The answer is (C) as the closest idea of the natural time process in contrast to the modern world's concept of time.

71.   **(C)**   The fact that we can make day into night and vice versa shows the ability to tamper with nature (C). We shall never have control over nature (witness earthquakes and hurricanes) nor can we elongate the day no matter what we do with shift work and biological rhythms. Read the passage carefully to gain not just the understanding but also the symbolic quality of what Rifkin has to say.

72.   **(E)**   Rifkin clearly states "experience can only be simulated but no longer savored" which suggests that in the old time world we could savor life to the fullest...now we simply try to copy life (E).

73.   **(D)**   The natural rhythm of the sentence here draws attention to the artificial rhythms Rifkin describes (D); the other choices undercut what Rifkin says about the new time world, or go too far as in suggesting a satisfying climax.

74.   **(B)**   Choice (B) clearly makes us sound as if we are part of the high-tech machines Rifkin regrets in the new time world. The other choices express more of the regret...here we sound like little automatons "zipping" along in life.

75.   **(A)**   Line 1 suggests that sleeping does not mean "peacefully slumbering," "opening up a dream world," or simply "closing one's eyes" — choices (B), (E), and (D), respectively. Line 15 reinforces that statement and suggests ignorance ("knows nothing"). "Dreaming" — choice (C) — almost makes it because we do daydream as escape from reality; but (A) better describes the paraphrase of "sleeping" in this passage, and "dreaming" does not differentiate day and night dreams. "Deliberately ignoring reality" — choice (A) has support in "while the others suffered" and in "he knows nothing, let him sleep on."

76.   **(B)**   Unless we stretch quite a bit to irony, choices (E) and (A) immediately drop out of the realm of possibility. Nothing is comic here, and the same can be said for cheer. Sinister — choice (D) — means evil, bad, or corruptive; it too does not apply exactly. Choice (C), sober, comes close to the mood of the piece; but bleak — choice (B) — describes the passage almost completely. Sober means realistic, upright, not drunk, and perhaps a bit on the melancholic side; bleak, however, means relatively hopeless, desperate, depressing, etc. Taken as a whole, even with the mention of "To-morrow" (line 2), little hope shows up in this passage.

77. **(E)** Normally, we would think birth is the beginning of life (II). But then if we look at a glass with water at the halfway point, do we see it as half-full or half-empty? If you will allow a mixed metaphor, the image of the grave-digger as obstetrician or midwife, certainly suggests the glass is half empty. Furthermore, life, as defined by the distance between the mother astride of a grave and the grave itself, allows for little time or comfort. Therefore, life, as embodied in the metaphor, is also a struggle. So, the best answer is (E), which comprises both statements I and III.

78. **(B)** This one should be fairly obvious, the correct exception being choice (B). Certainly at the end no hope appears. "I can't go on!" emphasizes the apparent pessimism and despair — choices (A) and (D). Likewise, the speaker appears both confused (C) and ambivalent (E), as noted in the pauses and the references to sleeping, as well as the final "What have I said?"

79. **(D)** In the immediate context of the phrase, choice (D) makes the most sense. We do not think when we act out of habit; so if life is miserable, we simply dull ourselves to it and go on living — or at least that seems to be the speaker's suggestion. As used here, "deadener" kills only our spirit or our thought, not our physical presence, so (A) is not correct. Likewise, (B) means the exact opposite. Choice (C), fun, in this context seems out of place and, therefore, incorrect. Finally, if habitual behavior allows us to plod through life, it does not slow us down any further than we already are, so (E) does not quite work.

80. **(D)** The ladies are "deep and debonair" (line 6), so they are covering their true feelings. The pink paint also covers "the innocence of fear" (line 7). There is no indication in the poem of any embarrassment shown by the Ladies' League members.

81. **(C)** The cruelty of the ladies is in their true lack of feeling for the people they intend to serve. The ladies are prepared to treat the poor as they would an animal such as the wrens. They are not prepared to distinguish the good from the desperate from the criminal in the poor people they encounter: this "barbarously fair" (line 10) love is cruel because it is so impersonal. Also, because the ladies are out to make themselves feel better about having money, they are convinced it is their "social obligation" to serve those worse off.

82. **(C)** The narrator has nothing but contempt for the ladies of the league. The narrator does not reveal self-serving pity (A) nor patronizing understanding (B). There is disappointment (D) and shock (E) but no amusement. The overriding tone is one of bitter derision for the ladies from the Ladies' Betterment League.

83. **(A)** The intention of the ladies is good, but the reality is that their actions hurt. The ladies intend to be fair, but their fairness is barbarous (B). Their sweetness is abortive to their efforts (E). They coddle but assault anew (C) and (D) in their efforts. Choice (A) shows no contrast as the intentions and feelings of the ladies are deep and smoothed over by a comfortably thick facade.

84. **(E)** The ladies should have had a social consciousness long ago. Age 50 is a bit late for turning "moral." Probably the women have been wealthy all their lives, as evidenced by their dress and sleek bodies, so (C) is not a viable answer. Choice (B) is not a good choice because even children can deal with different lifestyles. There is no evidence the ladies are ashamed of themselves (D), and (A) is never a good excuse for not helping others.

85. **(B)** The ladies wish "to be a random hitching-post" (line 21), an occasional place for someone to seek help. They also wish to be a "random and handy hem" (line 22) for someone who is crying, "for wet eyes" (line 22). There is no sense of an organized or steady help for the poor, just an occasional visit or commiseration.

86. **(C)** Choice (A) is incorrect because it comes from a failure to recognize and understand the simile "like the jerk of a chain," which may suggest a chain gang, but which is not meant to be taken literally. Choice (B) is incorrect because it is inconsistent with previous observation by the narrator about "the careless, powerful look" Ethan had. Choice (C) is correct because his physical handicap creates a noticeable contrast with his "careless, powerful look." Choice (D) is incorrect because Ethan is clearly identified as one of the taller "natives." Choice (E) is incorrect because it, too, stems from a misreading of the line just as choice (A) does.

87. **(A)** Choice (A) is a correct interpretation of the figurative expression "lank longitude." Only this interpretation makes sense in the context where the "natives" are compared to the shorter and heavier "foreign breed" who have recently settled there. Choice (B) is incorrect be-

cause it interprets "longitude" in a sailing context, which it does not have here. Choice (C) is incorrect because nothing in the passage supports the idea of the "natives" being prejudiced towards their own kind. Choices (D) and (E) are incorrect because they are unsupported in the passage.

88. **(D)** Choice (A) is incorrect because Ethan's appearance is more a matter of genetics, i.e., his size and height, than it is due to his residence in the town. Choice (B) is incorrect because it is contradicted by lines 3–4. Choice (C) is incorrect because Ethan retains these aspects of his appearance in spite of his personal history. Choice (D) is correct because the look on his face is a direct result of his personal history. Choice (E) is incorrect because the passage does not support it.

89. **(E)** Choice (A) is incorrect because it is not supported by anything in the passage. The word "degenerate" carries moral overtones unsuitable for describing weather in this passage. Choice (B) is incorrect because these artifacts of the outside culture are not degenerate in and of themselves as much as the cultural changes they encourage and convey. Choice (C) is incorrect because it is contrary to the meaning of lines 23–24. Choice (D) is incorrect because it erroneously connects the new age and the recurring season of winter. Choice (E) is correct because the trolley, the bicycle, and rural mail delivery opened the village to outside corrupting influences that had not been experienced previously.

90. **(B)** Choice (A) is incorrect because the narrator expresses no amusement toward Ethan and there is no distrust expressed towards Ethan's motives. Choice (B) is correct because the sight of Ethan pulls the narrator up sharply and arouses his curiosity. Choice (C) is incorrect because the narrator expresses no sarcasm towards Ethan. He does not view Ethan as someone deserving criticism. Choice (D) is incorrect because Ethan's appearance intrigues the narrator but he has yet to learn anything about the man to evoke sympathy. Choice (E) is incorrect because the narrator is struck by this unusual man but there is nothing in his description to suggest a worshipful attitude.

ANSWER SHEETS

CLEP ANALYZING AND INTERPRETING LITERATURE – TEST 1

1. Ⓐ Ⓑ Ⓒ Ⓓ Ⓔ		31. Ⓐ Ⓑ Ⓒ Ⓓ Ⓔ		61. Ⓐ Ⓑ Ⓒ Ⓓ Ⓔ	
2. Ⓐ Ⓑ Ⓒ Ⓓ Ⓔ		32. Ⓐ Ⓑ Ⓒ Ⓓ Ⓔ		62. Ⓐ Ⓑ Ⓒ Ⓓ Ⓔ	
3. Ⓐ Ⓑ Ⓒ Ⓓ Ⓔ		33. Ⓐ Ⓑ Ⓒ Ⓓ Ⓔ		63. Ⓐ Ⓑ Ⓒ Ⓓ Ⓔ	
4. Ⓐ Ⓑ Ⓒ Ⓓ Ⓔ		34. Ⓐ Ⓑ Ⓒ Ⓓ Ⓔ		64. Ⓐ Ⓑ Ⓒ Ⓓ Ⓔ	
5. Ⓐ Ⓑ Ⓒ Ⓓ Ⓔ		35. Ⓐ Ⓑ Ⓒ Ⓓ Ⓔ		65. Ⓐ Ⓑ Ⓒ Ⓓ Ⓔ	
6. Ⓐ Ⓑ Ⓒ Ⓓ Ⓔ		36. Ⓐ Ⓑ Ⓒ Ⓓ Ⓔ		66. Ⓐ Ⓑ Ⓒ Ⓓ Ⓔ	
7. Ⓐ Ⓑ Ⓒ Ⓓ Ⓔ		37. Ⓐ Ⓑ Ⓒ Ⓓ Ⓔ		67. Ⓐ Ⓑ Ⓒ Ⓓ Ⓔ	
8. Ⓐ Ⓑ Ⓒ Ⓓ Ⓔ		38. Ⓐ Ⓑ Ⓒ Ⓓ Ⓔ		68. Ⓐ Ⓑ Ⓒ Ⓓ Ⓔ	
9. Ⓐ Ⓑ Ⓒ Ⓓ Ⓔ		39. Ⓐ Ⓑ Ⓒ Ⓓ Ⓔ		69. Ⓐ Ⓑ Ⓒ Ⓓ Ⓔ	
10. Ⓐ Ⓑ Ⓒ Ⓓ Ⓔ		40. Ⓐ Ⓑ Ⓒ Ⓓ Ⓔ		70. Ⓐ Ⓑ Ⓒ Ⓓ Ⓔ	
11. Ⓐ Ⓑ Ⓒ Ⓓ Ⓔ		41. Ⓐ Ⓑ Ⓒ Ⓓ Ⓔ		71. Ⓐ Ⓑ Ⓒ Ⓓ Ⓔ	
12. Ⓐ Ⓑ Ⓒ Ⓓ Ⓔ		42. Ⓐ Ⓑ Ⓒ Ⓓ Ⓔ		72. Ⓐ Ⓑ Ⓒ Ⓓ Ⓔ	
13. Ⓐ Ⓑ Ⓒ Ⓓ Ⓔ		43. Ⓐ Ⓑ Ⓒ Ⓓ Ⓔ		73. Ⓐ Ⓑ Ⓒ Ⓓ Ⓔ	
14. Ⓐ Ⓑ Ⓒ Ⓓ Ⓔ		44. Ⓐ Ⓑ Ⓒ Ⓓ Ⓔ		74. Ⓐ Ⓑ Ⓒ Ⓓ Ⓔ	
15. Ⓐ Ⓑ Ⓒ Ⓓ Ⓔ		45. Ⓐ Ⓑ Ⓒ Ⓓ Ⓔ		75. Ⓐ Ⓑ Ⓒ Ⓓ Ⓔ	
16. Ⓐ Ⓑ Ⓒ Ⓓ Ⓔ		46. Ⓐ Ⓑ Ⓒ Ⓓ Ⓔ		76. Ⓐ Ⓑ Ⓒ Ⓓ Ⓔ	
17. Ⓐ Ⓑ Ⓒ Ⓓ Ⓔ		47. Ⓐ Ⓑ Ⓒ Ⓓ Ⓔ		77. Ⓐ Ⓑ Ⓒ Ⓓ Ⓔ	
18. Ⓐ Ⓑ Ⓒ Ⓓ Ⓔ		48. Ⓐ Ⓑ Ⓒ Ⓓ Ⓔ		78. Ⓐ Ⓑ Ⓒ Ⓓ Ⓔ	
19. Ⓐ Ⓑ Ⓒ Ⓓ Ⓔ		49. Ⓐ Ⓑ Ⓒ Ⓓ Ⓔ		79. Ⓐ Ⓑ Ⓒ Ⓓ Ⓔ	
20. Ⓐ Ⓑ Ⓒ Ⓓ Ⓔ		50. Ⓐ Ⓑ Ⓒ Ⓓ Ⓔ		80. Ⓐ Ⓑ Ⓒ Ⓓ Ⓔ	
21. Ⓐ Ⓑ Ⓒ Ⓓ Ⓔ		51. Ⓐ Ⓑ Ⓒ Ⓓ Ⓔ		81. Ⓐ Ⓑ Ⓒ Ⓓ Ⓔ	
22. Ⓐ Ⓑ Ⓒ Ⓓ Ⓔ		52. Ⓐ Ⓑ Ⓒ Ⓓ Ⓔ		82. Ⓐ Ⓑ Ⓒ Ⓓ Ⓔ	
23. Ⓐ Ⓑ Ⓒ Ⓓ Ⓔ		53. Ⓐ Ⓑ Ⓒ Ⓓ Ⓔ		83. Ⓐ Ⓑ Ⓒ Ⓓ Ⓔ	
24. Ⓐ Ⓑ Ⓒ Ⓓ Ⓔ		54. Ⓐ Ⓑ Ⓒ Ⓓ Ⓔ		84. Ⓐ Ⓑ Ⓒ Ⓓ Ⓔ	
25. Ⓐ Ⓑ Ⓒ Ⓓ Ⓔ		55. Ⓐ Ⓑ Ⓒ Ⓓ Ⓔ		85. Ⓐ Ⓑ Ⓒ Ⓓ Ⓔ	
26. Ⓐ Ⓑ Ⓒ Ⓓ Ⓔ		56. Ⓐ Ⓑ Ⓒ Ⓓ Ⓔ		86. Ⓐ Ⓑ Ⓒ Ⓓ Ⓔ	
27. Ⓐ Ⓑ Ⓒ Ⓓ Ⓔ		57. Ⓐ Ⓑ Ⓒ Ⓓ Ⓔ		87. Ⓐ Ⓑ Ⓒ Ⓓ Ⓔ	
28. Ⓐ Ⓑ Ⓒ Ⓓ Ⓔ		58. Ⓐ Ⓑ Ⓒ Ⓓ Ⓔ		88. Ⓐ Ⓑ Ⓒ Ⓓ Ⓔ	
29. Ⓐ Ⓑ Ⓒ Ⓓ Ⓔ		59. Ⓐ Ⓑ Ⓒ Ⓓ Ⓔ		89. Ⓐ Ⓑ Ⓒ Ⓓ Ⓔ	
30. Ⓐ Ⓑ Ⓒ Ⓓ Ⓔ		60. Ⓐ Ⓑ Ⓒ Ⓓ Ⓔ		90. Ⓐ Ⓑ Ⓒ Ⓓ Ⓔ	

CLEP ANALYZING AND INTERPRETING LITERATURE – TEST 2

1. Ⓐ Ⓑ Ⓒ Ⓓ Ⓔ	31. Ⓐ Ⓑ Ⓒ Ⓓ Ⓔ	61. Ⓐ Ⓑ Ⓒ Ⓓ Ⓔ
2. Ⓐ Ⓑ Ⓒ Ⓓ Ⓔ	32. Ⓐ Ⓑ Ⓒ Ⓓ Ⓔ	62. Ⓐ Ⓑ Ⓒ Ⓓ Ⓔ
3. Ⓐ Ⓑ Ⓒ Ⓓ Ⓔ	33. Ⓐ Ⓑ Ⓒ Ⓓ Ⓔ	63. Ⓐ Ⓑ Ⓒ Ⓓ Ⓔ
4. Ⓐ Ⓑ Ⓒ Ⓓ Ⓔ	34. Ⓐ Ⓑ Ⓒ Ⓓ Ⓔ	64. Ⓐ Ⓑ Ⓒ Ⓓ Ⓔ
5. Ⓐ Ⓑ Ⓒ Ⓓ Ⓔ	35. Ⓐ Ⓑ Ⓒ Ⓓ Ⓔ	65. Ⓐ Ⓑ Ⓒ Ⓓ Ⓔ
6. Ⓐ Ⓑ Ⓒ Ⓓ Ⓔ	36. Ⓐ Ⓑ Ⓒ Ⓓ Ⓔ	66. Ⓐ Ⓑ Ⓒ Ⓓ Ⓔ
7. Ⓐ Ⓑ Ⓒ Ⓓ Ⓔ	37. Ⓐ Ⓑ Ⓒ Ⓓ Ⓔ	67. Ⓐ Ⓑ Ⓒ Ⓓ Ⓔ
8. Ⓐ Ⓑ Ⓒ Ⓓ Ⓔ	38. Ⓐ Ⓑ Ⓒ Ⓓ Ⓔ	68. Ⓐ Ⓑ Ⓒ Ⓓ Ⓔ
9. Ⓐ Ⓑ Ⓒ Ⓓ Ⓔ	39. Ⓐ Ⓑ Ⓒ Ⓓ Ⓔ	69. Ⓐ Ⓑ Ⓒ Ⓓ Ⓔ
10. Ⓐ Ⓑ Ⓒ Ⓓ Ⓔ	40. Ⓐ Ⓑ Ⓒ Ⓓ Ⓔ	70. Ⓐ Ⓑ Ⓒ Ⓓ Ⓔ
11. Ⓐ Ⓑ Ⓒ Ⓓ Ⓔ	41. Ⓐ Ⓑ Ⓒ Ⓓ Ⓔ	71. Ⓐ Ⓑ Ⓒ Ⓓ Ⓔ
12. Ⓐ Ⓑ Ⓒ Ⓓ Ⓔ	42. Ⓐ Ⓑ Ⓒ Ⓓ Ⓔ	72. Ⓐ Ⓑ Ⓒ Ⓓ Ⓔ
13. Ⓐ Ⓑ Ⓒ Ⓓ Ⓔ	43. Ⓐ Ⓑ Ⓒ Ⓓ Ⓔ	73. Ⓐ Ⓑ Ⓒ Ⓓ Ⓔ
14. Ⓐ Ⓑ Ⓒ Ⓓ Ⓔ	44. Ⓐ Ⓑ Ⓒ Ⓓ Ⓔ	74. Ⓐ Ⓑ Ⓒ Ⓓ Ⓔ
15. Ⓐ Ⓑ Ⓒ Ⓓ Ⓔ	45. Ⓐ Ⓑ Ⓒ Ⓓ Ⓔ	75. Ⓐ Ⓑ Ⓒ Ⓓ Ⓔ
16. Ⓐ Ⓑ Ⓒ Ⓓ Ⓔ	46. Ⓐ Ⓑ Ⓒ Ⓓ Ⓔ	76. Ⓐ Ⓑ Ⓒ Ⓓ Ⓔ
17. Ⓐ Ⓑ Ⓒ Ⓓ Ⓔ	47. Ⓐ Ⓑ Ⓒ Ⓓ Ⓔ	77. Ⓐ Ⓑ Ⓒ Ⓓ Ⓔ
18. Ⓐ Ⓑ Ⓒ Ⓓ Ⓔ	48. Ⓐ Ⓑ Ⓒ Ⓓ Ⓔ	78. Ⓐ Ⓑ Ⓒ Ⓓ Ⓔ
19. Ⓐ Ⓑ Ⓒ Ⓓ Ⓔ	49. Ⓐ Ⓑ Ⓒ Ⓓ Ⓔ	79. Ⓐ Ⓑ Ⓒ Ⓓ Ⓔ
20. Ⓐ Ⓑ Ⓒ Ⓓ Ⓔ	50. Ⓐ Ⓑ Ⓒ Ⓓ Ⓔ	80. Ⓐ Ⓑ Ⓒ Ⓓ Ⓔ
21. Ⓐ Ⓑ Ⓒ Ⓓ Ⓔ	51. Ⓐ Ⓑ Ⓒ Ⓓ Ⓔ	81. Ⓐ Ⓑ Ⓒ Ⓓ Ⓔ
22. Ⓐ Ⓑ Ⓒ Ⓓ Ⓔ	52. Ⓐ Ⓑ Ⓒ Ⓓ Ⓔ	82. Ⓐ Ⓑ Ⓒ Ⓓ Ⓔ
23. Ⓐ Ⓑ Ⓒ Ⓓ Ⓔ	53. Ⓐ Ⓑ Ⓒ Ⓓ Ⓔ	83. Ⓐ Ⓑ Ⓒ Ⓓ Ⓔ
24. Ⓐ Ⓑ Ⓒ Ⓓ Ⓔ	54. Ⓐ Ⓑ Ⓒ Ⓓ Ⓔ	84. Ⓐ Ⓑ Ⓒ Ⓓ Ⓔ
25. Ⓐ Ⓑ Ⓒ Ⓓ Ⓔ	55. Ⓐ Ⓑ Ⓒ Ⓓ Ⓔ	85. Ⓐ Ⓑ Ⓒ Ⓓ Ⓔ
26. Ⓐ Ⓑ Ⓒ Ⓓ Ⓔ	56. Ⓐ Ⓑ Ⓒ Ⓓ Ⓔ	86. Ⓐ Ⓑ Ⓒ Ⓓ Ⓔ
27. Ⓐ Ⓑ Ⓒ Ⓓ Ⓔ	57. Ⓐ Ⓑ Ⓒ Ⓓ Ⓔ	87. Ⓐ Ⓑ Ⓒ Ⓓ Ⓔ
28. Ⓐ Ⓑ Ⓒ Ⓓ Ⓔ	58. Ⓐ Ⓑ Ⓒ Ⓓ Ⓔ	88. Ⓐ Ⓑ Ⓒ Ⓓ Ⓔ
29. Ⓐ Ⓑ Ⓒ Ⓓ Ⓔ	59. Ⓐ Ⓑ Ⓒ Ⓓ Ⓔ	89. Ⓐ Ⓑ Ⓒ Ⓓ Ⓔ
30. Ⓐ Ⓑ Ⓒ Ⓓ Ⓔ	60. Ⓐ Ⓑ Ⓒ Ⓓ Ⓔ	90. Ⓐ Ⓑ Ⓒ Ⓓ Ⓔ

CLEP ANALYZING AND INTERPRETING LITERATURE – TEST 3

1.	Ⓐ Ⓑ Ⓒ Ⓓ Ⓔ	31. Ⓐ Ⓑ Ⓒ Ⓓ Ⓔ	61. Ⓐ Ⓑ Ⓒ Ⓓ Ⓔ
2.	Ⓐ Ⓑ Ⓒ Ⓓ Ⓔ	32. Ⓐ Ⓑ Ⓒ Ⓓ Ⓔ	62. Ⓐ Ⓑ Ⓒ Ⓓ Ⓔ
3.	Ⓐ Ⓑ Ⓒ Ⓓ Ⓔ	33. Ⓐ Ⓑ Ⓒ Ⓓ Ⓔ	63. Ⓐ Ⓑ Ⓒ Ⓓ Ⓔ
4.	Ⓐ Ⓑ Ⓒ Ⓓ Ⓔ	34. Ⓐ Ⓑ Ⓒ Ⓓ Ⓔ	64. Ⓐ Ⓑ Ⓒ Ⓓ Ⓔ
5.	Ⓐ Ⓑ Ⓒ Ⓓ Ⓔ	35. Ⓐ Ⓑ Ⓒ Ⓓ Ⓔ	65. Ⓐ Ⓑ Ⓒ Ⓓ Ⓔ
6.	Ⓐ Ⓑ Ⓒ Ⓓ Ⓔ	36. Ⓐ Ⓑ Ⓒ Ⓓ Ⓔ	66. Ⓐ Ⓑ Ⓒ Ⓓ Ⓔ
7.	Ⓐ Ⓑ Ⓒ Ⓓ Ⓔ	37. Ⓐ Ⓑ Ⓒ Ⓓ Ⓔ	67. Ⓐ Ⓑ Ⓒ Ⓓ Ⓔ
8.	Ⓐ Ⓑ Ⓒ Ⓓ Ⓔ	38. Ⓐ Ⓑ Ⓒ Ⓓ Ⓔ	68. Ⓐ Ⓑ Ⓒ Ⓓ Ⓔ
9.	Ⓐ Ⓑ Ⓒ Ⓓ Ⓔ	39. Ⓐ Ⓑ Ⓒ Ⓓ Ⓔ	69. Ⓐ Ⓑ Ⓒ Ⓓ Ⓔ
10.	Ⓐ Ⓑ Ⓒ Ⓓ Ⓔ	40. Ⓐ Ⓑ Ⓒ Ⓓ Ⓔ	70. Ⓐ Ⓑ Ⓒ Ⓓ Ⓔ
11.	Ⓐ Ⓑ Ⓒ Ⓓ Ⓔ	41. Ⓐ Ⓑ Ⓒ Ⓓ Ⓔ	71. Ⓐ Ⓑ Ⓒ Ⓓ Ⓔ
12.	Ⓐ Ⓑ Ⓒ Ⓓ Ⓔ	42. Ⓐ Ⓑ Ⓒ Ⓓ Ⓔ	72. Ⓐ Ⓑ Ⓒ Ⓓ Ⓔ
13.	Ⓐ Ⓑ Ⓒ Ⓓ Ⓔ	43. Ⓐ Ⓑ Ⓒ Ⓓ Ⓔ	73. Ⓐ Ⓑ Ⓒ Ⓓ Ⓔ
14.	Ⓐ Ⓑ Ⓒ Ⓓ Ⓔ	44. Ⓐ Ⓑ Ⓒ Ⓓ Ⓔ	74. Ⓐ Ⓑ Ⓒ Ⓓ Ⓔ
15.	Ⓐ Ⓑ Ⓒ Ⓓ Ⓔ	45. Ⓐ Ⓑ Ⓒ Ⓓ Ⓔ	75. Ⓐ Ⓑ Ⓒ Ⓓ Ⓔ
16.	Ⓐ Ⓑ Ⓒ Ⓓ Ⓔ	46. Ⓐ Ⓑ Ⓒ Ⓓ Ⓔ	76. Ⓐ Ⓑ Ⓒ Ⓓ Ⓔ
17.	Ⓐ Ⓑ Ⓒ Ⓓ Ⓔ	47. Ⓐ Ⓑ Ⓒ Ⓓ Ⓔ	77. Ⓐ Ⓑ Ⓒ Ⓓ Ⓔ
18.	Ⓐ Ⓑ Ⓒ Ⓓ Ⓔ	48. Ⓐ Ⓑ Ⓒ Ⓓ Ⓔ	78. Ⓐ Ⓑ Ⓒ Ⓓ Ⓔ
19.	Ⓐ Ⓑ Ⓒ Ⓓ Ⓔ	49. Ⓐ Ⓑ Ⓒ Ⓓ Ⓔ	79. Ⓐ Ⓑ Ⓒ Ⓓ Ⓔ
20.	Ⓐ Ⓑ Ⓒ Ⓓ Ⓔ	50. Ⓐ Ⓑ Ⓒ Ⓓ Ⓔ	80. Ⓐ Ⓑ Ⓒ Ⓓ Ⓔ
21.	Ⓐ Ⓑ Ⓒ Ⓓ Ⓔ	51. Ⓐ Ⓑ Ⓒ Ⓓ Ⓔ	81. Ⓐ Ⓑ Ⓒ Ⓓ Ⓔ
22.	Ⓐ Ⓑ Ⓒ Ⓓ Ⓔ	52. Ⓐ Ⓑ Ⓒ Ⓓ Ⓔ	82. Ⓐ Ⓑ Ⓒ Ⓓ Ⓔ
23.	Ⓐ Ⓑ Ⓒ Ⓓ Ⓔ	53. Ⓐ Ⓑ Ⓒ Ⓓ Ⓔ	83. Ⓐ Ⓑ Ⓒ Ⓓ Ⓔ
24.	Ⓐ Ⓑ Ⓒ Ⓓ Ⓔ	54. Ⓐ Ⓑ Ⓒ Ⓓ Ⓔ	84. Ⓐ Ⓑ Ⓒ Ⓓ Ⓔ
25.	Ⓐ Ⓑ Ⓒ Ⓓ Ⓔ	55. Ⓐ Ⓑ Ⓒ Ⓓ Ⓔ	85. Ⓐ Ⓑ Ⓒ Ⓓ Ⓔ
26.	Ⓐ Ⓑ Ⓒ Ⓓ Ⓔ	56. Ⓐ Ⓑ Ⓒ Ⓓ Ⓔ	86. Ⓐ Ⓑ Ⓒ Ⓓ Ⓔ
27.	Ⓐ Ⓑ Ⓒ Ⓓ Ⓔ	57. Ⓐ Ⓑ Ⓒ Ⓓ Ⓔ	87. Ⓐ Ⓑ Ⓒ Ⓓ Ⓔ
28.	Ⓐ Ⓑ Ⓒ Ⓓ Ⓔ	58. Ⓐ Ⓑ Ⓒ Ⓓ Ⓔ	88. Ⓐ Ⓑ Ⓒ Ⓓ Ⓔ
29.	Ⓐ Ⓑ Ⓒ Ⓓ Ⓔ	59. Ⓐ Ⓑ Ⓒ Ⓓ Ⓔ	89. Ⓐ Ⓑ Ⓒ Ⓓ Ⓔ
30.	Ⓐ Ⓑ Ⓒ Ⓓ Ⓔ	60. Ⓐ Ⓑ Ⓒ Ⓓ Ⓔ	90. Ⓐ Ⓑ Ⓒ Ⓓ Ⓔ

CLEP ANALYZING AND INTERPRETING LITERATURE
Optional Free-Response Section

Practice Test I

TIME: 90 Minutes
Two Essays†

DIRECTIONS: You are presented with two free-response questions. In the first essay, you are asked to discuss poetry printed on these pages. In the second essay, you should apply a general literary statement to a work of recognized literary merit that you have read.

Question 1

Discuss one major theme explored in the following poem. You may choose any theme that you like, but support your statements with examples from the poem.

Now as I was young and easy under the apple boughs
·About the lilting house and happy as the grass was green,
       The night above the dingle starry,
          Time let me hail and climb,
       Golden in the heydays of his eyes,   5
And honored among wagons I was prince of the apple towns
And once below a time I lordly had the trees and leaves
       Trail with daisies and barley
       Down the rivers of the windfall light.

And as I was green and carefree, famous among the barns   10
About the happy yard and singing as the farm was home,

†Note the different spin between the two questions: the first asks you to respond to poetry presented in the test book; the second asks you to apply a general literary statement to a work of "recognized literary merit" that you have read. In both cases, steer clear of vagaries; favor the specific and concrete. Each of our model essays represents the kind of effort that would earn its writer the highest score on the Optional Free-Response Section of the CLEP Analyzing and Interpreting Literature exam. Consult your registration bulletin for details.

In the sun that is young once only,
      Time let me play and be
  Golden in the mercy of his means,
And green and golden I was huntsman and herdsman, the   15
        calves
Sang to my horn, the foxes on the hills barked clear and cold,
      And the sabbath rang slowly
  In the pebbles of the holy streams.

All the sun long it was running, it was lovely, the hay   20
Fields high as the house, the tunes from the chimneys, it
        was air
    And playing, lovely and watery
        And fire green as grass.
    And nightly under the simple stars   25
As I rode to sleep the owls were bearing the farm away,
All the moon long I heard, blessed among stables, the night-
        jars
    Flying with the ricks, and the horses
      Flashing into the dark.   30

And then to awake, and the farm, like a wanderer white
With the dew, come back, the cock on his shoulder: it was all
    Shining, it was Adam and maiden,
      The sky gathered again
    And the sun grew round that very day.   35
So it must have been the birth of the simple light
In the first, spinning place, the spellbound horses walking
        warm
    Out of the whinnying green stable
      On to the fields of praise.   40

And honoured among foxes and pheasants by the gay house
Under the new made clouds and happy as the heart was long,
    In the sun born over and over,
      I ran my heedless ways,
      My wishes raced through the house high hay   45
And nothing I cared, at my sky blue trades, that time allows
In all his tuneful turning so few and such morning songs
    Before the children green and golden
      Follow him out of grace,

Nothing I cared, in the lamb white days, that time would   50
      take me
Up to the swallow thronged loft by the shadow of my hand,

In the moon that is always rising,
> Nor that riding to sleep
I should hear him fly with the high fields   55
And wake to the farm forever fled from the childless land.
Oh as I was young and easy in the mercy of his means,
> Time held me green and dying
Though I sang in my chains like the sea.

Reprinted with permission from *The Collected Poems of Dylan Thomas, 1934–1952.* New Directions Books: New York, 1953, pp. 178–180.

Model Essay 1

One of the overarching themes of the preceding poem is time, specifically how time is an uncontrollable force that ultimately leads to the destruction of the poet. Various methods are employed so that the force of time is portrayed as subtle, but destructive nonetheless. The recurrent motifs and images used in the poem first illustrate the happy, innocent youth of the poet, but when these same images then refer to the destructive power of time, the whole poem becomes a warning about time's relentlessness.

Since time is such an unstoppable force within the poem, it is interesting to note how time is utilized within the poem. The first five verses of the poem constitute the description of the poet's childhood, frozen in time. The language reinforces this lack of movement of time; many of the stanzas begin with "and," indicating that the poem is a description of a moment in time. The destructive force of time is not meant to be noticed until the last stanza of the poem.

Within that moment as represented in the first five stanzas, the imagery supports the poet's own belief that he is in control of his world. The poet calls himself "prince of the apple towns" (line 6), as well as "...huntsman and herdsman" (line 15), suggesting dominance over the fields in which he plays. This is further reinforced by his statement that he "...lordly had the trees and leaves" (line 7). Often these images are taken to the height of power; each day when the poet awakens is "Shining...like Adam and maiden" (line 33). By equating each day with the day of Creation, the poet betrays his refusal to believe that time does in fact move inexorably forward.

This fact is evident through several interesting phrases in the poem. The poet undermines his own authority with his statement that all of his happiness occurred "once below a time" (line 7), that is, when time did not display its power—or perhaps, more precisely, when that power was not recognized or acknowledged. As the poet shifts from his carefree days of youth toward death, he admits that "time allows...so few and such morning songs" (lines 46-7). What the poet failed to appreciate about the beauty of youth he now longs for, now that he no longer has the gift.

The most effective technique used by the poet in the illustration of the destructive force of time is in its personification. The word "time" is always followed with active verbs ("Time let me hail and climb...," line 4; "Time let me play and be...", line 13); the poet's relationship with time is submissive. He is clearly too enthralled in his own youth to pay the passage of time any heed; it is only in retrospect that the poet notices his youthful activity was merely permitted, not an illustration of control over one's life. The true nature of the poet's relationship with time is meant to go unnoticed in the midst of the idyllic description of nature and beauty. However, the line "Time held me green and dying" (line 58) shows the power that time has over the poet, and the poet's impotence over it. Time's power is reinforced through the use of "chains" in the last line, chains which have suddenly appeared to trap the poet now that the presence of time has become visible to him.

While the beauty of nature and youth are important themes within the poem, what is more important is the idea that such things are temporary. This poem wonderfully and chillingly underscores the permanence of time, even in the moments when beauty and youth seem to be enough to overcome it. The poet can do nothing but "sing" while at the same time acquiescing to time as a force. The reader of this poem eventually realizes that it is all he or she may do as well.

Analysis of Model Essay 1

In analyzing this essay and the other model essays that follow, it is well to keep in mind what would be the most efficient, logical way to write this kind of response. When writing your essays, the most important thing to remember is that you will be writing under a strict time limit. Therefore, it is vitally important that you make the best possible use of your time. Outline your thoughts, but don't make your outline too elaborate; you should not spend more than 10 minutes preparing it. Your response will have three basic parts: an introductory paragraph, the body of your essay (four to six paragraphs), and a closing paragraph. You only have time to discuss one major argument in your paper, so the body of the paper should be concerned with presenting the details of the argument (one paragraph for each detail).

Keep in mind that the people who check this exam will be looking for a well-organized, well-written essay. Therefore, do not be too concerned with looking for a new interpretation of a work. A straightforward analysis that illustrates your knowledge of literary terms and devices will be your best bet for a good score.

In this essay, note how the writer states a thesis—"how time is an uncontrollable force"—and pursues this theme methodically by staying close to the text, providing careful citations, and continually building toward a self-assured conclusion. The writer brings in and then dismisses an alternate theme in the final paragraph ("While the beauty of nature and youth are important themes...."), something that normally should be eschewed to avoid undercutting or diluting your own argument. In this case, however, the essay's confident point-of-view overrides any possible distraction that this could cause.

Question 2

Think of a novel that you have read which used a first-person narrator. Discuss the importance of first-person narration within that novel, specifically with regard to how the first-person narrator affected the plot, tone, and other literary elements of that story. Try to be as specific as possible.

Model Essay 2

Alice Walker's novel The Color Purple is a strong example of the literary usefulness of a first-person narrator. An epistolary novel, The Color Purple is written in the form of a series of letters composed by the protagonist, Celie. Celie writes her letters in hopes of finding a sympathetic response in a world that does not seem to care about her. The claustrophobic atmosphere of the novel is supported by the narrative point-of-view; the reader shares in Celie's loneliness. This feeling of loneliness permeates the novel and is the driving force behind the plot and other stylistic elements of the novel.

The first sentence of the novel is a warning to Celie from her stepfather; Celie has just been raped by her stepfather, and he says to her that telling anyone but God will kill her mother. So the only release that Celie has in her plight is the letters that she writes to God about what she must endure. In a short period of time, Celie's children are taken away from her, and she is quickly given in marriage to the farmer Mr.____, and must work and care for his family while receiving no love in return. Since Celie is abandoned at an early age, the isolation theme is very powerful and is reinforced through narrative technique. Celie has no one to communicate with, save God and the reader. This isolation causes Celie to fail to understand the significance of her interactions with others. Attempts to get Celie to stand up for herself by other women are lost on her, though evident to the reader. When Celie's sister, Nettie, is driven away from her, Celie begins to write letters to Nettie instead of God. However, Celie does not receive any response, so she still has no open lines through which she can communicate her feelings.

The first time this pattern of behavior changes is with the introduction of Mr.____'s lover, Shug Avery. The narrative perspective is very important here: since the reader is forced to look through Celie's eyes, tantalizing pieces of information about Shug are sparingly given. Since Celie is not allowed to leave the house, she cannot learn much about Shug, and neither can the reader. What Celie does learn, however, makes her want to know more; Celie's excitement foreshadows the importance of Shug as a character in the novel. Indeed, Shug is the character who allows

Celie to feel love for the first time, and it is through this love that Celie may communicate with Shug about herself. For the first time, Celie reveals to another character within the text what she has only previously revealed in her letters. As a result, Shug finds out about Celie's letters to her sister, and lets her know that the responses to these letters have been hidden by Mr.____. The discovery of Nettie's letters is the true climax of the novel because once these letters are found, Celie realizes that others will listen to her and she no longer lives in an isolated world.

Once Celie finds out someone has actually taken the trouble to write back to her, she knows that she does not have to worry about being alone. Indeed, once the letters are discovered, the narrative perspective shifts; the reader is now given letters written by Nettie as well as Celie. This shift serves two purposes. First, the new perspective shows the love that Celie has always had but never realized. Secondly, Nettie's struggles in Africa serve to complement Celie's struggles with her husband; she is no longer alone in her suffering. What happens to Celie now becomes the struggle of all the women in the novel, and with this newfound support, Celie can start a new life on her own.

After this occurs, there is far less tension in the novel; the second half of the novel is devoted to Celie's continuing success in her business and the opening of new relationships and new lines of communication. This pattern culminates in the reunion of Celie with her long-lost children, taken away from her at birth. While the whirlwind of activity which leads to this reunion is almost too much for the reader, the narrative is carried along by Celie's joy at finally having something to do after so many years of repression and stagnation. The importance of Celie's point-of-view is evident in the denouement of the novel; the happiness and fullness of Celie's life is all the more wonderful because the reader has had such vivid descriptions of Celie's life without family or friends. Without a first-person narrator, the depths of Celie's loneliness could not have been shown in a manner understandable to the reader.

When a novel employs a first-person narrator, there is usually a better understanding of the inner workings of a single character, at the expense of other characters. In The Color Purple, this approach is very effective because Alice Walker is interested in presenting a world in which one woman is oppressed and cut off from those with whom she most desires to have contact. The portrayal of Celie's anguish and despair is best served by having Celie tell her own story. As a result, her subsequent victory is all the more uplifting to the reader.

Analysis of Model Essay 2

In this type of essay, you are expected to provide your own work to discuss. This essay not only tests how well you can analyze a work that you have read but also gives the scorers insight into the kind of material you have read.

While writing a variety of essays based upon this topic might help you prepare, there is no better preparation than having read and being familiar with a variety of works read either in previous literature classes or on your own.

Once again, do not panic when called upon to choose a work to discuss. As long as you can support your statements with examples from the work being discussed, your interpretation of the work should be fine. So pick a work that you know very well—better still, pick a novel or poem that you've discussed in your literature class. By writing about a work with which you are very familiar, you can maintain confidence in your interpretation while concentrating on writing in an interesting style.

Do not be too concerned if you do not have a photographic memory. Since you obviously will not have the book with you, you will not be expected to provide direct quotes from the work being discussed. You should have a solid understanding of the major characters and the plot of the work, but since an essay of this type will again focus on a major theme or characteristic of the novel, you should concern yourself with presenting a general overview of the novel. Each paragraph in the essay should be focused with the presentation of a supporting idea, which could be a summary of a character, image, or plot point from the novel. In the sample essay, the ideas are arranged in the same way events are presented in *The Color Purple*; analyzing the novel from beginning to end while offering a running analysis is a fine way to organize your ideas. The most important thing to remember while writing an essay of this nature is that you are illustrating that (a) you are familiar with the work that you chose and (b) you are capable of providing a general analysis of that work.

The writer of the above essay displays keen insight into the psychological and circumstantial states of the protagonist. Concisely and persuasively, the writer makes a case for the importance—and power—of first-person narrative by showing how Celie deals with and ultimately surmounts her "anguish and despair."

Practice Test II

TIME: 90 Minutes
Two Essays

DIRECTIONS: You are presented with two free-response questions. In the first essay, you are asked to discuss a poem printed on these pages. In the second essay, you should apply a general literary statement to a work of recognized literary merit that you have read.

Question 1

This question refers to the following excerpt from Shakespeare's *Romeo and Juliet*. Discuss the imagery of light and darkness in these lines from Juliet's soliloquy in Act III, scene ii.

Come, night; come, Romeo; come, thou day in night;
For thou wilt lie upon the wings of night
Whiter than new snow upon a raven's back.
Come, gentle night; come, loving, black-browed night;
Give me my Romeo; and, when he shall die,
Take him and cut him out in little stars,
And he will make the face of heaven so fine
That all the world will be in love with night
And pay no worship to the garish sun.

Reprinted with permission from *The Penguin Romeo and Juliet*, edited by John E. Hankins, Penguin Books, New York, NY (1970), pp. 91-92.

Model Essay 1

Romeo and Juliet is one of William Shakespeare's most widely known tragedies. It deals with themes of forbidden, young romantic love. The protagonists, Romeo and Juliet, are children of two feuding families, the Montagues and the Capulets. (Romeo is a Montague. Juliet is a Capulet.) They meet and fall in love. However, their romance must ensue in secret because a marriage between the two youths would never be agreed to by either family. Set in 16th-century Italy, when most marriages were arranged, the play makes a bold statement for its time in favor of romantic love. Throughout the play the dominant image is light (sun, moon, stars, fire) contrasted with darkness (night, mist, smoke, clouds). The above lines from Juliet's soliloquy contain metaphors that exemplify the imagery of light versus darkness.

In this soliloquy there are several metaphors contrasting light and dark. Firstly, Romeo is referred to as the "day in night." In subsequent lines, Juliet compares Romeo to new snow on a raven's back. Lastly, Romeo is compared to stars in the night sky. While it is common for writers of sonnets and romances to use metaphors comparing the beloved to a source of light, within this drama, Shakespeare revises this tradition by contrasting light and dark. Nearly any time that light is mentioned, darkness is contrasted against it.

The contrasting of light and dark goes on throughout this tragedy. In another speech, Romeo calls Juliet a "rich jewel in an Ethiop's ear." Near the end of the tragedy, Juliet's body is said to be illuminated and seems to glow in the dark vault. Perhaps Shakespeare's use of these contrasting images is a means by which the audience is made to understand the depth of the lovers' feelings for one another. That is, in this particular soliloquy Romeo is made to seem even brighter to Juliet because in the metaphors she uses, he is contrasted against dark images. A bright light seen in the dark seems brightest of all. However, the imagery may reveal more than this alone.

Some literary critics have noted that the imagery of light contrasting dark in this play alludes to danger. Just as the light in these metaphors is related to darkness, the lovers' happiness is overshadowed by the circumstances of their romance. Romeo and Juliet must meet in secret at night and finally, they come to a tragic end in which both die. The metaphors that employ a contrast between light and dark foreshadow the lovers' death. The brightness of their love is eventually snuffed out by the darkness of death.

Juliet's stirring soliloquy is a beautiful example of Shakespeare's ability to effectively use the imagery of light contrasted with darkness in Romeo and Juliet. In these lines from Act III, scene ii, Juliet's choice of metaphor enables the audience to grasp the depth of her love for Romeo. More importantly, the metaphors foreshadow the danger the two lovers will face. The poetry and imagery of this play is moving and Juliet's soliloquy is a fine example of that. The image of Romeo cut out in little stars to make everyone fall in love with night lives in one's mind. The image encapsulated in the soliloquy resonates strongly even in our modern age, as seen, for example, in Robert Kennedy's characterization of his brother John after his assassination. All that was "light" was now dark. But Robert Kennedy, in quoting these very lines, declared that even in death his brother still shone brightly.

Analysis of Model Essay 1

In its ability to sufficiently discuss the imagery between light and darkness in the soliloquy, the essay would receive a high score on the CLEP. The introductory paragraph gets the reader oriented by providing a brief summary of the play. The final two sentences of the paragraph introduce the thesis for the essay.

The writer does a good job of supporting her point by providing examples from scenes in the play. One particular instance can be found in paragraph three, in which Romeo is quoted as calling Juliet a "rich jewel in an Ethiop's ear."

The concluding paragraph sums up the theme of the soliloquy and ends with a 20th-century image of light contrasted with darkness. This kind of ambitious conclusion engenders some risk in terms of the writer's ability to tie up loose ends, but when done in a disciplined, focused way adds depth and texture to the essay.

Question 2

Write an essay about a short story that could be described as a "rite of passage" story. Within the essay, you should define "rite of passage" and point out ways in which the short story you are using fits this definition.

Model Essay 2

Most short stories can be categorized to fit into one or more of these types: allegorical tale; formula story; fable; historical fiction; rite of passage story; myth. A "rite of passage" story is one in which the protagonist gains a new level of understanding or a different perspective throughout the course of the tale. This occurs as a reaction to the events of the story. "Reunion" by John Cheever is a rite of passage story about a young man named Charlie who becomes disillusioned with his alcoholic father after meeting him for lunch.

When the story opens, Charlie has not seen his father for three years, since his parents' divorce. Having an hour or so to spare at Grand Central station, Charlie makes a date to meet his father for lunch there. In anticipation of meeting him, Charlie is somewhat excited. He states that he is happy to be seeing him again. Like most young men, Charlie is seeking a role model in his father. To illustrate, Charlie says that when he is grown, he expects to be like his father.

When they actually meet, father and son shake hands. The father puts his arm around Charlie. At this point Charlie vividly describes his father's smell. He says that it is whiskey, shoe polish and aftershave lotion combined. Charlie's description here is childlike. He is experiencing his father like a small child would. At the same time, Charlie is feeling sentimental about seeing his dad again. He tells the reader that he wishes he and his father could be photographed together. He wants a record of their meeting. This bespeaks how much this reunion means to the son. Charlie wants to mark the occasion for posterity.

Unfortunately, lunch quickly disintegrates into a disaster. Because of his father's drunken rudeness, Charlie and his dad are hastened out of one restaurant after another until finally the hour is up and Charlie must catch his train. At each restaurant the father orders gin both for himself and his underage son. It becomes obvious from his behavior and slurred speech that Charlie's father has been drinking. Charlie does not have any sort of moral commentary on his father's behavior, which could indicate that it is a common occurrence. Perhaps Charlie has always seen his father behave this way.

By reporting the facts of his father's behavior without any commentary on it, Charlie reveals that he has disconnected himself from his father. This is a more mature stance than Charlie took in the beginning of "Reunion." Earlier, Charlie admits his father has faults, but even still Charlie expects to be like him as a man. It is almost as if Charlie believes he is destined to be like his dad. Now he is realizing he has a choice about this. Just because he is genetically linked to his father does not mean that Charlie is predestined to be like him. With this realization, Charlie has managed to take a great leap in the direction of "growing up."

Observing his father's behavior with a new level of maturity after three years have passed, Charlie comes to see his father in a new light. He has become disillusioned with him over the course of the hour-long reunion. By the end of the story, Charlie says that this meeting was the last time he ever saw his father. This decision not to see his father again could be related to Charlie's fear of becoming like his father. By completely disassociating himself from this unlikely role model, Charlie hopes to direct his own life in a different direction than his father's life has taken.

Because Charlie goes from anticipating a joyous father-and-son reunion to the realization of his father's limitations, John Cheever's "Reunion" can be called a "rite of passage" story. By story's end, a disillusioned young man has replaced Charlie's earlier childlike characterization. This "rite of passage" story is a commentary on what everyone eventually goes through when they begin to see their parents for who they really are. Fortunately, for most people this experience is not as troublesome as the one played out in "Reunion."

Analysis of Model Essay 2

For any essay to receive a high score on the CLEP it must be clear and well-organized. The writer answers the first part of the question by defining a "right of passage" story and then providing a thesis for the essay. In the subsequent paragraphs, specific examples in the short story are cited to support the thesis.

Notice the prudent use of transitional words and phrases like "To illustrate," "Unfortunately," and "By story's end."

Heeding the College Board's advice against using unnecessary plot summaries, the writer avoids this potential pitfall by focusing on critical commentary of the work. The essay succeeds in describing Charlie's changing views of his father from the moment they meet at Grand Central Terminal until the end of the meeting. The concluding paragraph is effective in restating the overarching theme of the short story and tying that into the thesis.

Practice Test III

TIME: 90 Minutes
Two Essays

> **DIRECTIONS:** You are presented with two free-response questions. In the first essay, you are asked to discuss a poem printed on these pages. In the second essay, you should apply a general literary statement to a work of recognized literary merit that you have read.

Question 1

Read these final lines from "Song of Myself" by the American poet Walt Whitman. Identify and discuss the major themes of this excerpt.

52

The spotted hawk swoops by and accuses me, he complains of my gab and my
loitering.

I too am not a bit tamed, I too am untranslatable,
I sound my barbaric yawp over the roofs of the world.

The last scud of day holds back for me,
It flings my likeness after the rest and true as any on the shadow'd wilds,
It coaxes me to the vapor and the dusk.

I depart as air, I shake my white locks at the runaway sun,
I effuse my flesh in eddies, and drift it in lacy jags.

I bequeath myself to the dirt to grow from the grass I love,
If you want me again look for me under your boot-soles.

You will hardly know who I am or what I mean,
But I shall be good health to you nevertheless,
And filter and fibre your blood.

Failing to fetch me at first keep encouraged,
Missing me one place search another,
I stop somewhere waiting for you.

Model Essay 1

Walt Whitman, an American poet of the mid-19th century, was concerned with creating a uniquely American verse. <u>Leaves of Grass</u>, in which "Song of Myself" is contained, is his attempt at writing an American epic. He embraced American ideals like equality, freedom, love of nature, and individualism. He also elevated the common man and his labor. Whitman tried to incorporate these ideals into his poetry. He was profoundly influenced by the philosophy of Ralph Waldo Emerson, another transcendentalist. Like Emerson, Whitman tends to seek answers in nature to life's spiritual questions. "Song of Myself" is one of Whitman's best-loved poems. Written and revised over the course of several years, it extols his ideals. The major themes in this final section from "Song of Myself" are that life is perpetual and man is a part of nature.

Whitman identifies with nature. This is revealed in the first lines of this section. The hawk has been given a human trait—the ability to speak to the poet. Then, Whitman saying, "I too am not a bit tamed," identifies with the animal. Further, Whitman shows his primitive nature when he sounds his "barbaric yawp." By first comparing the hawk to a human and then comparing himself to an animal, readers come away with the idea that Whitman is connected to nature on an equal footing. That is, he does not view himself as being above nature. And further, mankind is part of nature, not greater than the animals and plants but of equal value.

In the next lines the poet uses several metaphors to expand on his theme that life is ongoing or perpetual. In particular, Whitman speaks of what will happen to his body after his death. Whitman's shadow becomes vaporous. He says "I depart as air." Next, Whitman writes, "I effuse my flesh in eddies, and drift it in lacy jags." This last metaphor evokes a beautiful image of a stream that Whitman has become part of flowing over and around rocks, swirling and undulating. Further, the poet bequeaths himself to dirt. He wants to "grow into the grass I love." Through these images Whitman is presenting his philosophy regarding the cyclical nature of life. The atoms in Whitman's body will not depart this earth for some unknown heaven, but will infuse the earth with more energy and life-sustaining force. The individual body will die, but the molecules it contains can nourish plant and animal life forevermore.

One can see that Whitman does not fear death. Death for him is a new beginning. It is a rebirth. In his time, the mid-19th century, this was a radical idea. Most Americans being Christian believed in a spiritual after-life in heaven. For Whitman it is enough to become "the grass I love." In fact, in these final lines from "Song of Myself," Whitman seems overjoyed at the prospect of being reborn into nature after his body dies. One comes away with the idea that, for Whitman, being grass is just as wonderful as being human.

Many of the themes of "Song of Myself" are reflective of Emerson's transcendentalist ideology. This final section of the poem extols the transcendentalist themes that life is ongoing and humanity is part of nature. Seeing a need for an American bard, Whitman set out to become that. His intent in writing <u>Leaves of Grass</u>, in which "Song of Myself" is contained, was to create an American epic. He has met with much criticism for this. There are those who believe he falls short of his goal. However, his influence on modern American poetry cannot be denied. His language and meter are ahead of their time—more like what is associated with poets of the 20th century. Whether these modern poets admire Whitman or not, they must surely admit that his influence is far-reaching, even to future American poets.

Analysis of Model Essay 1

This essay embraces all the qualities associated with a high-scoring essay. The thesis is clearly spelled out. A well-organized body follows. The writer explains the lines of the poem clearly and cogently, carefully avoiding glib generalities or empty philosophizing. The essay offers a critical assessment of the poem while taking care to develop the thesis. In the fourth paragraph, a concise explanation is given as to why Whitman did not fear death. In addition, the writer displays his broader knowledge of poetry by linking the thoughts of Emerson to Whitman.

Question 2

The Right of Nature and Law of Nature are themes that run through much of great literature. Write an essay in which you explain how a particular author in a particular novel, short story, or play deals with these themes. Draw a distinction between the two and explain the relationship between them.

Model Essay 2

Thomas Hobbes, in his *Leviathan,* distinguishes between the Right of Nature, which basically looks only to self-interest, and the Law of Nature, which looks to the common good. But because self-interest ultimately depends on the common good, the Law of Nature must take priority over the Right of Nature.

By "Right of Nature," Hobbes means the liberty to preserve one's life through any means the individual's reason deems necessary. Under the Right of Nature, no external force may restrain man from taking any action he pleases to defend or preserve himself.

In contrast, a Law of Nature is based not on Liberty, but obligation, and forbids man to do things that would destroy his life or destroy the means of preserving his life. Both Right and Law derive from reason, but the former derives from an individual's reason whereas the latter derives from a broader perspective.

To fully understand the relationship between the two, it is necessary to understand Hobbes's conception of the human condition. Because he believes man's natural condition is a state of war, it follows that the Right of Nature would entitle men to destroy one another, in which case individual and group security are impossible. Hence a broader perspective is needed to create security. That broader perspective suggests that all men should pursue peace, which is Hobbes's first Law of Nature. Only when peace cannot be achieved may the Right of Nature—to protect oneself—be exercised. Furthermore, Hobbes derives a second Law of Nature from the first; in order to preserve peace and protect himself, man must be willing to give up unrestrained liberty if he wishes others to give up unrestrained liberty in their actions toward him. What Hobbes argues for, then, is a social contract that recognizes not only the desirability but also the necessity of subordinating individual self-interest to the group interest, even from the narrow perspective of self-preservation. In a constant state of war in which each individual does as he pleases, no individual will prosper. Hence, the Right of Nature cannot take priority over the Law of Nature if chaos is to be avoided.

Analysis of Model Essay 2

This question asks the student to explain the distinction between two complex concepts. That the student can do this in the course of displaying mastery of a sophisticated work like *Leviathan* would surely impress any reader. There are several stages in Hobbes's explanation, and the student must demonstrate a firm grasp of each of them. Moreover, the two concepts spring from certain assumptions and depend on other background ideas that must be explained or clarified. Finally, the relationship between the two concepts is more subtle than first appears, and the student must make sure that he clarifies that relationship.

In the sample essay, the writer provides a brief explanation of the essential difference between "Law of Nature" and "Right of Nature" and states the ultimate relationship between the two in the first paragraph. The second paragraph then explains, in clear, contemporary English and in more detail, what Hobbes means by Right of Nature. The third paragraph explains what Hobbes means by Law of Nature, contrasting the source of the Law of Nature with the source of the Right of Nature. The relationship between the two, briefly stated in the writer's first paragraph (that the Law of Nature must take priority over the Right of Nature because self-interest ultimately depends on the common good), is complex, involving several steps; hence, the writer appropriately spends more time on this aspect of the question than on any other part of the essay. The writer explains that the relationship between the two depends on an understanding of a prior concept (Hobbes's conception of the human condition) and on several conclusions that follow from that concept. Finally, the writer restates the central argument of the excerpt in language that Hobbes himself might not recognize but which makes Hobbes's chief position clear. Only by tracing the several stages of Hobbes's argument can the student arrive at an adequate explanation of the two concepts that the question asks the student to analyze.

INSTALLING REA's TEST*ware*®

SYSTEM REQUIREMENTS

Pentium 75 MHz (300 MHz recommended), or a higher or compatible processor; Microsoft Windows 95, 98, or later; 64 MB Available RAM; Internet Explorer 5.5 or higher.

INSTALLATION

1. Insert the CLEP Analyzing & Interpreting Literature TEST*ware*® CD-ROM into the CD-ROM drive.
2. If the installation doesn't begin automatically, from the Start Menu, choose the RUN command. When the RUN dialog box appears, type d:\setup (where *d* is the letter of your CD-ROM drive) at the prompt and click OK.
3. The installation process will begin. A dialog box proposing the directory "Program Files\REA\CLEP_AIL" will appear. If the name and location are suitable, click OK. If you wish to specify a different name or location, type it in and click OK.
4. Start the CLEP Analyzing & Interpreting Literature TEST*ware*® application by double-clicking on the icon.

REA's CLEP Analyzing & Interpreting Literature TEST*ware*® is **EASY** to **LEARN AND USE**. To achieve maximum benefits, we recommend that you take a few minutes to go through the on-screen tutorial on your computer. The "screen buttons" are also explained here to familiarize you with the program.

SSD ACCOMMODATIONS

Our TEST*ware*® can be adapted to accommodate your time extension. This allows you to practice under the same extended-time accommodations that you will receive on the actual test day. To customize your TEST*ware*® to suit the most common extensions, visit our website at *www.rea.com/ssd*.

TECHNICAL SUPPORT

REA's TEST*ware*® is backed by customer and technical support. For questions about **installation or operation of your software**, contact us at:

> **Research & Education Association**
> Phone: (732) 819-8880 (9 a.m. to 5 p.m. ET, Monday–Friday)
> Fax: (732) 819-8808
> Website: http://www.rea.com
> E-mail: info@rea.com

Note to Windows XP Users: In order for the TEST*ware*® to function properly, please install and run the application under the same computer-administrator level user account. Installing the TEST*ware*® as one user and running it as another could cause file access path conflicts.

USING YOUR INTERACTIVE TEST*ware*®

Exam Directions

The **Exam Directions** button allows you to review the specific exam directions during any part of the test.

Stop Test

At any time during the test or when you are finished taking the test, click on the **Stop** button. The program will advance you to the following screen.

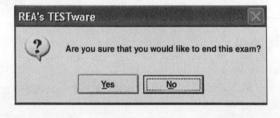

This screen allows you to quit the entire test, or return to the last question viewed prior to clicking the **Stop** button.

Back / Next Buttons

These two buttons allow you to move successfully between questions. The **Next** button moves you to the next question, while the **Back** button allows you to view the previous question.

Mark/Q's List

If you are unsure about an answer to a particular question, the program allows you to mark it for later review. Flag the question by clicking on the **Mark** button. The **Q's List** button allows you to navigate through the questions and explanations. This is particularly useful if you want to view marked questions in Explanations Mode.

View Scores

Three score reports are available: Chart, Summary and Detail (shown below). All are accessed by clicking on the **View Scores** button from the Main Menu.

Explanations

In Explanations mode, click on the **Q & A Explanations** button to display a detailed explanation to any question. The split window shown below can be resized for easier reading.

Congratulations!

By studying the reviews in this book, taking the written and computerized practice exams, and reviewing your correct and incorrect answers, you'll be well prepared for the CLEP Analyzing & Interpreting Literature exam. Best of luck from everyone at REA.